The Devil's Whore

The Devil's Whore

Reason and Philosophy
in the Lutheran Tradition

Jennifer Hockenbery Dragseth
Editor

IA BOOKS

THE DEVIL'S WHORE
Reason and Philosophy in the Lutheran Tradition

Cover image: Ancient English Church Stained Glass © iStockphoto.com/RMAX
Cover design: Alisha Lofgren

ISBN : 93-82661-18-2

Book Team
President : Vijay Sharma
Sr. Vice President : Puneet Singh (London)
Vice President : Kanika Sharma (London)
Pre-Press : P. K. Mishra
Vice-President Marketing : Agnel Henry

Published and Digitally Printed in India in 2014 with permission from the copyright holder by:
Indo American Books (IA Books)
2261, Ground Floor, Hudson Line, Kingsway Camp
Delhi 110009, INDIA. Ph.: 91-011-42870094
Email: sales@iabooks.com
Web: www.iabooks.com

"Indeed, that man Luther is the master of us all."

—Søren Kierkegaard, *The Journal of Søren Kierkegaard*

CONTENTS

CONTRIBUTORS

Oswald Bayer is professor emeritus of systematic theology at the Protestant Faculty of the University of Tübingen. He was, from 1986 until 2007, editor of *Neue Zeitschrift für Systematische Theologie und Religionsphilosophie*. English translations of his works include: *Theology the Lutheran Way* (2007), *Freedom in Response: Lutheran Ethics: Sources and Controversies* (2007), *Martin Luther's Theology: A Contemporary Interpretation* (2008), and *A Contemporary in Dissent: Johann Georg Hamann as a Radical Enlightener* (2011).

Dennis Bielfeldt is president and professor of theology at the Institute of Lutheran Theology. He has authored numerous articles on Luther and the Lutheran tradition, on issues within the theology and science discussion, as well as on more strictly philosophical topics. He is coauthor, with Paul Hinlicky and Mickey Maddox, of *The Substance of the Faith: Luther's Doctrinal Theology for Today* (Fortress Press, 2008). Bielfeldt, who is retired from being professor of philosophy and religion at South Dakota State University, lives and works in Brookings, South Dakota.

Troy Dahlke teaches religion and philosophy at St. Andrew's Episcopal School in Potomac, Maryland. He holds degrees from Concordia University, St. Paul (BA), Yale Divinity School (MAR), and the University of Virginia (MA). He lives with his wife and two sons in Fairfax, Virginia.

Jennifer Hockenbery Dragseth is associate professor of philosophy at Mount Mary College in Milwaukee. She received her AB in philosophy and classics from Bowdoin College and her MA and PhD in philosophy from Boston University, where she wrote her dissertation on Augustine's understanding of the nature and vocation of philosophy. She has written several articles on the relationship between philosophy and theology in Augustine, Hildegard von Bingen, Luther, Nietzsche, Wittgenstein, and John Paul II. She is on the steering committee for the Martin Luther and Global Lutheranism Consultation for the American Academy of Religion.

Sarah E. Fredericks, assistant professor of philosophy and religion studies at the University of North Texas, studies the relationship of religion, particularly Protestant Christianity, to environmental issues. Her work has focused on energy sustainability, the ethics embedded in international environmental policy documents, and environmental justice. Fredericks teaches a variety of philosophy and religion courses including philosophy of religion, religion and science, ethics of science, and Christianity and philosophy.

David J. Gouwens is professor of theology at Brite Divinity School. He is author of *Kierkegaard's Dialectic of the Imagination* (1989) and *Kierkegaard as Religious Thinker* (1996). With Lee C. Barrett, he is coediting *The Paul L. Holmer Papers*, to be published in three volumes by Cascade Books in 2011. Included will be Holmer's previously unpublished book on Kierkegaard; a selection of Holmer's seminal essays on Kierkegaard, Wittgenstein, theology and faith, and emotions and virtues; and a volume of Holmer's sermons, addresses, and prayers.

Christine Helmer is professor of religious studies and adjunct professor of German at Northwestern University. She is the author of *The Trinity and Martin Luther* (1999) and has edited (and coedited) books as well as written numerous articles in the areas of Luther studies, Schleiermacher studies, biblical theology, philosophy of religion, and systematic theology. Her most recent publications include the edited collection *The Global Luther: A Theologian for Modern Times* (Fortress Press, 2009) and an essay on Friedrich Schleiermacher's theology and philosophy in *The Blackwell Companion to Nineteenth-Century Theology* (ed. David Fergusson, 2010).

Paul R. Hinlicky, Tise Professor of Lutheran Studies at Roanoke College, teaches Christian theology and is author of *Paths Not Taken: Fates of Theology from Luther through Leibniz*, *Luther and the Beloved Community: A Path for Christian Theology after Christendom*; and *Divine Complexity: The Rise of Creedal Christianity*.

David M. Hockenbery is emeritus dean of arts and sciences and professor of humanities, Columbus State Community College. He received his PhD from The Ohio State University, studying under Harold J. Grimm. In addition to Luther and the history of ideas, his previous research has been on the social and intellectual history of the Radical Reformation in Nuremberg. He taught previously at Baylor University and Capital University. He also teaches on the history of Islamic thought.

John F. Hoffmeyer is associate professor of systematic theology at the Lutheran Theological Seminary at Philadelphia. He is the author of *The Advent of Freedom: The Presence of the Future in Hegel's Logic* and the translator of numerous theological books from German into English. His current teaching concentrations are trinitarian theology, Christian ethics, Christology, and theological engagement with consumer society. He is an ordained pastor in the Evangelical Lutheran Church in America.

Denis R. Janz is Provost Distinguished Professor of the History of Christianity at Loyola University in New Orleans. In addition to several books on Luther, he has published numerous essays and reviews. Most recently he served as general editor for Fortress Press's acclaimed seven-volume *A People's History of Christianity*. A second, revised edition of his *A Reformation Reader* appeared in 2008.

Gregory Johnson is associate professor and chair of the philosophy department at Pacific Lutheran University. He works in the area of political philosophy, where he attempts to bring together insights from the European tradition (especially nineteenth-century figures, hermeneutics, and existential phenomenology) with issues pertinent to contemporary practical life (such as war, violence and peace, and the task of political ethics). Before being awarded the PhD in philosophy, he earned degrees in theology.

Pauline M. Kaurin holds a PhD in philosophy from Temple University and is a specialist in military ethics, just war theory, philosophy of law, and applied ethics. She is assistant professor of philosophy at Pacific Lutheran University and teaches courses in military ethics, warfare, business ethics, and philosophy of law. Recent articles include "When Less Is *Not* More: Expanding the Combatant/Non-Combatant Distinction" and "With Fear and Trembling: A Qualified Defense of Non-Lethal Weapons."

Carter Lindberg is professor emeritus of church history at Boston University School of Theology. He previously taught at Susquehanna University and College of the Holy Cross. He was research professor at the Institute for Ecumenical Research, Strasbourg, France (1979–1982), and St. John's Summit Visiting Professor of Church History at the Lutheran Theological Seminary at Philadelphia (2005). Recent publications include *Love: A Brief History through Western Christianity* (2008), *A Brief History of Christianity* (2005), and a second, revised edition of *The European Reformations* (2010).

Christian Lotz is associate professor of philosophy at Michigan State University. He is the author of *From Affectivity to Subjectivity: Revisiting Edmund Husserl's Phenomenology* (2007–2008) and *Vom Leib zum Selbst: Kritische Analysen zu Husserl und Heidegger* (2005). He has coedited four books and published articles on various topics and philosophers in European philosophy in major U.S. and German journals. His current research interests are in German philosophy, aesthetics, philosophy of culture, and theories of subjectivity.

Mary Elise Lowe is assistant professor of religion at Augsburg College. Her teaching and research focus on contemporary theology, particularly theological anthropology, with special attention to new views of the human person, sin, and human sexuality. Lowe brings the insights of Luther's thought into conversation with emerging theology in critical and creative ways. She has written several articles and is the author of *The Human Subject and Sin: The Anthropology of Pannenberg, Ruether, and Fulkerson*. She holds a PhD from the Graduate Theological Union.

Martin E. Marty is Fairfax M. Cone Distinguished Service Professor at the University of Chicago, where for thirty-five years he taught in three faculties. Author of numerous books, he is an ordained minister serving in the Evangelical Lutheran Church in America. While he is an historian by profession, he has written numbers of books relating to theology, philosophy, and interpretation of culture.

Charles Peterson is pastor of Trinity Evangelical Lutheran Church (ELCA) in Columbus, Ohio. He received the MDiv degree from the Lutheran School of Theology at Chicago in 1991 and has served parishes in Pennsylvania and Wisconsin. He is a doctoral candidate in philosophy at Marquette University. His dissertation, *Philipp Melanchthon's* Commentrius de anima *of 1548*, will examine the relationship between philosophy and theology in Melanchthon's thought through a presentation of Melanchthon's view of human nature.

Gregory R. Peterson is professor of philosophy and religion at South Dakota State University, where he currently serves as program coordinator. His primary area of research is in religion and science and ethical theory, with special attention devoted to the biological and cognitive sciences and their implications for religious and philosophical approaches to human nature. Author of over thirty articles on religion and science in books, encyclopedias, and journals, he has published the book *Minding God: Theology and Cognitive Science* (Fortress Press, 2002) and is coeditor of the forthcoming *Routledge Companion to Religion and Science*.

William R. Russell specializes in the history and theology of the Lutheran confessional writings, as well as the life and work of Martin Luther. He has addressed academics and nonspecialists in a wide variety of settings. His seven books, five translations, and dozens of articles have appeared in print, online, and on CD-ROM. Russell has BA and PhD degrees from the University of Iowa and the MDiv from Luther Seminary. He is presently resident scholar at the Collegeville Institute for Ecumenical and Cultural Research.

Lea F. Schweitz is assistant professor of systematic theology/religion and science at Lutheran School of Theology at Chicago and the director of the Zygon Center for Religion and Science (www.zygoncenter.org). She teaches courses in theology, philosophy of religion, Lutheran confessions, and religion and science. Her research is in early modern theological anthropology and questions of faith and reason. She is working on projects that explore the connections between the Lutheran heritage and our understandings of human nature.

Gary M. Simpson is professor of systematic theology at Luther Seminary, St. Paul, where he is also director of the Center for Missional Leadership. He is author of *War, Peace, and God: Rethinking the Just War Tradition*; *Critical Social Theory: Prophetic Reason, Civil Society, and Christian Imagination*; and editor of *Missional Church and Global Civil Society*. He is currently writing *Natural Law, Public Theology, and Global Civil Society*.

Mary J. Streufert directs the Justice for Women program in the Evangelical Lutheran Church in America in Chicago. As contributor and editor, she published *Transformative Lutheran Theologies: Feminist, Womanist, and Mujerista Perspectives*, in addition to articles and chapters on Christology, soteriology, power, and method. Her current research continues to unfold connections between Schleiermacher and feminist thought. She holds a PhD from Claremont Graduate University.

David Vessey is assistant professor of philosophy at Grand Valley State University, specializing in nineteenth- and twentiety-century European philosophy. He received his BA from St. Olaf College and his PhD from the University of Notre Dame. He was a Fulbright Scholar at the Husserl Archives in Leuven, Belgium, and has been a visiting scholar at the University of Notre Dame, the University of Oregon, and the University of Chicago. He has published a number of articles on Hans-Georg Gadamer's hermeneutics, especially as they compare to other philosophical traditions.

Markus Wriedt holds a joint appointment as professor of historical theology/church history at Goethe University, Frankfurt/Main, and Marquette University, Milwaukee. He specializes in reformation history and theology with special attention to its late medieval relationships and patristic sources. He is editor of several important volumes in Reformation studies and is author of over 250 articles in professional journals, lexica, collections, and some books. He is currently doing research for a history of Reformation educational reform and its theological roots.

EDITOR'S PREFACE

Sixty years ago Jaroslav Pelikan ended his first book, a monograph on the influence of Luther on philosophy, with the hope that "twentieth century Lutheranism may produce Christian thinkers of the ability and consecration necessary for that task [of working out a Christian philosophy]."[1] It is now the twenty-first century. This book renews the call for such work.

My first call to the topic came not from Pelikan, whom I read later, but from my dissertation directors. I had written a thesis analyzing and ultimately advocating for Augustine's understanding of the nature and vocation of the philosopher. My two readers, the Roman Catholic Matthew Lamb and the Methodist Robert Neville, came to an agreement; my read of Augustine was thoroughly Lutheran. Despite my Lutheran pedigree—my grandfather was an American Lutheran Church pastor, my father was a Reformation historian, my husband was seeking ordination in the Evangelical Lutheran Church in America—I was surprised to hear that my read of Augustine was Lutheran. After all, I was a philosopher and thus believed that I read from a neutral standpoint. And frankly, I had not read much Luther beyond the Small Catechism, so I failed to see how his writing could have influenced me. I saw myself as a classicist, owing much more to Plato than to the late medieval Luther. But as I began to read Luther, at my husband's urging, I came to realize that Neville and Lamb had been right. I did read Augustine like a Lutheran. Moreover, I generally thought like a Lutheran and wrote like a Lutheran. But I was not sure where to go with this. There was no session at the American Philosophical Association on Lutheran philosophers. There was no Society or Association for Lutheran Philosophers. And when I went to those clubs for Christian philosophers I found thoughtful and faithful Calvinists and Roman Catholics but not many Lutherans.

Frustrated, I began looking for contemporary Lutheran philosophers in earnest. Unlike my first love Augustine, who saw Lady Philosophy as a seductive lover, a caring mother, and a feminine version of Christ, Luther claimed philosophy was no lady but merely a lovely whore or, worse, Satan's grandmother. Still, Lutheran philosophers had dominated nineteenth-century continental thought. The topic needed more inquiry in the current century. I began reading what I

---

[1] Jaroslav Pelikan, *From Luther to Kierkegaard: A Study in the History of Theology* (St. Louis: Concordia, 1950, 1963), 120.

could find written in English. There were some pieces by theologians like Pelikan, but virtually nothing by contemporary American academic philosophers. My father took a sabbatical to investigate the issue. My friend Cheryl Peterson, a Lutheran systematic theologian, took me to the American Academy of Religion and introduced me to a myriad of Lutheran and non-Lutheran professors of religion who were as interested in philosophy as in religion. Her husband, Charles Peterson, my father, David Hockenbery, and theologian David Gouwens came together to present a panel on the quandary of Lutheran philosophy at the 2008 national meeting of the AAR through the Martin Luther and Global Lutheranisms Consultation led by Deanna Thompson and Hans Hillerbrand. Sarah Hinlicky Wilson, editor of *Lutheran Forum*, published the papers given at that AAR panel.

At once, many scholars (philosophers but also historians, theologians, and professors of religion) came forth eager to research and write on the paradox of Lutheran philosophy. Three sections of inquiry emerged: those interested in understanding the philosophical formation of Luther and his subsequent formation of the discipline of philosophy; those interested in investigating Lutheran influence on major continental philosophers who were devoutly, or not so devoutly, Lutheran; and those interested in a new direction in twenty-first-century philosophy that would claim Lutheranism as an influence. The result is this book, a collection of essays from thinkers in several disciplines seeking to promote new interest in the question of Luther and philosophy. Each essay presents an angle or idea that is important to the general topic. No essay makes a holistic claim about what Lutheran philosophy is or should be. The essays reveal a Luther who is rich and complex philosophically, whose thought influenced much of continental philosophy from ethics to metaphysics, and whose ideas continue to bear fruit in our own century. In the end, the essays point the reader to new ideas, new questions, and hopefully a new line of inquiry for Lutherans and non-Lutherans, clergy and laity, historians of ideas and philosophers, professors and students.

All books, but especially volumes of collected essays, depend on the work of many people. I am grateful for the support of Mount Mary College, the Catholic women's college where I work and teach. MMC not only gave me resources to pursue this project; more importantly, the college gave me the unusual freedom to investigate outside of my area of study (ancient and early medieval philosophy) in order to indulge in a new area of research for me and for the discipline. The gift of this freedom of inquiry is what is best about the Catholic philosophical tradition. The support of family is often acknowledged in book prefaces; however, I must note that my husband provided academic as well as familial support, often times lending his knowledge of Luther and his skill at editing as well as free access to his collection of *Luther's Works*. A special note must go to my father, who I now recognize was teaching me Luther from the cradle. More formally, the fruits of his research from his last sabbatical are presented in the introduction to this volume. He also edited several of the essays in the book and generally helped the formation of the volume. I also wish to thank Paul Hinlicky and Carter Lindberg, who took an early interest in the project, providing encouragement, suggesting and recruiting contributors, and advocating for the volume's publication. A final thanks, of course, to Fortress Press and its editors, Michael West, Susan Johnson, and David Lott, for their work, advice, and confidence in the project.

Introduction

David M. Hockenbery

As we move toward the five hundredth anniversary of the beginning of Martin Luther's assault upon and ultimate destruction of the monolithic institution of the Roman Catholic Church with the posting of his Ninety-Five Theses for Debate on October 31, 1517, this collection of essays has been assembled to analyze some obvious and perhaps not-so-obvious connections between Luther's revolutionary theology and the historical development of philosophy on the European continent and to explore concepts on the development of contemporary philosophy done by Lutherans today. The purpose of this introduction is to supply context to the essays that follow and to serve as a guide to those readers who may not be experts on Luther, philosophy, or the history of ideas.[1]

An issue that one might legitimately raise about the topic: if it is true that more has been written by and about Martin Luther than any other historical figure, then surely there must be a great deal already written about the topic at hand. If one has taken even a survey course in the history of philosophy, however, I would wager that one did not come away with the impression that Luther was a major figure *in* the history of philosophy. I would even guess that Luther's name is absent from most current textbooks on the history of philosophy.

Apparently for professional philosophers or historians of philosophy, Luther is but a minor figure in its development. Perhaps it is a mere oversight that the professionals did not happen to notice that Gottfried Leibniz, J. G. Hamann, J. G. Herder, Immanuel Kant, J. G. Fichte, Friedrich Schelling, G. W. F. Hegel, Ludwig Feuerbach, Søren Kierkegaard, and Friedrich Nietzsche were all Lutherans, and many of these same men formally studied Lutheran theology in Lutheran seminaries in Lutheran universities. Almost all were the sons of Lutheran pastors. This could be, of course, sheer coincidence. But it is at least worth looking into the idea that Luther's thought had more than a modicum of influence on the intellectual development of the above-named key players in Western philosophical development.

Yet, it is also not true that nothing has been written on the topic. One of the first to call attention to Luther's influence on at least German philosophy after the advent of modern philosophy was the romantic poet Heinrich Heine. Writing in exile in France, Heine penned a disjointed, unfinished, and sometimes odd little gift to the French literary world in 1831, entitled *Religion and Philosophy in Germany*, for the purpose of "interpreting Germany to the Frenchmen." His premise was that one could not understand the German people without knowing something of the impact of Luther on German society. His book was to be a corrective to the prejudices of the French against the Germans. While often insightful, Heine's work is not systematic and was never finished.[2]

In more recent times, Jaroslav Pelikan published a tome in 1950 that was a consequence of teaching in the philosophy department at Valparaiso University, entitled *From Luther to Kierkegaard*. One might also say of this book that it was unfinished. While well versed in the history of Lutheranism and Lutheran thought, Pelikan's interest was as a theologian. His opening paragraph belies the author's admitted weakness in the study: "Luther's great accomplishment was not philosophical, nor yet theological but evangelical." That is also what Pelikan in his career wished to be.[3]

Aside from these two works, almost nothing that is available in English has been devoted to the topic at hand. This helps explain the lack of attention to the topic in the English-speaking world and the absence of references to Luther in English-language histories of philosophy.

As one might expect, German scholars have devoted considerable attention to the intellectual history of Lutheran thought. But one might also say of these scholars, as Pelikan said of himself, that their interest in Luther is primarily theological, religious, and evangelical rather than philosophical. While one can cull a great deal on the topic from reading the great German Lutheran historians of the twentieth century, especially Werner Elert, Heinrich Bornkamm, and Gerhard Ebeling, ultimately, one needs to read Luther.

Luther's Problem

Any discussion of Luther and his influence must begin with at least a brief look at his background, his religious or theological problem, and his solution to that problem. To understand Luther, and ultimately his theology, one must acknowledge two essential aspects of his person. First, Luther was, as characterized by the psychoanalyst Eric Erikson, a *homo religiosus*.[4] He was one who agonized over the question of human existence and who suffered with and for the suffering world around him. For Luther, this world simply did not make sense and human existence was indeed meaningless. His interest was, in this context, however, religious and theological, not psychological.

Following a near-death experience in a lightning storm while returning to college for law school after a visit home, Luther forsook his family and a potentially rewarding career as a lawyer to enter, significantly, an Augustinian monastery. If Luther's problem was that he had to become sinless to be saved before a righteous god, he reasoned, how much sinning could one do in a monastery? To paraphrase Luther's great American biographer, Roland Bainton, "A fine idea that was."[5]

Second, Luther was a person of enormous intellect. There were two intellectual giants of the early sixteenth century in Europe, Erasmus of Rotterdam and Martin Luther. One of the greatest errors made in attempting to appreciate, if not understand, Luther fully is to underestimate his enormous intellectual capacity. His contemporary enemies made that mistake, and it was fatal for the Roman Church. Because he later referred to Aristotle as that "damned" pagan and "reason as the Devil's whore" did not mean that Luther did not understand Aristotle.

Luther's Intellectual Background

There were three major influences afoot in northern Germany, which exercised essential influence on Luther's intellectual development: lay piety and mysticism, humanism, and scholastic nominalism.

Lay piety was a largely urban movement of an educated middle class. It emphasized ethical communal life based upon Christ's teaching in the Sermon on the Mount. Its greatest influence was from Thomas á Kempis's *The Imitation of Christ*. Considering Luther's view of himself as a sinner, one can imagine how successful he felt he could be in imitating the life of Christ. In fact, his inability to be like Christ, prior to and then in the monastery, only worsened his feelings of worthlessness and meaninglessness, what Luther called his *Anfechtungen*—anxiety, trials, despair.

On the other hand, lay piety had an intellectual, if not fully philosophical, underpinning that gave substance to its existential way of life. This was mysticism, as expressed most notably in the sermons of Johann Tauler. More important was an anonymous work that Luther discovered and published in 1516 as the *German Theology*,[6] calling it the most important influence on him outside of Scripture and Augustine. The students and faculty at the University of Erfurt, where Luther studied as an undergraduate, were steeped in this late medieval German mysticism. I would suggest that the underlying Platonic nature of those works worked an intellectual influence on Luther as well.

Humanism, like lay piety, was a movement of the urban laity. However, the significant urban laity that fueled humanism was the aristocratic middle class. The focus of humanism was on ethics and aesthetics. They found the answers to their questions not in the theology of the medieval church but in the philosophy of the pre-Christian classical Greeks. In the process, they recovered and reconstructed virtually all of the Platonic dialogues known to modern scholarship and much of the works of Aristotle. Of course, discovering the works of the Greeks is one thing, reading them is something else. The humanists had to learn Greek and in the process became masters of language study and linguistics. In the movement known as Christian humanism, the study of classical Greek necessarily turned to the study of Koine Greek and, ultimately, to the study of Aramaic and Hebrew.

The Platonic influence in Christian humanism culminated in the "philosophy of Jesus" of Erasmus of Rotterdam. The identification of Christ as the love of God in Christian humanism was a major influence on Luther, or at least allowed the Christian humanists to understand Luther's interpretation of Augustine's views. The traditional view that Luther hatched the egg that Erasmus laid is not without merit, but the egg was fertilized by real philosophical understanding on the part of both the Christian humanists and Luther.

The third influence on Luther, and for many the most relevant, was nominalism. Nominalism was developed by William of Ockham (1280–1349), a Franciscan scholar in England, on the basis of the Aristotelianism of John Duns Scotus, also a Franciscan and Englishman. Nominalism, or the *via moderna*, stood against the scholastic realism, *via antiqua*, which reached its culmination in the great synthesis of the Dominican scholar Thomas Aquinas. As Thomist theology/philosophy became the orthodox theology of the Roman Church, nominalism was suppressed. In the rebellious atmosphere of fifteenth-century Germany, it was revived by Gabriel Biel and held sway at the University of Erfurt when Luther arrived as a student.

Underpinning Luther's theology is a synthesis of these three intellectual movements of the early sixteenth century. I would contend that Luther's synthesis is also a philosophic synthesis underpinning the development of Continental, especially German, philosophy.

Luther's Epistemology

The debate between the realists and the nominalists focused on the nature of reality and epistemology. When there was a contradiction between what one knows through sense perception and what one knows through revelation, the scholastic realists posited that revelation accepted through faith is superior to knowledge gained from reasoning through sense perception. However, scholastic realism fully believed that all apparent contradictions between reason and revelation could be reconciled through the correct application of Aristotelian logic. Neo-Platonism, positing that reality stems from the participation of individual things in the *a priori* Idea, or the ultimate reality, became the cornerstone of the scholastic synthesis. The existent universe is ontologically necessary, part of the nature of God's being. Things are what they are because they are part of or participate in the very nature of God and they cannot be otherwise.

Nominalism, as developed by William of Ockham and then by Gabriel Biel, argued that one learns only through sense perception, period. Or, better, the only thing one knows for sure is what one learns through sense perception. What is beyond sense perception we ought not to believe. For the nominalists, the concept of *a priori* ideas cannot be proven nor are they necessary. The only *a priori* idea that matters is God, and trying to define God is impossible because one cannot know God in reality. The only reality one can know is in particular things, which one knows from sense perception. Particular things are what they are not because of the nature of reality as an emanation of God but because God wills them that way. The created universe is contingent upon God's will. To speculate beyond this is to detract from the reality of things and, more importantly, to suggest the power of God is limited.

Luther's Religious Synthesis and Its Consequences

Most are aware of Luther's religious solution to the problem of justification. He came upon this solution, his so-called *tower experience*, while studying for his lectures on the book of Romans. There, the words of Paul's letter to the Romans, "The righteous man shall live by faith alone" (Rom. 1:17), became for Luther the doctrine of "justification by faith alone." That the tower experience should be considered more of a philosophic insight than a religious revelation is apparent from Luther's inability to pinpoint when it occurred and subsequent historians' inability to do so as well.

The corollaries to *justification by faith*, which led to the destruction of the medieval Catholic Church, were the *priesthood of all believers* and *Scripture as sole authority*. From these religious axioms stems Luther's social ethics, which Luther first delineated in the revolutionary pamphlets of 1520, *On the Freedom of a Christian* and *An Address to the Christian Nobility of the German Nation*. I would contend that these treatises, and more specific ones that followed, had not only an immediate impact upon German Lutheran society but also a rather direct influence on German and subsequent philosophy.[7]

Luther's Philosophic Synthesis

Luther's philosophic synthesis begins with the acceptance of the nominalist position. The Judaic God in his full majesty is beyond human comprehension; this God is unknown and unknowable to humans' limited sense perception and reason. For Luther, the only thing we can know of God is as God revealed himself in the person of Jesus Christ, and Jesus, in this world, is the only way that we can think about God. We accept Christ as the love of God in faith. We know him as portrayed in Scripture. This is central to Luther's being because it is only Christ, the love of God, which gives meaning to individual existence. Everything else is knowable only through sense perception.

With the widespread acceptance of this religious position in Europe, there are profound and immediate philosophical consequences. Three are most profound:

1. *The role of civil law and civil authority.* The revealed God, Christ, only teaches one how to live in relation to one's neighbors or, rather, how one will live when one has accepted Christ in faith. It says nothing of how secular society should best be organized or governed. In 1520 Luther informed the secular authorities of Europe that it was their responsibility to establish civil authority. One can extrapolate much on this from Christian teaching, but ultimately this must be a rational construct. This was one thing that Aristotle was pretty good at. In this alone, Luther

opened the door to the true study of Aristotle. It was not coincidental that Luther's first teaching post at the University of Wittenberg was lecturing on Aristotle's *Nicomachean Ethics*.

2. *Science*. When Luther asserted that one can learn about reality only through sense perception, he sanctioned the development of modern science. It is rarely remarked in the history of science that Copernicus's *On the Revolution of the Heavenly Bodies* was first published and introduced in 1543 by Andreas Osiander, whom many consider the first orthodox Lutheran theologian. While Luther thought Copernicus's cosmology was wrong, he could hardly argue with Osiander's position, following Luther himself, that it was incumbent upon us to understand the created universe in exploring the "kernel of the nut and the germ of the wheat and the marrow of the bone."[8] This support and encouragement of empirical study by Lutheran theology would be a blessing to humanist scientific inquiry already being scrutinized by the inquisitors of the Roman Church.

3. *Nominalism*. Luther's nominalism anticipated the radical nominalism of Thomas Hobbes in England. It was always a logical option for Luther that if we can know for certain only what we learn through sense perception, perhaps the only reality is what we know through sense perception. Indeed, that this was a logical step in the nominalist argument was a major contributing factor in Luther's continuing *Anfechtungen*. The *Table Talks* are replete with Luther's own questioning of his theology. "Who knows," he would say, "if it is true." It also meant that Luther's concept of faith became a desperate act of affirming individual meaning. If you will, against reason and appearance, faith required a radical and irrational leap.

What enabled the emergence of radical nominalism was Luther's destruction of the authority of the Roman Church. England quickly followed suit in eliminating the authority of Rome in England, but the English Reformation never was truly enacted as a theological movement. Thus, Luther's theology did not act as a restraint against the emergence of radical nominalism and its ultimate triumph in the form of British empiricism as it did on the continent, where it could refute any ultimate conflict between science and religion and could ameliorate the gross materialism that must follow from the pure empiricist tradition.

Lutheranism after Luther

There is in Luther a logical contradiction between the Judaic concept of God as omniscient and omnipotent and Luther's formulation of the visible God in the historical Jesus. This is the problem of predestination, which early came to the fore in the Luther-Erasmus debates on the freedom of the will. Where the humanist Erasmus argued, "God must be Good," Luther argued, "Let God be God." When Erasmus pointed out the logical contradiction, Luther's response was that was God's problem, not his.[9]

Simply speaking, Luther's theology could not be systematized in the Aristotelian sense. During his lifetime, Luther was able to keep the problem of predestination at a distance from the core of his theology by the magnitude of his sheer personality. It was left to Philipp Melanchthon to systematize what he could of the theology. When Luther's restraining influence was removed with his death, Melanchthon's interpretation and systemization of Luther became increasingly more humanistic and logical and less existential. Further, as Melanchthon compromised with Catholic theologians, he became embroiled in bitter disputes with theologians within Lutheranism. While these disputes between liberal and orthodox interpretations of Luther occupied Lutheran thought for the next one hundred years, nominalism, in the form of empirical science, not only grew to dominance in England but spread back to the continent as well.

Rationalism and Lutheranism

In addition, religious conflict was manifested in religious war to such a point that religion itself, at least as represented by the institutional churches, fell into disfavor. The question that haunted Luther, "What kind of a God is this?," emerged anew in the form of religious and then philosophic skepticism, as first put forth by the French essayist Michel de Montaigne, in the French Wars of Religion.

Out of literary and religious skepticism emerged a systematic philosophic skepticism, and the birth of modern rationalist philosophy, in the works of the Frenchman René Descartes. While Descartes, mathematically and logically, was able to prove the existence of the *ideal* universe—initially in the person of his own subjective existence—and then the material universe, he could not necessarily demonstrate how these universes interacted, if they interacted at all.

The problem of Cartesian dualism exercised enormous influence on the future development of European philosophy, if unequally in England and in France. Descartes is modern, said Heinrich Heine, for after Descartes, "Philosophy no longer needed to solicit from theology permission to think for itself."[10]

In explaining the different influence of Descartes on the continent than in England, Heine said, "John Locke had gone to the school of Descartes and from him had learned all that an Englishman can learn—mechanics, analytical method, and the art of reckoning. There was but one thing he could not understand, innate ideas."[11]

Where Locke pursued the materialistic side of Descartes, the Lutheran Leibniz pursued the idealistic side. It was Leibniz who first broke through the stagnation of Lutheran quarrelling.[12] Leibniz attempted to create a new Lutheran (nay, Christian) synthesis with his concept of universal harmony. Using Descartes's tools, Leibniz sought to harmonize reason and revelation mathematically. German rationalism was born.

The German Language

The mention of Leibniz may not be central to the story of the impact of Luther's thought on formal philosophy, although Leibniz referred to Luther's treatise on "The Bondage of the Will" as, if not the last word on the subject, the best to date. However, the Lutheran impact is furthered, at least tangentially, as it was picked up by Leibniz's disciple Christian Wolfe. One of Luther's great accomplishments was the creation of the German language through his translation of the Scripture into the vernacular. Luther consciously created a language that was precise in its ability to describe the thing or convey the meaning of an event or teaching. By translating Leibniz into Luther's German, Wolfe was aiding the establishment of German as the most precise philosophical language since classical Greek.

Luther's focus on the word to get at the Word reverberates through all German philosophy. This would seem apparent from Immanuel Kant to Martin Heidegger. While Heine emphasized this point, the influence was most clearly delineated by the philosopher and poet Johann Gottfried von Herder, who wrote of Luther, "It is he who awoke and set free the sleeping giant of the German language; it is he who cast out the trade in mere words of scholasticism like the tables of the money changers; through his Reformation, he made a whole nation able to think and to feel."[13]

Nineteenth-Century Philosophy

Immanuel Kant, 1724–1804

Against the empiricism of Locke as it culminated in the Scottish philosopher David Hume, and against the rationalism of Leibniz who sought a new scholastic synthesis of reason and revelation, stepped onto the scene the first great modern German philosopher, Immanuel Kant. Quite significantly, Kant began where Luther began, by recognizing the limitations of human reason. He, of course, had tools that Luther did not have at his disposal in terms of the historical development of deductive and inductive logic and the mathematical methods of Descartes. However, his conclusion in *The Critique of Pure Reason* (1781) would seem to be pure Luther, that is, to demonstrate that one can learn only through sense perception does not demonstrate that the only reality is what one learns through sense perception.

We can know only phenomena, things as they appear to us, but we can also safely assume that there are *noumena*, things as they are in themselves. While God is noumenal and we can know nothing concerning God, this does not preclude the possibility—nay, the necessity—of religion to give social man purpose.

While not much attention has been paid to it in the professional philosophic community, Kant's discussion of *Religion within the Limits of Reason Alone* (1793) was Kant's attempt to reinstate the Lutheran theological position to primacy in Europe against the deism that had taken over in both England and the continent.

Georg Wilhelm Friedrich Hegel, 1770–1831

On the heels of Kant, stepping into the German scene was Hegel. As a young man writing *The Positivity of the Christian Religion,* Hegel argued that the religion of Jesus was essentially ethical in its orientation. This is pure Lutheran social ethics.

In *The Spirit of Christianity* Hegel critiqued Kant's theories of morality in light of the religious ethic of Jesus. His conclusion was that Kant's emphasis on duty and the domination of reason over inclination was contrary to the spirit of Jesus who taught that only a deed that is freely performed is good. Again, this is pure Luther. But Hegel derived his principles not from faith but from speculation. As Pelikan argues, "In Hegel the secularization of Lutheran theology is virtually complete."[14]

One can also argue that in the *Philosophy of History* and the *Phenomenology of Mind* Hegel was making an exposition of the Trinity. God is both transcendent but also immanent in history. It is decidedly not Lutheran, of course, that for Hegel God is the unfolding of World Spirit in history and there is no longer required a unique act of God in Jesus Christ for validation. However, the Hegelian dialectic would appear to have clear roots in the dynamic tension presented in Luther's attention to opposing theological and existential constructs, beginning with philosophy and theology but focusing on letter and spirit, law and gospel, law of nature and law of obligation, person and work, faith and love, the kingdom of Christ and the kingdom of the world, freedom and bondage, and God hidden and revealed. Ontologically, Luther saw the human as being in a constant state of nonbeing, being, and becoming. While this dialectical tension is most clearly apparent in Hegel, it is also obvious in the whole range of Lutheran-influenced German philosophers from Fichte and Schelling to Schleiermacher, Kierkegaard, and Nietzsche.[15]

Søren Kierkegaard, 1813–1855

This brings us to Søren Kierkegaard and those who followed in the existentialist tradition. As Pelikan argues, Kierkegaard recovered the mysticism or immediacy of God in Luther that was seemingly lost in Hegel's rational system that made truth external to experience. In Hegel, the individual is lost to the rational universe. There is no meaning for individual existence. In Kierkegaard, while there is no "reason" to believe that "my" life has meaning, I can affirm "my" meaningfulness through a radical leap of faith. I would contend that Kierkegaard's Leap of Faith is nothing but Luther's desperate clinging to justification by faith.

Contemporary Philosophy

It is our hope that as scholars continue to read and write about Luther in anticipation of the anniversary of the posting of the Ninety-Five Theses, as well as think about the vocation of the academy and philosophy, there will be rewarding effort invested in researching anew the published works, manuscripts, correspondence, and memoirs of the Continental philosophers. The investigation should not be limited to the few, albeit major, voices discussed here.

Finally, the goal of this book is not simply to retrace Luther's influence on past philosophers. Rather, to quote Gerhard Ebeling in his introductory lecture to Luther's thought in 1964, "The question we have to answer as we stand here before the university (community) is this: why has more attention been paid in the intellectual conflicts of the present day, particularly those which take place in the field of philosophy, to Augustine, Thomas Aquinas and Kierkegaard amongst thinkers from the past than to [Martin] Luther?"[16] Or, as more succinctly put by my dear friend, the late Heiko Oberman, following an early Sunday morning of watching American evangelical television, "The Lutheran Hour is yet to come."[17]

PART I

PHILOSOPHY AND LUTHER

CHAPTER 1

Philosophical Modes of Thought of Luther's Theology as an Object of Inquiry

Oswald Bayer
Translated by Jeffrey G. Silcock

The fact that I am not a philosopher but "only" a theologian and yet am addressing a philosophical topic is no accident. Rather, it makes palpably clear what I consider is the greatest deficiency in this area of research in the twentieth century.[1]

"Philosophy has paid no attention at all to the strong upsurge in Luther research over the last few decades—a striking sign of the strange way in which philosophy and theology . . . in Protestantism coexist in relative isolation." This is how Erwin Metzke begins his report on "Luther Research and the History of German Philosophy," which appeared in the *Journal of the German Philosophical Society*, 1934/35.[2] In 1948 the same author wrote an essay on "Sacrament and Metaphysics" that examined the state of Luther studies on the place of the bodily and material in Christian thought. The first sentence of the essay is telling: "Luther's theology on the whole was given only scant attention by philosophy, despite its profound intellectual impact."[3]

That judgment, unfortunately, is all too true. To be sure, Leibniz refers to Luther several times in his *Theodicy*,[4] Schelling expressly responds to *De Servo Arbitrio* ("The Bondage of the Will") in his treatise on human freedom,[5] and it can also be shown that Hegel's philosophy does not just pay lip service to Luther but feeds off the spirit of Luther and Lutheranism.[6] Indeed, scholars have tried to show that this is also true of the philosophy of Kant[7] and Fichte.[8] In sum, seen in the mirror of German *Geistesgeschichte*,[9] Luther is a broad field. Not only the Reformation but also the person of Luther will always be important for the history of ideas as well as for the history of philosophy, as exemplified in Wilhelm Dilthey.[10] Yet reference to Luther or discussion about him in a philosophical and systematic context that does justice to his intellectual significance is rarely found among philosophers. We find it, for example, in Arthur Schopenhauer,[11] but especially in Ludwig Feuerbach,[12] and of course, under entirely different circumstances, in Søren Kierkegaard.[13] In the twentieth century—and here dialectical theology has to accept a fair share of blame[14]—the indifference of the philosophers only increased. The few exceptions are men like Martin Heidegger,[15] Erwin Metzke, Friedrich Brunstäd,[16] and Rudolf Malter.[17]

What is the origin of this scandalous indifference that damages philosophy and theology, church and culture? Luther has been clearly labeled a despiser and enemy of thought and philosophy, apparently because of his remark that reason is a "whore."[18] Consequently, a philosopher like Karl Jaspers, who inclined to Erasmian humanism, can only sound a warning against Luther: "The atmosphere that emerges from this man is strange and philosophically noxious."[19] Karl Popper made a significant remark over dinner when he was in Tübingen to receive the Lucas prize on May 26, 1981. He told me that originally he had intended to embark on a crusade against Luther's martial-sounding phrase *mundus tumultuetur* ("the world is thrown into a state of tumult") from his *De Servo Arbitrio*[20] and to take up the cudgels for Erasmus and his *Querela Pacis* ("The Complaint of Peace," 1521).[21] But he changed his mind out of deference to the Evangelical Theological Faculty, which was responsible for awarding the prize, and decided not to proceed with his plan to launch a scathing attack against Luther. Herbert Marcuse, however, did go ahead and publish his tirade against Luther.[22]

But why should a philosopher take seriously an enemy and despiser of logic, thought, and reason? Is it not enough, if he deigns to look at him at all, to summarily dismiss him as a "misologist"[23] or, following Thomas Mann, as a "bull-necked, godly barbarian,"[24] or to say with Kurt Wuchterl, "[For] Luther, logic was a work of the devil. We are called to pray and worship, not to argue or think logically."[25]

These sorts of perceptions of Luther, where opportunities have been lost or ignored, are typical of the way in which virtually all important philosophical problems have been handled: not only the problem of the human will and its freedom or enslavement, the problem of evil, the question of the subject of a good act, the problem of epistemology (including the suspicion of projection), but also the problem of the constitution of the world and of being, the problem of ontology, the problem of the perception of space and time, and the problem of nature and history, and fundamentally the problem of the understanding of word and language.

But only through "a more thorough exploration of its historical genesis" would "philosophy necessarily arrive at the question: What aspects of an existential analysis, of an understanding of history and nature, are included in Luther's theology and what do they mean philosophically?"[26] These introductory remarks bring us closer to my assigned task.

The Task

Philosophical Modes of Thought?

"Philosophical modes of thought"! Are there also other than "philosophical" modes of thought? Are there, for instance, theological modes of thought, so that it would be necessary to define "modes of thought" more precisely by means of an adjective? Or do modes of thought fall *eo ipso* to the competence of philosophy? Is there a specifically theological way of thinking and, correspondingly, a specifically theological understanding of reality that, even though it does not follow the philosophical tradition and is in contradiction to it, would still always be a philosophical way of thinking?[27] To answer that question, we need to distinguish between Luther's explicit self-understanding and the way he actually does his theology. If the first will reclaim the modes of thought mentioned below as genuinely theological, then a study of the latter will show how fundamentally these modes of thought are in fact indebted to an engagement with philosophy.

Furthermore, it is not clear what is meant by "mode of thought" (*Denkform*). The conceptual history of the term in the German *Historical Dictionary of Philosophy*—which characteristically begins in 1787 with an examination of Kant's theory of the categories—concludes with the following statement that leaves us completely in the dark when it comes to defining our task: "At the present time, the term 'mode of thought' no longer has any conceptual precision. Today, it is used uncritically to designate various sorts of things and serves especially to describe styles of thought, mindsets, thinking techniques or methods of thought."[28] Be that as it may, the rest of the title of this lecture is fairly clear. It speaks of Luther's "theology," not just his "philosophy." It also speaks about the modes of thought of "the" theology of Luther, not only the modes of thought "in" Luther's theology. Finally, these modes of thought, whatever we understand them to be, need to be viewed as an "object" of inquiry, not as a "subject"[29] of inquiry or as a lens for viewing the data, as important and appealing as that might be to consider.

The stated task, as I understand it, is to inquire into the modes of thought of Luther's theology as identified by the history of philosophy, particularly those that are thoroughly characteristic of his theology and that are so essential to it that we could not imagine his theology without them.

Orientation to Aristotle's "Organon"

On the way to explaining what is to be understood by "mode of thought," I want to take my bearings from an institution: the arts faculty and its seven liberal arts, which had a lasting effect on the Master of Arts (*magister artium*) Martin Luther. The liberal arts include dialectics and philosophy, which Luther, however, did not want to see isolated from rhetoric and grammar. In fact, he gave grammar first place in the trivium.[30] For Luther, philosophy, and the questions it poses, is no mere accessory or ornament that decorates his life and work; nor is it a ballast that he would have to jettison. For him it is simply essential. A glance at a representative text, such as the theses for the "Disputation concerning Man" of 1536,[31] shows that Luther articulates his theology in close partnership with philosophy. This engagement with philosophy is not something secondary but constitutive.

The theses for the "Disputation concerning Man" are representative of Luther's entire theology and its philosophical modes of thought. In fact, they show that the philosophical tradition in which Luther is most at home, and that he affirms as well as negates, is the Aristotelian. Not that other traditions do not also have significance! We only have to think of the neo-Platonic tradition of the *via negationis*[32] or the way that Luther occasionally praises Plato himself.[33] Yet these other traditions, apart from the fundamental importance of the *via negationis* for the pre-Reformation Luther, are not as determinative for his theology as the Aristotelian traditions.

That it is necessary to speak of Aristotelian traditions in the plural, and in what sense, has been carefully shown by Theodor Dieter, who is himself both a philosopher and a theologian, in his *magnum opus, Der junge Luther und Aristoteles*.[34] The Aristotle that Luther refers to proves to be

> a multifaceted entity. Since Luther refers to the Aristotle that can be found in his works (today), and to the Aristotle that has been received and transformed by philosophy, as well as to the Aristotle of Scholasticism that been integrated with theology, his relation to "Aristotle," from a critically distanced perspective, can only be described by a *series of antitheses with different referents*. These forms of "Aristotle" differ from one other in somewhat far-reaching ways, despite the obvious commonalties; even a grave criticism of Aristotle in the Middle Ages can appear as an interpretation.[35] If we ignore this diversity and simply speak of "Aristotle" without any further qualification, we will be dealing with an abstract entity devoid of any specificity (which is gained through a particular context of thought).[36]

The institution, the basic university education in "dialectics" within the trivium, thus Aristotle's "Organon," produces a perspective that we cannot sidestep. The "Organon" begins with the Categories. These are the instruments for thinking and for bringing something into language as something. After the Categories comes the theory of the sentence: Περὶ ἑρμηνείας ("On Interpretation"). The third is the theory of the conclusion and demonstration (First and Second Analytic; I take both analytics together as a third).[37]

Apropos these first three parts of the "Organon," which are the main parts, I now propose to answer the question (which up till this point I have not yet answered): What could be meant concretely by "philosophical modes of thought" in the distinction between three levels of different meaning for Luther's theology? First, as far as the "Categories" are concerned, his denial of the validity of substance ontology in the areas of trinitarian theology, Christology, and soteriology, as well as its "regional"[38] affirmation, should be considered "an object of inquiry." Second, as far as the "sentence" is concerned, the linguistic-theological or linguistic-philosophical version of Luther's fundamental criticism of substance ontology in the fields of trinitarian theology, Christology, and soteriology should become a topic for discussion. In my judgment, these are the two most important "theological modes of thought" as well as the two most important "philosophical modes of thought." In brief and in sum, this is just another way of speaking of Luther's *ontological hermeneutic* or his *hermeneutical ontology*.

Third, Luther uses "modes of thought" that are different again, especially in his disputations, above all in dealing with figures of conclusion and types of demonstration. These have been examined especially by Graham White[39] but also by Heikki Kirjavainen,[40] Simo Knuuttila,[41] Reijo Työrinoja,[42] and others in their works on the history of philosophy, which are characterized by different ways of receiving the Aristotelian tradition.

In my stipulative definition of "modes of thought," I must take up at least two further aspects of this term, found throughout Luther's theology, besides the three just mentioned in connection with Aristotle's "Organon." First, there is the concept of movement and becoming,[43] which took shape in Luther's reception of the idea of motion in Aristotle's "Physics." Second, we must attend to the peculiar concept of knowledge, which can be explicated in relation to the Aristotelian teaching on the soul, Περὶ ψυῆς (*De anima*, especially book III).[44]

The final and most important part of this essay, which now follows, has five sections. These correspond to the five elements of my stipulative definition of the "modes of philosophical thought of Luther's theology." I would like to make a point of stressing that this approach is meant to provoke an attempt at falsification. Anyone who can demonstrate that there are more important "philosophical modes of thought of Luther's theology" that cannot be made to fit the five we have mentioned, or that fit them only with difficulty, will have achieved the falsification required by science.

The Execution

The final five sections correspond to the five elements of my stipulative definition of the "modes of philosophical thought of Luther's theology." This approach is meant to provoke an attempt at falsification. Anyone who can demonstrate that there are more important "philosophical modes of thought of Luther's theology" that cannot be made to fit the five we have mentioned, or that fit them only with difficulty, will have achieved the falsification required by science.

1. Substance and Relational Ontology

A relational ontology[45] as well as the concept of "being as communion"[46] are not characteristic of Luther as such. What is characteristic, rather, is the *distinction* Luther makes between the trinitarian-theological, christological, and soteriological realms, in which we do not think at all "in the category of substance but of relation"[47] and the realm in which the "being-in-itself" of the thing, and therefore substance ontology, prevails.[48] The fundamental difference between Luther and the post-Christian natural theology—especially a *theologia crucis naturalis*—typical of Hegel[49] on this decisive point cannot be emphasized clearly and sharply enough. He is hardly ever mentioned in contemporary mainstream theological discourse but rather is glossed over and forgotten. Today, therefore, there is no awareness of a monumental mistake in the recent history of philosophy and theology, which I have tried to draw attention to since my inaugural lecture at Bonn.[50]

In this connection I also have to criticize the otherwise commendable and remarkable works of the Roman philosopher Stefano Leoni.[51] Following in the footsteps of Enrico De Negri,[52] he takes relational and communal ontology in the sense of a single, universal, and consistent concept of being and rejects a "regional" ontology, which, in my opinion, Luther supports.[53]

2. *"Extremorum compositio"*[54]

Besides the mentioned distinction between substance and relational ontology, there is a specific linguistic-theological or linguistic-philosophical form of the relational or communal ontology characteristic of Luther's theology and its philosophical mode of thought.[55] On the surface, this linguistic form of Luther's ontology looks very similar to Hegel's "speculative sentence"[56] and his concept of the "concrete spirit,"[57] but it is of a different type, as can be shown from linguistic philosophy,[58] as for example in the later Wittgenstein.[59]

If we compare the facts to be considered in this second subsection to the second part of Aristotle's "Organon," where he writes about the sentence (Περὶ ἑρμηνείας), then we can see at once the contrast between Luther's explanations of the union of God and humanity, as well as bread and body, which are highly significant for theology and linguistic philosophy, and the λόγος ἀποφαντικός, the declarative sentence (or proposition). The sentence "this is my body" is not a declarative sentence, at least not semantically and pragmatically, and therefore, according to Aristotelian logic, it is not capable of being true.[60] With this promise and gift, two entities clearly separate from each other without the word that unites them are joined together, indeed united, into one. The body, however, is not "declared"[61] or signified by the bread. Luther is able to prove that a nonapophantic sentence is true, not only by referring to the linguistic usage of the Bible but also to ordinary language. He appeals to the reason inherent in the general use of language. This is a concrete example of Luther's correction to traditional Aristotelian logic and at the same time an example of his demonstration, based on grammar and rhetoric, that a sentence that is not a declarative sentence is capable of being true.[62]

The union of the dissimilar, which is most remarkable also philosophically, is not found *before* the reformational turn in Luther's theology.[63] Anyone who tries to determine the christological dimension of the reformational concept of *promissio* will see the constitutive role played by the promise in Reformation Christology and the way that it is closely interwoven with the new understanding of the Lord's Supper. The fact is that Luther discovered his reformational Christology and his reformational understanding of the Lord's Supper at the same time.[64]

The simultaneity of God and humanity, life and death, forgiveness and sin that the church proclaims in the public, oral, external "bodily" word speaks against a secret identity of these antitheses or of an immanent peripety. At this point philosophy and theology go their separate ways. For philosophy can think of the simultaneity only analytically, not synthetically (and if synthetically, then speculatively or existentially but not linguistically and concretely). It understands the "sign" as a representation of an absence, not the presentation of a presence. For "a philosophical sign is the mark of a thing that is absent; a theological sign is the mark of a thing that is present."[65]

The promise is the medium in which the *vere homo* and the *vere Deus* are inseparably united. This means the *est* that mediates the *vere homo* and the *vere Deus*—God's life and Jesus' death—cannot be understood predicatively or apophantically. It does not declare the meaning of an already fixed subject but is the movement in which the reality of both is established at the same time. It does not mean a significative copula but an effective one, in fact a synthetic one. If the natures need the *promissio* as a copula, then the copula in turn is determined solely by the natures—hence, Luther's identification of *verbum* and Christ himself as *Verbum*. What the *promissio*, the *verbum*, is, it is only as the presence of the *Verbum* in which God is human. All our christological speech about the *unio personalis* would for its part degenerate into a mere intellectual game or be nothing but a cipher for the hidden true nature of every human being, if we were to forget that it is nothing but the contemplation of that event that enters constitutively into the realm of the bodily word, which is both oral and public.

In this connection, we could investigate a remarkably seldom-asked question in Luther research: How does Luther, who before 1518 denied the world, arrive at his concept of worldliness and the essential worldly mediation of all spiritual reality?[66] For the "hermeneutical" form of the relational and communal ontology has to be characterized as a "bodily word" if considered from the standpoint of Christology and sacramental theology. Johann Georg Hamann can open our eyes to this, for instance, with his formula: creation is an "address to the creature through the creature."[67] If we read Luther through this lens, we will be surprised to discover what creation theology, specifically its ontological dimension, really means for his theology.[68]

3. Techniques of the Disputation

What would normally be set out here has already been briefly hinted at above.[69]

4. "*Semper in motu*": Becoming

Especially instructive for our topic is Luther's engagement with the Aristotelian theory of motion.[70] Since, as Luther sees it, sin is not completely driven out by grace in the blink of an eye, he comes to realize that a Christian has to be righteous and a sinner at the same time, and he has to give a new answer to the question of the duration of a person's existence in grace, since the concepts of *qualitas* and *habitus* are now no longer available to him. Luther understands the being of the justified as the motion of becoming justified.

Since the scholastic reception modified the Aristotelian theory of motion in many ways, it is only after a study of the reception of this theory in Thomas Aquinas and Ockham that we can say exactly which Aristotle Luther receives here and how he has modified him in the process: it is the Aristotle interpreted by Ockham. Luther now integrates the two motions that are strictly distinguished among the scholastics—the instantaneous movement from the existence of the sinner to the existence of the righteous (*e contrario in contrarium*) and the movement of the *augmentum gratiae seu caritatis*—and interprets them by means of the Ockhamist theory of motion. In this way we can understand a motion, also the intensification of a quality, as an infinite variety of moments of motion that are characterized by a combination of affirmations and negations. Against Ockham's intentions, but by his means, Luther explains being righteous as a growth of the believer and *at the same time* a constant transition from the being of the sinner to the being of the righteous. For being righteous, understood as motion, is the unity of the motions of fundamental importance. This presupposes the unity of time whose linguistic signal is the very frequent *semper*. The phrase *proficere est semper incipere* ("to progress is always to begin again") should never be understood, as often happens, to mean that the Christian always has to begin anew, like Sisyphus, from the same starting point. The phrase is almost a definition of motion and means that every point of motion as such is the endpoint of the preceding motion and the starting point of the further motion. The main point of the phrase is that the Christian should never cease from moving.

Also, the *partim–partim* phrase arises from the Aristotelian tradition: the object moved may be partly at the beginning (*partim in termino a quo*) and partly at the end (*partim in termino ad quem*). Luther adopts an Ockhamist interpretation of this phrase that deviates from the Aristotelian understanding: the object moved stands simultaneously under an affirmation and under a negation or an infinite number of negations (further moments of motion). Thus, the *partim–partim* is not in competition with the *simul* of being righteous and being sinner, even if Luther's use of the phrase is not uniform.

5. Luther's Reception of Aristotelian Epistemology

The idea, developed in the Aristotelian tradition, that a knowing subject (*Erkennendes*) and a known object (*Erkanntes*) are one, offers Luther the model of a nonsubstantial unity of a believer and the word that still permits us to declare: we are the word.[71] Also, the fact that the person who becomes the word is nothing in his or her own eyes can be accounted for by this model. It is evident from this that Luther at any given time takes up only those aspects of an Aristotelian idea that can clarify the theological matter to be considered without ever worrying about the consistency of the various aspects among themselves.

In these last two sections I have presented the results of the groundbreaking research of Theodor Dieter. His work *Der junge Luther und Aristoteles: Eine historisch-systematische Untersuchung zum Verhältnis von Theologie und Philosophie*[72] marks a new chapter in Luther research and, more specifically, makes a significant contribution to our question concerning the philosophical modes of thought of Luther's theology.

CHAPTER 2

Does Luther Have a "Waxen Nose"?

Historical and Philosophical Contextualizations of Luther

Christine Helmer

Luther's influence on the history of Western intellectual thought is, as the essays in this volume demonstrate, monumental. What would the Enlightenment be without Luther's radical notion of freedom (in Christ)? How might modern theories of subjectivity look without Luther's characterization of the self as existing simultaneously before God and others? How might contemporary secularization have developed without Luther's advocacy for worldly vocation and the common priesthood? The genealogy of Western modernity requires looking seriously at Luther, whose ideas extended far beyond his own preoccupation with religious and political matters, more than even he could ever have fathomed.

If Luther's effects on philosophy, culture, and the "modern temper" are significant, is there any relevance in studying how he was affected by the philosophical, cultural questions of his own early-sixteenth-century milieu? The question concerning the philosophical and culturing shaping of Luther's own ideas seems to undermine the claim of novelty concerning Luther's contributions to Western history. Yet this question is just as important as the question addressing the ways in which Luther's contributions have been contextualized philosophically in the history of the modern West. I begin with the recent developments in studies of Luther's thought that have contextualized his ideas in historical continuity with medieval philosophy. I then turn to "philosophical contextualizations" in order to show how different philosophical conceptualities frame Luther's thought in quite different ways. Both contextualizations underline the main point that the task of interpreting Luther requires self-critical attention to what the historical Luther has to say to us today.

Historical Contextualization of the Philosophical Luther

Happily, Luther scholarship over the past twenty years has taken steps to distinguish what Luther said from what he meant. The search for the "historical Luther" has contextualized Luther's thought in late-medieval spirituality, philosophy, and theology.

The result is a historical Luther who looks more medieval, more Catholic, more mystical, and more philosophically astute than before.[1] One contributing element to this development has been the attention paid to Luther's disputations. The disputation was one of two academic genres in the medieval university (the other being the academic lecture, which Luther used as the genre for his many commentaries on Scripture). The disputation is the genre that issued the earliest intimations of the Reformation; the Ninety-Five Theses from 1517 were an invitation to academic disputation. Luther continued to use this form right up to his last doctoral disputation, that of Petrus Hegemon in 1545, a few months before his death. The theses of Luther's various disputations and transcripts of actual encounters between respondent (*respondens*) and opponent (*opponens*) provide detailed evidence for Luther's working out of philosophical, historical-theological, and doctrinal issues in the language of the medieval intellectual elite.[2] Luther's use of Latin, his deployment of disputation's rules, and the process by which he applied the philosophical tools of logic, semantics, and metaphysics to a specific theological issue are aspects of Luther's philosophical knowledge and agility, on the one hand, and of his medieval inheritance, on the other. Graham White's pathbreaking work on doctrines in Luther's mature disputations, Theodor Dieter's study of Luther's in-depth relationship with Aristotle in the "Heidelberg Disputations" (1518), and my own investigation of Luther's use of William of Ockham's debates with Duns Scotus in articulating the doctrine of the Trinity show how Luther's thinking is characterized by distinct philosophical commitments.[3] The disputations reveal remarkable variety in Luther's appeals to philosophy. As further studies of the genre of disputation are undertaken, a more detailed picture of issue-specific continuity with, correction of, and elaboration of late-medieval philosophy will emerge.

The more historically useful attitude to Luther's approach to philosophy has likewise been the result of taking Luther's venomous polemics against philosophy with a few grains of late-medieval salt. The historical Luther's education at the University of Erfurt was a standard course as a *baccalaureus*. Luther would have studied the seven liberal arts (*artes liberales*)—the *trivium* was composed of logic, grammar, and rhetoric, and the *quadrivium* of geometry, arithmetic, music, and astronomy. This basic undergraduate education was in "philosophy" and preceded the study of the three higher (or postgraduate) programs in theology, jurisprudence, and medicine. Given the philosophical curriculum of his undergraduate years, Luther's later and allegedly negative evaluations of philosophy cannot be read in terms of a simple binary opposition between theology and philosophy, competing against each other for the sole truth of a subject matter. Rather, the rhetorical opposition must be interpreted as Luther's plea for distinguishing between a theological perspective that has Trinity and incarnation as its subject matter and a philosophical perspective that is preoccupied with temporal beings. Once the subject is appropriately circumscribed, then further theological work consists of selecting and applying the relevant rational tools in order to describe and analyze the subject matter. Luther's "Disputa-tion concerning the Passage: 'The Word Was Made Flesh (John 1:14)'" (1539) is often cited in support of his insistence on a fundamental antipathy between theology and philosophy. The second thesis sets the subject matter of the disputation, Christ's incarnation, in this light: "In theology it is true that the Word is made flesh; in philosophy the statement is simply impossible and absurd" (LW 38:239). Yet on a closer look, this thesis only initially circumscribes Christology as a correctly theolog-ical subject matter. The disputation's transcript shows that Luther goes on to ana-lyze in detail the appropriate application of philosophical resources both to philosophical and theological subjects. Christology is properly theological, but this designation in no way precludes philosophy in order to understand it.

Luther did not break with the intellectual commitment to reason as deployed in the service of understanding that he had inherited. Yet how can his fierce polemic pitting faith against reason be interpreted? After all, Luther did say that speculation in matters of faith would result in certain death by neck fracture.[4] One way to make sense of Luther's more outrageous claims privileging simple faith over convoluted reason is to see Luther against the backdrop of a specific medieval trajectory. The intellectual background to Luther's own thinking was nominalism, a late-medieval philosophical development, owing its origin to the English Franciscan William of Ockham. Ockham diverged from the Scholastic philosophical theory of universals by assigning universals to the mind. Mental concepts, rather than "forms" that co-exist with matter in really existing beings, constitute universals. Luther's own philo-sophical training at the University of Erfurt was in Ockham's *via moderna*, which was presented in opposition to the *via antiqua* of Dominican philosopher theologians Thomas Aquinas and Duns Scotus. Some of Luther's polemic against philosophy may be read as his participation in the late-medieval battle between two rival schools of thought.

A central subject of particular relevance to Luther's polemic had to do with the type of reason that can be applied to matters of faith. Where Scotus, to refer to a debate that Luther reiterated in a disputation on the Trinity, articulated proposi-tions concerning the formal and real distinctions in the inner Trinity, Ockham was able to claim only that the persons are "absolute things" (*res absoluta*), leaving aside the matter of what that meant to "the saints."[5] For Ockham—and subsequently for Luther—reason was capable of delineating the basic contours of theology's subject matter and of providing its elementary vocabulary. Further rational inquiry into the eternal nature of divine mysteries would consist of the category mistake between temporally structured human reason and the divine rationality that transcends time. Luther's commitment to reason in the sense of its minimal capacities for distin-guishing and identifying should be read in light of the increasing bifurcation be-tween reason and faith evident in the Scotus-Ockham trajectory. Luther contributes to this discussion by assigning faith to the personal terms of individual spiritual confidence in God's justification. Reason for Luther must be excluded from justification, as that activity is God's alone; it is not to be excluded from a person's understanding about God's agency, the reason for God's justifying activity, and the human attitude of receptivity. Reason is certainly not to be excluded from theology. The changing views in the Scotus-Luther trajectory concerning reason's capacities and limits ultimately pave the way for modern understandings of rationality. Confidence in metaphysical reason waned, but other aspects of knowing, such as empiricism, the significance of nonrational subjective contributions to knowledge, and plural epistemologies came to characterize the modern view of the relation of self to world and God.

So far: a historical investigation of the ways in which Luther's understanding of philosophy are contextualized by his own late-medieval milieu has helped us distinguish between Luther's polemic and his own philosophical habits. The historical Luther is required for understanding the philosophical Luther. Further careful work is needed in this area for a more comprehensive and complex picture of the philosophical Luther to emerge.

If historical contextualization can help us to know better the philosophical Luther, then what about the other way around? In other words, what about the philosophical frameworks operative in the history of Luther interpretation? Current consensus in epistemology holds that interpretative frameworks are constitutive of knowledge. Could it not be that philosophical commitments inform the way the historical Luther is viewed?

Philosophical Contextualization of the Historical Luther

If thinking were a static enterprise, then it would be easy to pin down the philosophical Luther historically. But thinking is dynamic. The past is constantly and dynamically related to the present. Figures from the past move and breathe in relation to investigating subjects, who themselves exist in moving time. In the case of a larger-than-historical figure such as Luther, a twin set of interpretative moves results in a nonstatic portrayal. Luther's effect on others is studied by a history of effects (*Wirkungsgeschichte*), while subjective individual and cultural conceptualities can critically be studied as they shape Luther's later reception (*Rezeptionsgeschichte*). In view of the latter, the question concerning Luther and philosophy is how philosophical and cultural interpretative dynamics have shaped the ways in which the "historical" Luther is viewed. To put this another way, Luther's waxen philosophical nose is due in part to retroactive shaping.

One example will help shed light on the contrast when different theologians interpret the same topic. Luther's hidden God (*Deus absconditus*) has fascinated, even terrified, theologians throughout the centuries. Its impact can be compared across generations of Luther interpreters, sometimes yielding surprisingly different results. The striking contrast in understanding this notion between Albrecht Ritschl (1822–1889) and current-day German theologian Oswald Bayer is a good example of this divergence. Ritschl grants the hidden God's negligible status in Luther's theology; Bayer takes it seriously as a crucial aspect of Luther's doctrine of God. The reason for the difference between these two interpretations is not solely Luther's rhetoric. Rather, different interpretations have to do with the subjective framing on the parts of interpreters' philosophical and cultural commitments. The difference in this case begins with a neo-Kantian perspective.

The theologian emblematic of a neo-Kantian interpretation of Luther is Albrecht Ritschl. Under the influence of neo-Kantianism, Ritschl situates aspects of Luther's thought into a particular philosophical mold. Justification (*Rechtfertigung*), for Ritschl, is rendered in the neo-Kantian understanding of spirit's victory over nature that effects a subsequent step, "reconciliation" (*Versöhnung*), which gives evidence of this fundamental change in circumstance. Ritschl's prohibition of a mystical account of justification coheres with his rejection of a "substance metaphysic."[6] For Ritschl, subjective change must be empirically perceivable. A theology that does justice to Kant's modern philosophical restriction of experience to perception must explain God's activity in the heart of the human believer without recourse to occult and imperceptible realities. Ritschl demonstrates a characteristic Lutheran indebtedness to Kant on this issue of the soul's noumenal status and makes the same claims for the hidden aspect of the divine nature. The God who is "exlex," who is "bound by no law . . . is the motto of Scotism and of Nominalism adopted by Luther," Ritschl complains.[7] The ascription of hiddenness smuggles metaphysical error into the doctrine of God. By this Ritschl means that a metaphysical account of an occult reality with no perceptible effects is illegitimate on neo-Kantian grounds. It is philosophically more acceptable and theologically more indicative of Luther's true reformation intention to determine God by viewing the effects of divine agency. God's love is revealed in God's work of justifying the sinner. There is no philosophical need or theological benefit in appealing to hiddenness here. If Luther had been conceptually consistent in his doctrine of justification, Ritschl argues, he would have excised the dangerous idea of divine hiddenness, and Ritschl, who saw himself as "completing" Luther's Reformation, performed this theological surgery.

Oswald Bayer, in contrast, assigns to the divine hiddenness a constitutive role in Luther's theology. The *Deus absconditus* is the "referent" of particular experiences of human existence: suffering, evil, and death cry out for explanation, says Bayer, but are met with brutal and terrifying silence. These are the experiences that merit talk of God's hiddenness. Hiddenness is sharply counterposed with revelation. Bayer assigns two words, law and gospel, to the *Deus revelatus*. The complete content of revelation is the Trinity; the triune God who justifies the sinner is the unquestionable "God of the gospel." Yet the trinitarian God of the gospel is dynamically related to the trinitarian God of the law, the incomplete revelation of God's judgment on human works that is necessarily and only completed in the gospel. When Bayer situates the relation between *Deus absconditus* and *Deus revelatus* in his systematic representation of Luther's theology, he does so by separating that aspect of God that remains silent when the "why" of existential evil is cried out from the divine twofold speech in law and gospel. The result is that divine hiddenness is assigned to the systematic locus of the *"general teaching about God, to be distinguished from the teaching about the Trinity, describes the non-Christian person."*[8] Although it is unclear what Bayer means here in an empirical sense, he moves on to include non-Christians together with "the experience of every single one of us" when confronted with inexplicable suffering and evil.[9] Human nature does not recognize God as revealed in either law or gospel. Hiddenness means crushing silence—no comfort, no cross.

Bayer's position on the necessary placement of hiddenness in the systematic doctrine of God is shaped by particular philosophical commitments. Like Ritschl, Bayer rejects the applicability of the metaphysical category of substance to Luther's God. Luther's God is too dynamic, according to Bayer, too alive, to be pressed into the metaphysical mold of an eternal, unchanging essence. Bayer can resort to the terminology of a "change, a turning, in fact: an unheard overthrow (Hos. 11:8)" to argue that Luther explodes the Greek notion of an enduring essence with the biblical-prophetic idea of a God who changes from wrath to love.[10] The biblical language of change is to be taken literally. The metaphysic that is required by the distinct theological subject matter represents a new development in philosophy.

Yet metaphysics is still inadequate to capture Bayer's philosophical commitments. The conceptuality structuring his work is the philosophy of language, particularly indebted to speech-act theory. The three distinct aspects of God—law, gospel, hiddenness—are categorized from the speech-act theoretical perspective. The Trinity's complete revelation of mercy is spoken in the present tense in the promise that also contains the fulfillment of forgiveness. The incomplete but necessary revelation of God's judgment on sin is spoken in the word of law. God's hiddenness, in contrast, is not referred to any speech; it is silence. Bayer takes seriously the *Deus absconditus* as the reality of the absence of speech. Bayer could have moved in the direction indicated by Ritschl, meaning he could have subscribed to a metaphysic of effect. This would have precluded positing an occult reality in the absence of effects. Instead, Bayer refers silence to the reality of hiddenness. There are two distinct realities of God in this account: the Trinity and the reality referred to by a "general anthropology" that cannot be identified with the Trinity. Bayer formulates his position against those theologians who attempt to preserve a metaphysical unity to the Trinity in relation to a hidden divine aspect: "It is one of the grandiose blunders of the more recent history of both philosophy and theology that an attempt has been made to conceptualize this almighty nature theologically as trinitarian."[11] The result of Bayer's preserving the hidden God from trinitarian determination is a metaphysical dualism that cannot be resolved, at least on this side of heaven. The Trinity as the sole identification of the Christian God with speech and gospel is metaphysically distinct from the hidden God who is silent when the psalmist cries out, "How long?" (Ps. 13:1). This hiddenness is terrifying in its systematic-theological necessity.

My point is not so much to adjudicate between more or less correct interpretations of Luther. Rather, it is to emphasize the fact that interpretations of Luther are themselves contextualized philosophically. Scholarship cannot definitively give us the historical Luther. At best, we can use historical tools to get at Luther's philosophy, and conversely, we can use philosophical knowledge in order to get at reasons for why interpretations of Luther are the way they are. Whether neo-Kantian, language-philosophical, or classic metaphysical, philosophical contextualizations of the present engage with the past in order to yield knowledge.

Conclusion

Thinking appropriately about the past requires a critical perspective. When studying a historical figure as rhetorically explosive and intellectually influential as Luther, careful attention must be paid to the historical Luther. Scholarly care in recent years for Luther in his historical setting has resulted, as shown here, in detailed studies outlining his philosophical commitments and his furthering of philosophical questions. Yet attention to the past must also be critical of the present as well as self-reflective. Interpretations of Luther shaped by philosophical and cultural commitments and scholarly results implicitly convey these commitments. A critical consideration of both the historical Luther's philosophical practices that lie beneath his rhetoric and the philosophical conceptualities that his interpreters bring along with their questions informs the methodologically responsible approach to Luther today.

Perhaps the best way to promote the ethics of Luther scholarship is to dedicate one's scholarly efforts to historical and philosophical contextualizations. By this, a lively conversation with this figure from the past who continues, in our conversations with him, to speak to the present can carry on. And maybe we can discover something that we have not noticed before.

CHAPTER 3

"Putting on the Neighbor"

The Ciceronian Impulse in Luther's Christian Approach to Practical Reason

Gary M. Simpson

Everyone should "put on" his neighbor and so conduct himself toward him as if he himself were in the other's place.[1]

Cicero was the wisest man.[2]

What has long been noticed but little analyzed is Luther's relationship with his "beloved Cicero," as one interpreter has again recently remarked.[3] I will explore a key feature of Cicero's relationship with his philosophical predecessors in order to highlight one reason for Luther's love affair with this "wisest man." The twinkle in Luther's eye makes good sense when we consider Cicero's peculiar wisdom within the context of Luther's christological formulation of Christian love as "putting on" one's neighbor. In particular, Cicero's innovation in the Greek rhetorical tradition provided Luther with a kind of philosophical venture capital for his christologically tinged approach to practical reason.

Faith and Practical Reason

Luther's "The Freedom of a Christian" remains a mother lode for the intricate and richly textured relationships of faith, love, and practical reason, which were much contested in Luther's day and before, as in our own.[4] Indeed, in the very last paragraph he summarizes the predicament that confronts practical reason[5] or "natural reason," as he calls it there.[6] When the ubiquitous questions of our moral life arise, practical reason becomes "superstitious." That is, practical reason erroneously presumes the quite commonly held "opinion," which moreover is "trained and confirmed . . . by the practice of all earthly lawgivers," that its calling is to lead us toward righteousness in God's sight, toward justification.[7] Luther sought to emancipate practical reason from such "false opinions concerning works, that is, from the foolish presumption that justification is acquired by works"[8] by having us "*theodidacti*, that is, those taught by God [John 6:45]."[9]

In Luther's *Lectures on Galatians* (1531, 1536), he promulgates the first com-mandment of his theology, so to speak: *ne confundatur mores et fides* ("let not moral-ity and faith be confounded")—"both are necessary, but both must be kept within their limits." As he notes in a 1522 sermon:

> [I]t is necessary to make a distinction between God and men, between spiritual and temporal things. In human af-fairs man's judgment suffices. For these things, he needs no light but that of reason. . . . But in divine things, the things concerning God, and in which we must conduct ourselves acceptably with him and must secure [eternal] happiness for ourselves, human nature is absolutely blind, staring stone-blind, unable to recognize in the slightest degree what these things are.[10]

Luther emphasizes that this distinction between the passive righteousness of faith and the active righteousness of love and reason is "easy to speak of," but "in experience and practice it is the most difficult of all, even if you exercise and practice it diligently."[11] When reason trespasses its terrestrial limits, aspiring to occupy the throne in matters of salvation, Luther's rhetoric is unsparing. Reason, so enthroned, transmogrifies into "the lovely whore," the "arch-prostitute," "the Devil's whore," and the "Devil's bride."[12] For this reason, exclaims Luther in his "Disputation against Scholastic Theology," "Virtually the entire [*Ni-comachean*] *Ethics* of Aristotle is the worst enemy of grace. This in opposition to the scholastics."[13]

As we will see, a Ciceronian form of practical reason, when—like love—formed by faith in Christ, can render a salutary service to the Christian love of neighbor.[14] Practical reason, when formed by faith, shares characteristics akin to Luther's famous "reason illumined by faith" that grasps the beauty and joy of that "fortunate exchange,"[15] which "couples Christ and me more intimately than a husband is coupled to his wife."[16] Here we encounter forms of "another reason," of an emancipated reason that Luther calls "the reason of faith."[17] The purpose, therefore, of the Christian vocation to rightly distinguish faith and reason in ex-perience and practice is so that in everyday life they might be rightly related and coordinated. Cicero's oratorical model of practical reason made it a ready candi-date for such coordination. Before turning to it we will attend briefly to Luther's cruciform communion Christology and its ramifications for the relationship of faith and good works of neighbor love.

"Putting On" the Neighbor

Luther sought to reestablish the relationship between faith and love and thus to undo the distorted relationship that had come to dominate medieval piety expressed theologically in Aquinas's formula, "faith formed by love." Luther claimed, to put it briefly, that Christian living is doubly ecstatic. Christians live "beyond" themselves in a twofold way: "a Christian lives not in himself, but in Christ and in his neighbor. . . . He lives in Christ through faith, in his neighbor through love."[18] Faith, whose form is Christ himself,[19] is our all-sufficient sociality in relationship with God, and love is our all-sufficient sociality in relationship with neighbors.[20] Indeed, it is the sufficiency of faith in Christ, this "living 'spring of water welling up to eternal life' [John 4:14],"[21] that begets love's sufficiency in relationship with neighbors. Because "every good tree produces good fruit" [Matt. 7:17],[22] therefore, "[l]ove is true and genuine where there is true and genuine faith."[23]

Christian love entails that "the good things we have from God should flow from one to the other and be common to all."[24] In this earthly commonwealth formed by love, the explicit focus lies on "what I see is necessary, profitable, and salutary to my neighbor."[25] While love, overflowing from faith, provides the willing spontaneity to meet the neighbors' and their neighborhoods' needs, it does not yet by itself provide the moral epistemology, so to speak, for how one discerns these needs and what will meet them. Historically, such discernment is the calling, service, and capacities that practical reason provides for love, provisions of which Luther is quite aware.[26]

Luther employs the oft-used biblical, and Pauline, metaphor of "put on," as with clothing, relative to our neighbors. Indeed, we "put on" Christ (Rom. 13:14) in our baptisms (Gal. 3:27) because in Luther's cruciform sociality Christ has "so 'put on' us and acted for us as if he had been what we are,"[27] that is, sufferers and sinners.[28] More so yet, Christ's putting on sufferers and sinners furnishes both the possibility and the form of a Christian's putting on one's neighbor "as if he himself were in the other's place."[29] We become "Christ to my neighbor," "Christ to the other," "Christs to one another"[30] by putting on their life-world, sharing their place, attending to their needs from within their situation. Here Luther's exploration of cruciform communion Christology emits a moral epistemological imagination, so to speak, for practical reason.

The Love Affair with Cicero

Luther had high regard for "worldly wisdom" relative to the moral life.[31] God "writes it [God's moral wisdom and law] upon the hearts of all human beings . . . [and] from this natural knowledge have originated all the books of the more sensible philosophers, such as Aesop, Aristotle, Plato, Xenophon, Cicero, and Cato."[32] Indeed, God

> is a gentle and wealthy Lord. He casts much gold, silver, wealth, dominions, and kingdoms among the godless, as though it were chaff or sand. Thus he casts great intelligence, wisdom, languages, and oratorical ability among them, too, so that His dear Christians look like mere children, fools, and beggars by comparison.[33]

In his *Lectures on Genesis*, Luther also reveals his own preference for worldly wisdom: "Let the older ones learn Cicero, to whom, to my surprise, some prefer Aristotle as a teacher of morals."[34] Already in his first appointment at the University of Wittenberg (October, 1508–March, 1509) he had lectured four hours a day on Aristotle's *Nicomachean Ethics* for a course on moral theology. He always held Book 5—justice and *epieikeia*—and Book 6—prudence—of *Nicomachean Ethics* in high regard, but he still considered Cicero "supreme in human wisdom."[35] "Aristotle's [*Nicomachean*] *Ethics* is fair," he confessed, "but Cicero's *Offices* [*On Duties*] is better."[36] It is no accident, then, that even in his last preserved written words Luther cites Cicero.[37] Here we will examine one aspect of Cicero's work—there are others—that endeared him to Luther: oratory and civic life.

Oratory and Civic Life

The first Ciceronian impulse for Luther's approach to practical reason resides in the civic vocation of Cicero's innovative understanding of rhetoric. Here we will probe three facets of Ciceronian rhetoric that are crucial (there are others): the bond of wisdom and eloquence, the vocation of oratory in civic life, and the relationship between oratory and consent. Cicero took on the dispute between Plato and the sophists who both, though from opposite points of view, held to the incompatibility of philosophy, reason, and wisdom, on the one hand, and rhetoric, on the other. From his earliest reflections as a twenty-year-old or so to his last book written in the year that he died, Cicero sought to heal the breach inherited from the Greeks between philosophy and rhetoric, between reason and speech, between wisdom and eloquence. This was an artificial, indeed illusory breach, he argued, that undermined his own lifelong aspirations for a republican basis of society. "Wisdom without eloquence leads to very little of value for civic bodies, while eloquence without wisdom for the most part performs in an excessive fashion and leads to nothing," he claims in *On Invention*.[38] In *On Duties* he argues:

But it seems we must trace back to their ultimate sources the principles of fellowship and society that Nature has established among men. The first principle is that which is found in the connection subsisting between all the members of the human race; and that bond of connection is reason and speech, which by the processes of teaching and learning, of communicating, discussing, and reasoning associate men together and unite them in a sort of natural fraternity. In no other particular are we farther removed from the nature of beasts.[39]

Cicero was "the wisest man" precisely because, as Luther himself emphasized in 1532, he combined "wisdom and eloquence."[40] Luther was keen on this Ciceronian innovation to bring about not only a measure of "natural fraternity," which is the task of practical reason, but also to bolster Luther's waning though still hopeful yearnings for reform of the church. For instance, in his introductory remarks to Erasmus in *The Bondage of the Will* (1525) he goes so far as to employ the Ciceronian innovation. Luther would bring his gift of wisdom to the debate and bear Erasmus's "ignorance," and he pleaded that Erasmus would bear Luther's "lack of eloquence" by bringing his gift of it, in order "to render mutual service with our gifts, so that each with his own gift bears the burden and need of the other [Gal. 6:2]."[41] During the weeks leading up to the Diet of Augsburg (1530), Luther urged political authorities to excel in the virtue of peacemaking with its benefits "so eloquent and so wise."[42] On another, very different occasion, Luther, directly inspired by Cicero, raved that we come to trust Jesus because he alone is "the wisest among the sons of men" endowed with "the sweetest and loveliest lips," with "the loveliest mouth," "pleasant lips," indeed "superabundant in His lips" out of which "gushes forth . . . the sweetest and loveliest wisdom . . . sweet and delightful wisdom, worthy of such high praise."[43]

Luther's initial affection for Cicero commenced because of the "bond" that Cicero had forged between wisdom and eloquence. Luther's love intensified because Cicero understood oratory itself to be nothing less than wisdom and eloquence brought to bear on civic life for its well-being, and, from Luther's theological perspective as well, brought to bear on ecclesial life for its communion and salvation. Indeed, Cicero had argued that it was oratory itself that originally actualized human sociality and furthermore that it is only continual oratory that can sustain and strengthen civic life in its various dimensions. In this way oratory is itself the key mode of practical reason. The implications of Cicero's argument for Luther and his times were enormous and are routinely underestimated or even overlooked altogether.

Briefly stated, nineteenth- and twentieth-century historians of political philosophy have generally juxtaposed two dichotomous medieval and Reformation lines of thought relative to human sociality, and theologians have usually followed this consensus. Augustine set forth the first line of thought, epitomized in his well-known statement: "For there is nothing so social by nature, so anti-social by sin, as man."[44] Within the earthly city, humanity's fallen, perverted, sinful nature made anything but discord and strife hardly imaginable yet alone achievable. At best God instituted political authority as a negative counterforce to our fallen nature, with the task to bridle human corruption and to compel obedience to its order of coerced tranquility. Human sociality hardly crosses the threshold into the postlapsarian era, perhaps not at all. Aristotle fathered the second line of thought, according to this historical reconstruction, which Thomas Aquinas and his followers supposedly adopted wholeheartedly. Nature constitutes human beings as political animals and endows us with an internal telos whereby our natural inclinations and tendencies organically, directly, and inexorably lead to positive family, civic, and political structures and institutions. Robust notions of sin, or its philosophical equivalents, do not figure prominently in Aristotle's equation, save perhaps in a weak privational fashion.[45] Political historians, and theologians as well, have routinely placed Luther prominently and exclusively within the Augustinian line of "pure pessimism."[46]

Cicero, however, represents a third, clearly distinguishable, and readily available tradition from which Luther himself drew.[47] In Cicero's account of the origins of human sociality, Nature originally endowed humans with the potentiality for sociability residing in their capacities for reason and speech. This potentiality, however, stayed dormant, leaving human primordial existence scattered, savage, brutish, and devoid of morality, law, and civic associations. What humans needed and what emerged was a first orator who "transformed them [primordial humans] from wild beasts and savages into tame and gentle creatures on account of heeding speech and reason more diligently."[48] Furthermore, for Cicero, oratory's civic vocation must continue lest humans relapse to their primordial antisocial existence. For Luther and many others, this vision of sinful yet social contributed to his twofold realism about both human sin and God's continuing left-hand providence. The Ciceronian impulse continually nudged Luther away from the "pure pessimism" that he surely at times exhibited. Luther, therefore, regularly cited Psalm 127:1, which was also on his short list of verses that children should memorize,[49] when espousing God's real providence mediated through a variety of terrestrial "masks." Unsurprisingly, Luther at times interpreted these masks from the viewpoint of oratory.[50]

Especially in *On the Best Sort of Oratory* and *On Duties*, Cicero construed and exercised practical reason through his oratorical imagination. Here Cicero emphasized a third characteristic that kindled Luther's affection: the consent of the orator's audience. In the task of practical reason "[t]he supreme orator is the one whose speech instructs, delights, and moves the minds of his audience . . . To move them is indispensible."[51] The orator must therefore accommodate oneself to common idioms, customs, and speech. As Cary Nederman stresses, "whereas in all other arts that which is most excellent is furthest removed from the understanding and mental capacity of the untutored, in oratory the very cardinal sin is to depart from the language of everyday life and the usage approved by the sense of the community."[52] We can see this very dynamic at work in Luther's "On Translating," whereby the biblical translator must diligently "look the other in the mouth."[53] This priority on the audience resonates both with Luther's "new radical reevaluation of ordinary life"[54] and with his christological accent to "'put on' his neighbor and so conduct himself toward him as if he himself were in the other's place."

Cicero's oratorical, discursive, communicative imagination of practical reason is "overtly participatory" where the audience of fellow citizens is the final arbiter. The orator thereby defers to the audience rather than commands them.[55] According to Luther's christological imagination of Christian love, we "put on" our neighbors' circumstances and needs, and these then direct, discipline, and determine the situation-specific shape of Christian love. Luther usually reserved his more overt participatory intuitions and insights more for his conciliar approach to ecclesial life[56] than for his political approach to terrestrial rule. However, when he reflected on the moral aptitudes of rulers regarding distributive justice, he often played a participatory note.

Luther developed a suggestion first made by Augustine that Paul positioned love as the first fruit of the Spirit because love is really the only Christian virtue (Gal. 5:6; also Rom. 5:5; 1 Corinthians 13). As we "put on" our neighbors, Christian love "expands into all the fruit of the Spirit."[57] Whether the neighbor is within or without the Christian communion appears unimportant (Gal. 5:13-14; Rom. 13:8-10). Christian love operates like a pluripotent stem cell becoming—by means of an emancipated practical reason—whatever set of virtues neighbors, neighborhoods, and communities need for their welfare, thus setting out the breadth of Christian vocation in God's world.

Conclusion

Luther was surely not the only one of his age to be delighted, instructed, and moved deeply by this "wisest man." In this brief exploration we can more easily determine the extent and depth of Luther's delight and affectedness than we can the precise nature of the instruction that he took from Cicero. Various models of practical reason were commonplace in Medieval and Renaissance thinkers and numerous were delighted, instructed, and moved by Cicero.

I have suggested a Ciceronian impulse within Luther's approach to practical reason, though he never wrote a philosophical account on the subject matter.

Luther's metaphor of Christian love as "putting on" one's neighbors readily opens a door for and resonates with Cicero's participatory oratorical model of practical reason. The Ciceronian impulse also sheds light on his frequent lyrical raptures in favor of Aristotle's concept of *epieikeia*—the practical spirit of justice in complexities of real life—rather than Plato's preference for the pure letter of the law. Here, too, Luther regularly cites Cicero's commonplace, "More law, less justice [more injury]" ("*Summum ius summa iniuria est*"; *De officiis* I.10.33) in order to insist, "therefore equity [*epieikeia*, Greek; *aequitas*, Latin] is necessary."[58] But such an exploration must wait for another occasion to appraise Luther's love affair with this "wisest man."

Chapter 4

Luther and Augustine—Revisited

Markus Wriedt

It was more than a century ago that the Dominican religious Heinrich Denifle irritated Protestant researchers in the aftermath of the celebrations of the four hundredth anniversary of Luther's birth in 1883.[1] He asked them provocatively for the precise date and the content of Luther's Reformation breakthrough. With his immense knowledge of late medieval sources, Denifle sought to prove the heretical substance of Luther's theology by showing that main parts of Luther's arguments against Scholastic and curial theology did not match the authentic teaching of the theologians current for these years. Thus, he concluded that it was not Catholic theology and piety but Luther's vain and corrupted theology that led him to stray from and finally to break with Rome.

Coincidental with this polemic, a large number of handwritten sources of Luther's early theology had been found hidden in archives or embedded in Luther's vernacular yet to be edited and published in the newly begun critical edition of Luther's works, the Weimar Edition. No wonder so many more articles and books were to be published on the development of Martin Luther.[2] The question of how Luther dealt with ecclesiastical tradition especially became the pivotal point of confessional polemic. As much as Luther was found to be in line with late medieval tradition, one could say that the gap was not so great and Luther could be declared—more or less—Catholic. Such a perspective led to the demand to revisit the condemnations of Trent and its picture of Luther.[3] In opposition to this position, other researchers focused on the originality and singularity of Luther and his findings. His theology spoils the scholastic system of theology. In addition to the historical issues, both positions reflect the question of Lutheran identity and the relevance of today's confessional split.

Within this large context the question of Luther's use and understanding of Augustine became increasingly important. It seemed that Augustine was the key to Luther's theological development. The following article will look again to the broad evidence of quotations from and references to Augustine in Luther's writings. We will have to look very carefully at the context in which Luther used Augustine and in which context we inquire into the place of the Latin Church Father in the Reformer's oeuvre. Too often have the unspoken prejudices of a certain anti-Pelagian Augustinianism prefigured the results of later source-related research. Thus, I do not present here unknown or "new" sources but focus on a thorough, that is, methodologically reflected, hermeneutically justified approach to Luther's own description of Augustine's importance for his development. I will prove a twofold thesis:

- *Negatively*: former research was heavily affected by systematically prede-cided positions and confessional identity. Thus, Augustine became the *initium* and starting point of Luther's Reformation breakthrough, which in later years he overcame to develop his Reformation theology.

- *Positively*: I will focus on the authentic expression of Luther's self-description of 1545 and show that Augustine became, against the anxious expectation of the young religious, the orthodox seal of the theological exploration he had made by his own investigation on Scripture.

Late Medieval Augustinianism

There is certainly no theologian or philosopher who wrote between the fifth and the fifteenth centuries who was not greatly influenced in one or another way by the great Latin Church Father.[4] Augustine was seen as the manifest unity of occidental theology. Quotations had to be interpreted *pars pro toto*: they were seen in a larger coherence. Contradictions or opposition had to be interpreted in the light of the larger and higher unity. In Augustine's writings many theologians found an encyclopedic summary of biblical theology and its ecclesiastical tradition. Thus, Augustine represented both the breadth and depth of theology and the orthodoxy of theology. In this dimension his work marked the limitations of orthodox theology. Those who went beyond his understanding were in danger of leaving catholic and with it orthodox belief. Especially, Augustine's statements against Donatists, Manicheans, Pelagians, and so forth were not only the expression of an actual conflict but a dogmatic decision of eternal relevance.

Conflict arose where theologians were able to prove their individual positions with Augustine's sayings and writings and where their opponents could quote other parts of Augustine with the same assurance. The manifold work of the Church Father was no longer the subject of theology but had become an arbitrary source for different and even contradictory arguments. Thus, his successors became interpreters and validated their interpretation with arguments "from outside," that is, from sources other than Augustine. Augustine became a source for extremely different and often hardly comparable arguments. Thus, the claim *Augustinus totus noster est* served as an often-used phrase to exclude the reception (interpretation) of Augustine and his writings in the opponents' argument.

The broad variety of interpretations of Augustine in the Middle Ages can hardly be overstated. A good example can be found within the Augustine Reference within the Order of the Hermits of St. Augustine (hereafter Augustinians). They referred to the African Church Father as the seal of orthodoxy, as the ideal of a teacher, and as pastor. For a while a certain anti-Pelagian school seemed to explain why Luther became such an irascible defender of the late Augustine's interpretation of Paul. This *via Gregorii* was certainly not institutionalized, though a number of representative theologians can be named. However, it is not clear whether it was that stream of late medieval Augustinianism that influenced Luther's further development.

Certainly, the general vicar of the Observant branch of the Augustinians, Johann von Staupitz, played a major role within Luther's development. Although his reading—and understanding—of Augustine can hardly be explored through documentable quotations, it seems perfectly clear that he read Augustine without certain anti-Pelagian spectacles. He quoted—if ever—Augustine in the broader Augustinian understanding as the seal of orthodoxy and example of a teacher and a pastor. However, an anti-Pelagian sentiment can be found especially in the preaching of the later Staupitz (after 1517). This certainly was of special interest for the young Luther. But this should not be overexaggerated in the broader understanding in which Augustine served as an authority, which Staupitz knew and understood in his interpretation of Scripture. We have to bear in mind that Staupitz cannot be identified with a specific type of theology or Augustinianism within the Augustinians. He certainly supported Luther and thus had the effect of an *initium*, a catalyst or fertilizer—but certainly not as the founder of Reformation theology.

Luther and Augustine

Augustine always played a pivotal role in Luther's theology. He is one of the most quoted authorities.[5] Obviously, after 1509 Luther read the authentic Augustine in available editions, probably the famous Amerbach Edition from Basel. He annotated extensively[6] and used the Church Father often in his first lectures on the Sentences.[7] When he took over the position from Staupitz as lecturer on Scripture in Wittenberg in 1512, he continued in reading and quoting the major works of Augustine. His view of the Church Father's work took on a new dimension around 1515/16 when he read *De Spiritu et Littera* as a model for interpreting Paul from the perspective of an anti-Pelagian theologian.[8] As one can clearly see in his preparations to the lecture on Paul's letter to the Romans, he starts to identify his anti-Scholastic critique with Augustine's critique against Pelagius. Augustine as the seal of orthodoxy supports his position. Whether Augustine's description of

Pelagius is accurate is hardly relevant for Luther in his furor against the late medieval Scholastics.

Interestingly enough, if one compares what Luther prepared (WA 56) and what he actually presented in class (WA 57), one will find, astonishingly, that Luther skipped most of the critical passages. Obviously, he found himself not well enough prepared to irritate his students. On the other hand, it seems fairly clear that he understood his position as critical and in some points differing from what was known as mainstream Catholic theology. He understood his findings as "new" and was desperately in search of a proof for his orthodoxy.

Another point shows how much Luther developed his position without influence from medieval or antique authority: in the first seven chapters of his lecture on Paul's letter to the Romans he sketches out what later became his distinction between law and gospel. However, the terminology was not clear yet and Augustine served as interpreter and model for the distinction of *spiritus et littera*. This served as an important argument within his understanding of the law within the process of the justification of the sinner. That Luther worked out his position almost independently can be seen in the following chapters 8 to 15, in which the professor of Sacred Scripture quotes Augustine less often. But even in the previous chapters, Luther transforms the terminology and topic of Augustine in a remarkable and very individual way: "sin" in Romans 5:12; "the old humankind" in Romans 6:6; or the question of to whom the letter is addressed in the second chapter.

The distinction of *spiritus et littera* is specifically transformed to the later distinction of law and gospel, which shows most impressively the independence and autonomy in Luther's theological development. When in 1519 he referred to Romans 2:16 and claimed that this passage had not been understood correctly in the ecclesiastical tradition except by Augustine but only in his later, anti-Pelagian writings, Luther's self-esteem and sense of authority appeared very clearly: Luther knew what had to be said of a certain passage in Scripture and was now certain enough that he began to criticize even unquestioned authorities of the tradition. This confidence can also be found in another example, in his interpretation of the famous prologue to the Gospel of John in which he comments on Augustine's unclear neo-Platonic and philosophical interpretation. Obviously, Luther construed a hierarchy between Paul and Augustine: Paul became the paradigm for theological criticism against any authority from the contemporary Scholastics to early church tradition. In his later development Luther became more and more independent and varied his theological expression under the influence of actual debate and conflict. Thus, he was also able to critique Augustine even further than his early writings would lead us to expect. Still, Augustine held the position of the ultimate expression of Catholic orthodoxy to which Luther always felt absolutely loyal.

Previous Luther research has analyzed his Reformation breakthrough extensively. Especially the role of Augustine and his anti-Pelagian writings were debated intensely. Unfortunately, these discussions were led by the unquestioned presupposition that Augustine led Luther to Paul.[9] If one looks more closely at Luther's biographical sketch from the Preface to the edition of his Latin writings from 1545, one comes to another conclusion: thirty years after the fact, Luther described how he came to a new understanding of the message by reading and interpreting Romans 1:17. *Iustitia Dei* was understood and taught as active— justice of God that man never reaches. Luther turned this understanding upside down: *iustitia Dei* had to be understood passively, as justice that God grants the contrite sinner. That was revolutionary since it contradicted everything and everyone Luther had learned to honor as authoritative. However, he continued to follow this understanding: *hic me prorsus renatum esse sensi, et apertis portis in ipsam paradisum intrasse. Postea legebam Augustinum de spiritu et littera, ubi praeter spem offendi, quod et ipse iustitiam Dei similiter interpretantur.*[10] Let us forget about the question of when this happened and concentrate on the facts. It seems important that Luther later (*postea*) reached out to Augustine's *De Spiritu et Littera*, in which he found against all hope (*contra spem*) an important representative antecedent of his own thought in comparison to late medieval scholastic teachings of a "new" understanding of Scripture. We do not know how much later Luther turned his interest to Augustine. Undoubtedly, he hesitated to read the great authority of tradition. He was afraid to find no support. How great was his astonishment when he found Augustine on his side. The seal of orthodoxy now sealed the young professor's findings. What a surprise! The door to paradise was not only open because he had found a solution to his tribulations and anxiety but because he felt the burden of innovation and heterodoxy taken away from his shoulders. Who would be able to argue with Luther if Augustine supported his understanding? After this finding Luther became more and more confident to present this even in class and from the church pulpit.[11]

Conclusion: Luther and Tradition

The debate about reformation theology was, as long as it lasted, contaminated by the argument on both sides of "illegal or nonbiblical innovation" whether against Luther or his Catholic opponents. From the very first and right up to the end, Luther defended his writings as a "re-formation," as a return to the good old past.[12] This had a specific meaning. For Luther the apostolic church ended with the emperor Phokas and the popes who struggled for worldly power. Thus, the previous time was the true tradition, since it represented the consensus *quinque saecularis*, the unity of doctrine and piety of all Christians within the first five centuries.

Luther critiqued the Roman Church as innovative. The curial theologians had illegitimately developed new dogmatic statements and practices that could not be found in Scripture. The anti-innovative argument was thus closely connected to the Reformation phrase *sola scriptura*. This was one of the most important reasons Luther looked for supporting or identical arguments to his own exegetical findings within the writings of the Fathers of the Apostolic Church. Among these, Augustine was of exceptional authority and importance.

However, the witnesses of the early church had their validity in their close connection to Scripture. As long as the Fathers could prove their argument on the basis of the Old and New Testaments, Luther willingly followed. But the moment they introduced a "new"—that is, nonbiblical—argument Luther criticized them heavily. Within his anti-Roman polemics, the argument as based on the authority of the Fathers had a certain weight and importance. Luther's Reformation did not want to split the church but to lead the impious and biblically illegitimate practices and teachings of the Roman Church back to its good and authentic beginnings.

Within this discourse Augustine holds a particular position of great importance. He seals orthodoxy. He proves the validity of an argument. He connects the beginnings of the church with its contemporary continuation. Thus, Luther felt relieved when he found that this weighty and unquestioned authority could be found on his side. And even more—he could not understand why the Roman theologians would ignore the Augustinian foundation of his theology and determine it to be heretical. With his excommunication Luther felt Augustine excommunicated as well as he.

Thus, the Roman Church was no longer the apostolic see of truth but its corrupted counterpart: antichrist. However, this did not require separation and division. Luther was convinced that another pope and other bishops easily could return to the biblical truth. They needed only to read the right authorities, for instance, Augustine, and use them to understand the word of God correctly. Like Augustine, Luther did not want to surrender to arbitrary interpretations but only to the true word of God as represented in Scripture and to its true and authentic interpretation as given by the Fathers.[13]

Within the debate about the date and content of Luther's Reformation breakthrough, we are not able to give exact details. However, we might be able to change the answer for the question of "about" a bit. Augustine was not the *initium* but the most important witness from an undoubted ecclesiastical tradition that supported and even enforced Luther's hermeneutical discovery, first of the passive justice of God and second of the distinction of law and gospel. And as I write the phrase it will be obvious that Luther explored his understanding of Paul on his own. Augustine became the secondary source for his Reformation and confirmation of his position and self-esteem.

This does not necessarily deny the need for further research about Luther's relation to the preceding traditions. He was certainly deeply influenced by Tauler, by mystical theology, by humanist writers and even by scholastic authors. However, all their interpretations had to be proven on the basis of a clear and self-evident interpreting of Scripture. With this method Luther overcame traditional authority without denying its validity for the development of church, doctrine, and piety. Even in this attitude he felt closely related to Augustine and thus secure against the accusation of illegal innovation.

CHAPTER 5

Whore or Handmaid?

Luther and Aquinas
on the Function of Reason in Theology

Denis R. Janz

Is reason "the Devil's whore," as Luther said,[1] or is it theology's "handmaid," as Aquinas (almost) said?[2] The place of reason in the theologies of Martin Luther and Thomas Aquinas is an issue of enormous complexity and the subject of many excellent and penetrating studies. Yet old caricatures surrounding this subject stubbornly persist, outliving by many years the carefully nuanced scholarship that has long since discredited them. On one side, Luther continues to be depicted as a "fideist," deriding reason and banishing it from the enterprise of Christian theology. On the other, Thomas Aquinas is portrayed as a "rationalist," drastically exaggerating the ability of the human mind to "prove" the Christian faith to be true. The two live on in popular accounts of Christianity as antithetical exemplars of rationality's role.

Experts on Luther have long understood that the charge of "fideism" against Luther cannot be sustained. And there is a consensus among Aquinas experts that "rationalism" is a highly inappropriate way to describe his theological approach. Yet these respective groups of scholars themselves bear some of the blame for perpetuating the caricature of the other. Only in the last generation have Luther experts begun to look seriously at Thomas, and vice versa. As a result both groups of scholars have begun to speak with greater nuance about the other.

In this essay, I want to address this issue not by attempting to explain the relation of faith and reason in Luther or in Aquinas. That would require a book-length presentation, and besides, this has been done with great care and precision by Luther experts and Aquinas experts. Rather, what follows is a rehearsal of some of the basic evidence in refutation of both caricatures.[3]

Luther as "Fideist"?

We must admit: for a Christian theologian to take *sola fides* as his watchword and then to call reason "the Devil's whore" is to invite misunderstanding and

47

caricature. A good many observers, in his own day and ever since, were disin-
clined to read more deeply into Luther's massive and somewhat chaotic author-
ship. For them the verdict was obvious: Luther was a naïve literalist, a dogmatic
obscurantist, an anti-intellectual—in short, a "fideist." Even as acute an observer
as G. K. Chesterton could, while heaping encomiums on Aquinas, excoriate Luther for his denigration of reason.[4]   *speech/writing that praises*

Luther did indeed speak of reason as "the Devil's whore," and moreover,
added a considerable list of other, equally negative epithets. What is less well
known is that, with some regularity, he also spoke of reason as an inestimable gift
of God. This other side of the matter is what I want to highlight here.

Humans, Luther believed, were created with reason, "the power to understand and judge."[5] In fact, reason is itself the image of God with which Adam
was created.[6] Humans share this with the angels, and it is what differentiates them
from animals.[7] Rationality is the essence of what it means to be human. And humans did not lose this when Adam sinned: "After the fall of Adam, God did not
take away this majesty of reason, but rather confirmed it."[8]   *song of praise / triumph*

This noble gift of God is celebrated in a virtual paean to reason penned by
Luther in 1536: "it is certainly true that reason is the most important and the
highest in rank among all things and, in comparison with other things of this life,
the best and something divine. It is the inventor and mentor of all the arts, medicine, laws, and of whatever wisdom, power, virtue, and glory men possess in this
life. . . . It is a sun and a kind of god appointed to administer these things [earthly
affairs] in this life."[9]

All human matters, all things having to do with human life in this world, fall
under the jurisdiction of reason, and reason is competent to administer them. In a
sermon of 1522, Luther explains: "In temporal, human affairs human judgment
suffices. For these things we need no light but that of reason. Hence God does
not in the Scriptures teach us how to build houses, to make clothing, to marry, to
wage war, to navigate the seas, and so on. For these our natural light is sufficient."[10] One such "human affair," Luther argues in 1539, is the institutional
structure of the church. The Holy Spirit has not revealed anything about this because the Spirit "does not dabble in such matters as are subject to reason . . ."[11]
When it comes to all these mundane matters, Luther has high confidence in the
power of rationality, if only humans would use it.

Natural human reason can not only lead us to a knowledge of the moral
law,[12] but it can bring in addition a certain knowledge of God himself, as Luther
insists in his lectures on Jonah of 1526: "Such a light and such a perception [natu-
ral knowledge of God] is innate in the hearts of all men; and this light cannot be
subdued or extinguished."[13] And furthermore, the human person can even reason
his or her way to some of the divine attributes: that God is Creator, that God is
just,[14] and so forth. "That is as far as the natural light of reason sheds its rays—it

regards God as kind, gracious, merciful, and benevolent. And that is indeed a bright light."[15] All this humans can know about God prior to any revelation on God's part. Could we here go so far as to say that in a sense, for Luther, "reason serves faith"?

As for revealed truth, it does not stand in opposition to reason. Indeed, Luther insists, how could it? For, as we have seen, reason is God's image in us, and hence it could not possibly contradict truth revealed by God. "Although the Gospel is a higher gift and wisdom than human reason, it does not alter or nullify the intelligence of reason which God himself planted in us."[16] Though the two may seem to us to be at odds, this cannot actually be the case: "If anything is really contrary to reason, it is certainly much more against God also. For how can anything not be in conflict with heavenly truth when it is in conflict with earthly truth."[17] Luther's fundamental position is this: what is of God is rational, and what is rational is of God. This is what Luther meant when he said at the Diet of Worms in 1521: "Unless I am convinced by the testimony of the Scriptures or by clear reasons [ratio evidens] . . . my conscience is captive to the word of God."[18] What contradicts "clear reason" contradicts God's word, and vice versa.

How can these positive statements on reason be reconciled with the negative? Reason is a marvelous gift of God, but it has its limitations. What is disastrous, according to Luther, is when reason oversteps its bounds and attempts to be the supreme judge in matters of faith. It cannot play this role because it is in various ways defective. First, it is insufficient; it fails to give humans what they need to know: "reason does admittedly believe that God is able and competent to help and to bestow; but reason does not know whether he is willing to do this also for us."[19] In fact, on the basis of bitter human experience, reason often draws the opposite conclusion, namely that God does not love us. That is its first defect.

Its second defect is that when reason attempts to specify what God is like, it inevitably falls into error: "Reason is unable to identify God properly. . . . It knows that there is a God, but it does not know who or which is the true God. . . . [I]t rushes in clumsily and assigns the name God and ascribes divine honor to its own idea of God. . . . Nature knows the former—it is inscribed in everybody's heart; the latter is taught only by the Holy Spirit."[20] In trying to characterize God, reason overreaches its competence and inevitably ends up with an idol of its own making. Could we say here that, for Luther, in some sense "faith elevates reason"?

The third defect of reason is that it can give us no sure guidance in the human quest for salvation:

> Ask [natural reason] what is necessary to please God and to be
> saved, and it replies: "You must build churches, cast bells,

endow masses, hold vigils, make chalices, monstrances, pictures and ornaments; burn candles, pray this much, fast for St. Catherine, become a priest or a monk, walk to Rome or St. James Compostella, wear a hair shirt, torture yourself, and so on. These are good works, the right way and path to salvation. . . ." [I]t is impossible for us to please God thus.[21]

What reason tells us to do gets us nowhere. On all these properly theological issues—the path to salvation, the true nature of God, God's attitude toward us—reason is blind. This kind of knowledge can come to us only through revelation. And what comes to us through revelation cannot be made subject to reason. When reason sets itself up as the final arbiter of truth in such matters, it trespasses onto foreign territory.

The picture painted here is drastically incomplete: Luther had much more to say on the issue. And I have not touched on the precise ways reason functions in his theology. But the main contours of the picture are already clear. In summary, reduced to its bare bones, Luther's view of reason is as follows: reason is God's greatest gift to humanity. Its proper jurisdiction and competence extend to all human affairs. When it claims supremacy in matters of faith, however, it becomes "the Devil's whore," for these things transcend reason. By submitting to revelation, granting revealed truth a privileged epistemic primacy, reason becomes "enlightened reason." Faith, in this sense, "elevates reason." Enlightened reason, for its part, "serves" faith. Luther valued reason as a marvelous gift of God, one that God surely intended us to use, above all in coming to understand ourselves in relation to God. The charge of "fideism" is groundless.

Thomas as "Rationalist"?

Already in his own day, Thomas was accused of exaggerating the ability of the human mind to comprehend and demonstrate the mysteries of faith. Luther, two-and-a-half centuries later, heartily endorsed this charge against Thomas and emphatically denounced him on this basis. To speak of Thomas as an "Aristotelian" was already an indictment, in Luther's view: "Briefly the whole Aristotle is to theology as darkness is to light. This in opposition to the scholastics."[22] Aristotle was the inspiration for "the men at the Sorbonne [the scholastics] who allow such things as the forgiveness of sins and the mystery of the incarnation and eternal life to be deduced by logic."[23] Leading the way in this attempt to prove the articles of faith, Luther held, was the "teacher of all teachers," Thomas Aquinas.[24] Here was "the source and foundation of all heresy, error and obliteration of the gospel."[25]

I do not want to attempt in this context a summary description of the relation of faith and reason in Thomas.[26] Rather, I want to address a much narrower question. Thomas held that the most proper function of reason is to "prove."[27] When it comes to the Christian faith, what exactly did he think is "provable" by human reason?

We can begin by noticing that Aquinas uses the term *probare* ("to prove") in various ways. Taken in the narrow sense, the word implies strict logical demonstration, what he sometimes called "sufficient proof." But it can also be used in a much weaker sense, as when, he writes, "a reason is introduced, not as furnishing a sufficient proof of a principle, but as confirming an already established principle, by showing the congruity of its results." This, too, Aquinas calls a proof. Thus he writes that in this sense "reasons avail to prove the trinity," a shocking statement unless read in connection with the sentence immediately following: "We must not, however, think that the trinity of persons is adequately proved by such reasons."[28] In other words, what proof means here is that the principle in question possesses at least minimal intelligibility. Proving in this case is a far cry from logically demonstrating. Failure to recognize these very different uses of the term in Aquinas leaves the reader open to disastrous misunderstanding.

With this in mind, we turn directly to our question: What did Thomas think is "provable"? The foundational texts on this question are three passages that Thomas experts have come to regard, collectively, as Thomas's discourse on method: the *Summa contra gentiles* (I, chaps. 1-9); the *Summa theologiae* (1a, q.1); and the *Super Boetium de Trinitate*. I draw from this collection of writings several salient points.

First, all three passages insist that the truths of faith are not susceptible to proof. In the *Summa contra gentiles*, Aquinas argues that reason can "gather certain likenesses" of these truths, but such "likenesses" are "not sufficient so that the truth of faith may be comprehended as being understood demonstratively." Whatever weak arguments we can come up with along these lines, there should be "no presumption to comprehend or demonstrate."[29] In the final analysis, Aquinas states, "we believe [these truths] only through the revelation of God."[30] In the *Summa theologiae*, Aquinas reiterates that *sacra doctrina* "does not argue in proof of its principles, which are the articles of faith."[31] Again, we believe these "on the authority of those to whom the revelation has been made." This, and nothing else, constitutes the "incontrovertible proof" of the truths of faith.[32] And in the *Super Boetium*, the same point is made: "Human reasoning may be spoken of in two ways: in one way, it may be regarded as demonstrative, forcing the intellect to believe; and this kind of reasoning cannot be possessed in regard to those truths which are of faith."[33] In fact, Aquinas goes so far as to state that in this present life these truths of faith "are neither known nor understood by anyone."[34] The truths of faith, in short, can in no way be "proven," that is, logically demonstrated.

Moreover, Aquinas is concerned that even attempts to "prove" them would do more harm than good. He warns that for adversaries of the faith, "the very

means faith in general not just religious faith

insufficiency of these arguments would confirm them rather in their error, in giving them reason to think that we consent to the truth of faith for these poor reasons."[35] Elsewhere, in regard to the Trinity, he explains further why the very attempt to prove (and here he means to logically demonstrate) is misguided: "To dare to prove the Trinity by natural reason is to commit a double fault in faith." First, it shows a misunderstanding of what faith is, for, by definition matters of faith extend beyond reason. And second, it is strategically wrong, since unbelievers scorn such attempts.[36] Not only are such "proofs" impossible, but they should not be attempted.

Is there in fact any place in Thomas's theology for logically demonstrative proof? The best modern experts on Thomas agree that this is rare.[37] Perhaps the best-known instances of syllogistic demonstration are Thomas's arguments for the existence of God. Even here, however, experts now question whether these are proofs in the strict sense. Pesch, for instance, points out that each argument concludes with a statement about the Christian God: "and this everyone understands to be God," and so forth.[38] This "everyone" refers to Christians, those who already believe not merely in a metaphysical principle but in a saving God. The proofs for God, Pesch argues, are "in no way to be understood as a rational assent to a previously unknown God, but rather as reason's ultimate reaching toward a God who is already known in faith."[39] Thus, these arguments, which at first sight seem to be pure demonstrative syllogisms, already presuppose faith and function within faith. If Pesch is right about this, and I think he is, then nowhere in Aquinas's theology do we find a single proof in the strict sense.

In fact, Pesch argues, there is no such thing as autonomous reason in Aquinas.[40] Autonomous reason is basically a product of the Enlightenment; to read it back into Aquinas is anachronistic. Reason for Aquinas is always reason within faith. The act of reason that is proof takes place within faith. Proof, therefore, is never proof in the strict sense. Even those syllogisms that he called "demonstrative" function within the horizon of faith.

Conclusion

Old caricatures and tired clichés repeat the conventional wisdom: on the question of reason, a vast gulf supposedly separates these two representatives of the Christian tradition. But those who take seriously what Luther has to say about the glories of reason and what Aquinas has to say about the limitations of reason will reconsider. Perhaps the best answer to the question posed in the title of this essay is—Yes!

CHAPTER 6

Luther's "Atheism"

Paul R. Hinlicky

Twentieth-century scholarship rediscovered the provocative idea of Luther's atheism and treated it under the theme of the "hiddenness of God"[1] in the agony of existential decision.[2] In echo of Luther, Paul Tillich famously spoke of doubt as part of faith, understood as ultimate concern.[3] No one could rightfully deny this "existential" element in Luther nor should we want to deny it.[4] Far more interesting today, however, is the fact that Luther grounds this agony of decision in the divine Life itself[5] and thus locates the believer's agony in the gospel's specific narrative of "Trinitarian advent"[6] for cosmic reconciliation and human redemption.[7] That narrative grounding of theological discourse sets the table for a new dialogue with "postmodern" philosophy as between the rationalities of two narratives—not anything like Tillich's "method of correlation" in which ontological philosophy frames perennial questions that in turn theology existentially answers.[8] Indeed, Luther's theology, on one hand, challenges philosophy to give up conceits of disinterested objectivity and universal rationality and own up to its own historicity.[9] This new dialogue is possible from the side of theology in Luther's tradition, on the other hand, when theologians are willing to begin conversation at the point of greatest apparent difference: the experience of atheism.

Beginning at the Point of Difference

> Behold! God governs the external affairs of the world in such a way that, if you regard and follow the judgment of human reason, you are forced to say, either that there is no God, or that God is unjust; as the poet said: "I am often tempted to think there are no gods.". . . Is it not, pray, universally held to be most unjust that bad men should prosper, and good men be afflicted? Yet that is the way of the world. Hereupon some of the greatest minds have fallen into denying the existence of God, and imagining that Chance governs all things at random. Such were the Epicureans, and Pliny. And Aristotle, wishing to set his 'prime Being' free from misery, holds that he sees nothing but himself; for Aristotle supposes that it would be very irksome to such a Being to behold so many evils and injustices.[10]

It is surely a question worth pondering in historical perspective why the militant "atheistic humanism" that characterized so much of post-Kantian philosophy arose on the soil of Luther's Reformation.[11] No one expressed the new conviction with such eloquence and force as the early Marx:

> To be radical is to grasp things by the root. But for man the root is man himself. The clear proof of the radicalism of German theory [Marx is thinking of the young Hegelians], and hence of its political energy is that it proceeds from the decisive *positive* transcendence of religion. The criticism of religion ends with the doctrine that *man* is *the highest being for man*, hence with the *categorical imperative to overthrow all conditions* in which man is a degraded, enslaved, neglected, contemptible being.[12]

Marx had an answer, moreover, to the question about the source for this liberating inversion of dehumanizing theism: "Luther, to be sure, vanquished the bondage of devotion when he replaced it with the bondage of conviction. He shattered faith in authority while he restored the authority of faith. He transformed parsons into laymen and laymen into parsons. He freed man from outward religiosity while he made religiosity the innerness of man. He emancipated the body from its chain while he put the chains on the heart."[13] Luther appears here as the one who first emancipated humanity from an outward subservience to deity, only to reenslave the human heart with an inward conviction of deity's reality.[14]

Marx is relying on the account of Luther provided by Feuerbach, who had first argued that theology is alienated anthropology, that is, that divine perfections are but the idealized projections of the lost, fractured human essence under its condition of earthly degradation. In a justly famed introduction to a twentieth-century edition of Feuerbach's *The Essence of Christianity*, Karl Barth highlights this reliance on Luther: "Feuerbach for his own purposes could readily make use of Luther, and not without every appearance of justice."[15] Barth singles out two aspects of Luther's intellectual legacy that prepared the soil for Feuerbach. First, Barth notes, "Luther had a peculiar way of speaking of faith as an almost independent appearance and function of the divine *hypostasis*. Faith is able to do, and does everything." But faith, Barth assumes, is our human work; for Barth, it is a free response to the message of free divine grace. Barth's view is a highly dialectical one that gives God all the glory for the gift of grace yet never claims that faith is God in the act of grace or that faith captures God in grace. Second, Luther's Christology urges us "to seek deity not in heaven but on earth, in *man*, a *man*, the *man* Jesus." This leitmotif of Luther's doctrine of the incarnation "clearly suggests the possibility of an inversion of above and below, of heaven and earth, of God and man" (which, not incidentally, Barth immediately connects to Hegel). Against this slide down a slippery slope toward atheistic humanism first begun in Luther, Barth invokes the Reformed (but also Thomistic) doctrine of the *finitum non capax infiniti* as "adequate defense" to assure that "the relation to God is one that is in principle uninvertable."[16]

Catholic interpretation tends to follow a similar line. In the opening chapter on Feuerbach and Nietzsche in *The Drama of Atheistic Humanism*, Henri de Lubac, the eminent French theologian of the last century, notes that the "expression, 'the death of God,' had its place in the most traditional theology as signifying what happened on Calvary. Nietzsche had doubtless, on various occasions, heard Luther's chorale, 'God himself is dead'; he may even have joined the singing of it. Nor was he unaware of the use that Hegel had made of it" in the latter's "speculative Good Friday," that is, the death of the abstract, otherworldly God giving rise to the concrete, incarnate God, which is the this-worldly realization of reconciliation (a stance lately renewed with some force by Slavoj Žižek[17]). Lewis Ayres concludes his important contemporary study, *Nicea and Its Legacy* (in an entertainingly titled chapter, "In Spite of Hegel, Fire and Sword"), by arguing for the apophatic doctrines of divine simplicity and impassibility over against Hegel's criticism (deriving from Luther's critique of Aristotle, as per the excerpt above from "The Bondage of the Will") that "to maintain an account of the immutable God distinct from the world is to remain in the sphere of representation and to be alienated from the reality of the Spirit." Ayres's target is Hegel's provocative interpretation of the classical doctrine of the Trinity[18] for entailing divine passibility, so that "not only difference but also anguish and suffering are grounded in the differentiation of God."[19]

It is surely right that in some respects modernity's interest (among other interests) in *this* world, its *historical* redemption, and a spirituality of *courage and engagement* grounded in divine passion for righteousness, life, and peace—even if at the expense of traditional theism—may be traced to Luther's deliberate turn from the rationality cum theology of Athens[20] to the rationality cum theology of Jerusalem.[21] Moreover, theologians in the tradition of Luther have not been utterly silenced by the aforementioned line of criticism. I have argued that Luther's apparent hypostasizing of "faith" is in fact his very traditional trinitarian doctrine of the Holy Spirit as the bond of love both in the eternal life of God and in the temporal incorporation of believers into it.[22] Eberhard Jüngel took up Luther's Christology not to collapse theology into anthropology but rather to incorporate the experience of atheism into the incarnate life of God.[23] Theologians like Robert Jenson have found Luther's legacy important for purposes of de-Platonization, by which he means deliverance from a metaphysics of "persistence" to a metaphysics of "anticipation."[24] All such voices reject a false construction of divine transcendence on the model of the mind's putative independence of the body in favor of the Pauline eschatological-apocalyptic combat of the Spirit against the flesh.[25] This latter is a biblical model of apocalyptic imminence that Luther elevated to a criterion of genuine theology in his treatise against Erasmus, *De servo arbitrio* (from which the extract [I prefer "epigraph"] above is drawn).[26]

Does divine passibility[27] entail a dialectical self-cancellation in the concept of God (Hegel, as appropriated, for instance, by Feuerbach, Marx, Kojeve,[28] or Žižek)? The *finitum non capax infiniti* defense against this devolution involves a certain reading of Western theology going back to Augustine's belief that "the Platonists are closest to us" (*Confessions*, Book VII). Disputes between those more inclined to Plato's version of theism and those leaning toward Aristotle's version pale in comparison, however, to a master assumption operating here: that theologians should single out as best the philosophy that approximates what theology says and then take it as its own natural foundation in the realm of reason. But the context for Augustine's statement about the nearness of Platonism to Christianity was his struggle to free his thinking from corporal conceptions of the deity, in that these made the deity a part of, and so subject to, the cosmic system—which system in turn was treated as the operational eternity. Augustine's Bible instructed him, however, that "in the beginning God created the heavens and the earth." With the help of the doctrine of the Trinity ("begotten, not made"), Augustine took this to mean that the triune God *is eternally* the Father of God's own Son and breather of God's own Spirit, who as such *becomes* the Creator of an ontologically distinct creation, which is not, in turn, any kind of necessary emanation but a free decision and act. Although Augustine struggled with the implication that the *becoming* of God as Creator of genuine others involves God in *time*, God's trinitarianism marks, rather, an immense differentiation. The notion of divine infinity is that God as genuine Creator bounds the cosmos as God binds himself to it in a free act of love but is not bounded by it in a relation of lack, greed, or envy.

A latter-day Augustinian, Luther realized in his christological and pneumatological doctrines that this important notion of divine infinity as plentitude of charity (*esse deum dare est*)[29] does *not* entail the corollary that the finite is incapable of the infinite, *not* if the Almighty Father can originate, sustain, and fulfill a world other than himself, the eternal Son can become flesh in the fullness of time and remain this flesh forever, and the Lord and Giver of Life can be breathed into human hearts and bind them together in a beloved community as the true and future temple of God. So Luther can write: "at one and the same time . . . God is entirely present, personally and essentially, in Christ on earth in his mother's womb, yes, in the crib, in the temple, in the wilderness, in cities, in houses, in the garden, in the field, on the cross, in the grave, etc., yet nonetheless also in heaven in the Father's bosom."[30] Long before Hegel,[31] it was Luther who criticized the "false infinite" that thinks of the deity in "some circumscribed and determinate manner . . . for it is uncircumscribed and immeasureable, beyond and above all that is or may be . . . [yet, just so] essentially present at all places, even in the tiniest tree leaf."[32]

All this suggests that the question of Christian Platonism[33] is historically complex because there are various Platonisms, some more Socratic and skeptical, others more dogmatic and metaphysical, just as there are varied theological appropriations of Platonism, some systematic and others ad hoc.[34] Luther, in any case, thinks himself out of the semi-Pelagian theology-philosophy of the *moderni*,[35] that is, the Occamists,[36] with the help of Augustine. Philosophically he identifies himself with Renaissance Platonism over against the modernist-scholastic reading of Aristotle.[37] These historical nuances are important for correcting polemical narratives, alleging that "Western theology made its own, quite substantial contributions to modern nihilism" beginning with Luther's alleged Occamist irrationalism.[38] There is, to be sure, in Luther a critique of epistemology, that is, of self-grounding reason, and as alluded, a trinitarian revision of the antecedent metaphysics. The basis for that is the particular narrative—the agony in the garden and the cry of dereliction—that Luther read so closely.

The Spiritual Suffering of Christ

In amazement the prophet says: God has forgotten His own. So he describes the passion of Christ in a few words. He says nothing of the physical cross, but rather that for a little while the Son of man will be left hanging on God who has deserted him. Who can understand that? To be deserted by God is more evil than death. Think of Job. God boasts of His servant. Satan replies: He has good things. God permitted Satan to go after him, since he is able to do nothing unless the Lord allows. Now everything is burned away and the wife mocks him. Still the devil demands more: you have left him alive. Give me a piece of his soul. That's the blow. Now Job is totally abandoned, in trial, feeling hell without help from either men or angels. There is nothing to do but abandon oneself to God. No one knows this like Christ in the Garden. He is left in death, as if it were eternal. David writes concerning this: the divinity thus will hide itself, so that it is possible to say that there is no deity here. There is only the devil, hell, eternal fire and eternal death. He is a man, who is thus deserted, so that all the world says: God will never show Him regard. The deity has withdrawn, so that He fights all alone. In His agony there is not only sweat of blood but being abandoned, because He thought Himself deserted by God.

> There are thus according to David two kinds of suffering, the physical thirst and also the absence of consolation. If God Himself is absent, no one is able to be consoled, be there all the dancing and music in the world. That is Christ's true suffering.[39]

Seen in historical perspective, a critical innovation Luther makes within the theological tradition is to locate the trial of atheism within the life of faith, that is to say, within the life of Christ and those who participate in him.[40] Hence, the trial of atheism is not an alternative to Christian faith but part and parcel of its own dynamic, an indispensable moment in the divine Life's approach to us.[41] A certain "Christian atheism," to be sure, is as old as Justin Martyr, who scolded the emperor Marcus Aurelius: "We certainly confess that we are godless with reference to beings like these who are commonly thought of as gods, but not with references to the most true God, the Father of righteousness and temperance and the other virtues, who is untouched by evil. Him, and the Son who came after him . . . and the prophetic Spirit we worship and adore."[42] As may be seen in Justin's rebuke, the term *God* (or the concept *theism*) is notoriously equivocal; the question of theism or atheism on one level consists first in specifying the candidate for the title of deity under consideration. That is an abiding task. But in Luther's "atheism" the context is the *Christian's* faith, which is, for Luther, the gift of the Holy Spirit to believe with Jesus, that is, in Gethsemane, hoisted on the stake. Of this faith of the Crucified and his martyrs, Luther writes, "nothing in the world seems more uncertain than the Word of God and faith, nothing more delusive than hope in the promise. In short, nothing seems to be more nothing than God himself."[43] Such "faith"—"waiting on God" to show himself not the Nothing of present experience and its wisdom but the Something of the promised reign[44]—is, moreover, what differentiates theology as *new* language of the Spirit, according to Luther, from philosophy as the *old* language of common human experience and natural wisdom.[45]

Consider the above-cited stenographic record of a portion of Luther's christological sermon on Psalm 8:5a, "Thou will let Him be forsaken of God for a little while." Natural reason is not wrong. Law and nature are not illusory. Christ actually was accursed by God. The spiritual suffering of Christ was not only that men and angels regarded him as nothing and as abandoned by God but that Christ actually was abandoned, not only by the world but also by God. The cry of dereliction is as real as the imperial stake on which the man hung. For Luther this must be so. It provides the good reason, as he famously explained the second article of the Creed, why the redeemed—who otherwise would be abandoned to their sins, dead to God—will rise with Christ; because he has made his own the plight of his people before God, he was forsaken in their stead. Thus, the vindicated Lord is adorned with these same people, who have become his victory trophies.

What, then, are we to make of Luther's reckless language about the withdrawal of the deity in Christ's spiritual suffering in Gethsemane? The troublesome words are: *Divinitas sic occultabit se, ut dici possit nullam deitatem hic. Ibi Teufel, hell, ewig feur und ewig tod.*[46] Or again: *Die Gottheit hat entzogen.*[47] Such a notion might imply that the merit of Christ is that of an autonomous man who in agony abandoned himself to the God who had abandoned him—prefiguring Albert Schweitzer's mad, apocalyptic Jesus who hurled himself against the wheel of fate only to be crushed by it. In this way Jesus would have fulfilled in extremis a demand for faith and so compelled, as it were, God's recognition—or at least Schweitzer's admiration.[48] Christ's human merit in his trusting death would be the supererogatory good work par excellence.[49] Jesus as the perfect Kantian—he lived and died as if there were a God. In this way, he can be our existential model.

So which is it? Has the deity withdrawn? Or has the divine Son lost himself in lost humanity, who must then be found again in a new action of the Spirit, presenting him with his people to the Father? For Luther, both are true, but from different perspectives, those of philosophy and theology respectively.

> Now, all who regard and know Christ from a fleshly point of view are inevitably offended at him . . . since flesh and blood thinks no further than it sees and feels, and since it sees that Christ was crucified as a mortal man, it inevitably says, "This is the end; neither life nor salvation is to be found here; he is gone; he can help no one; he himself is lost." But he who is not offended at him must rise above the flesh and be raised by the Word so that he may perceive in the Spirit how Christ precisely through his suffering and death has attained true life and glory.[50]

Both perspectives see one and the same crucified Jesus. Both perspectives endure a trial of atheism. But each evaluates the experience differently and so constructs it, either as the dénouement of an illusion or as the surprising divine self-revelation. The fundamental difference is *axiological, not epistemological*; it is an incredible perception of goodness in the cross of Jesus (Nietzsche: "the creditor playing scapegoat for his debtor, from love—can you believe it?"[51]). Thus, faith is Luther's "divine faith," a sovereign gift and election of that same divine goodness (not Barth's "free" human act).

Yet the truthfulness of reason's perspective, which tells how things are in "the light of nature," is and remains presupposed. The resurrection to faith by the Spirit does not overcome the scandal of the cross but establishes it. There is not, as in epistemology, some rock-bottom objectivity that grounds knowledge in the way things really are—since the way things really are is flux of becoming, not ground of being, let alone heavenly thought placidly thinking itself. Human knowledge—both theology and philosophy—is always the temporal action of some definite perspective in one and the same world of human experience. Neither theologian nor philosopher cannot extract themselves into some superior posture of transcendence but only come to see things differently on the plane of immanence so that we act differently within it. The possibility of Luther's kind of theology, then, depends on the One who has broken into the strong man's house (Mark 3:27).

Neither Theism nor Atheism but Trinitarianism

The just-cited text about the two perspectives on the cross comes from one of two great treatises of Luther against Zwingli,[52] to which by way of conclusion I would call attention. Here Luther takes up Zwingli's objection and replies: "Why, this would make God's glory an altogether worldly and carnal thing, just as it would be inglorious for a worldly king to be hanged or crucified. But the glory of our God is precisely that for our sakes he comes down to the very depths, into human flesh, into the bread, into our mouth, our heart, our bosom."[53] God's "transcendence" here is not imagined as disembodied mind resting sweetly above it all but as imminence, as drawing near, coming close (cf. Mark 1:15). "Revelation" here is not depicted as a fixed and supernaturally secured worldview but as the subversion of all fixed ideas of the status *quo ante* by this imminence breaking into its midst, binding up the strong man to plunder his goods. "All tropes in Scripture signify the true, new object and not the simile of this new object"[54]— the latter simile would make the new object an immanent representation of some other still, distant object or an expressive symbol of self-transcendence. But atheism, too—rather, atheism and theism alike—are transformed to signify the "true, new object": the God whose glory is to come down into the depths, whose reign approaches in *man*, a *man*, the *man* Jesus. The true opposite of theism, then, is not atheism—atheistic humanism perpetuates the false transcendence it denies to God by claiming it for Promethean humanity. Trinitarianism is the true opposite of mere theism, gained at Gethsemane by its atheistic negation, when Jesus in obedience to God was forsaken by God in order to find us. Trinitarianism means to *think* God as the beloved community, which as a life, not a thing, has sought and found the way to us godless, pious and impious alike, and won us in and for the agony of love, wresting us free from the philosophical apathies of theism and atheism alike.

CHAPTER 7

Luther's Philosophy of Language

Dennis Bielfeldt

The philosophy of language deals with the nature of linguistic meaning. While concern about linguistic meaning is relevant to all areas of philosophy, sustained, self-conscious reflection on language as philosophy's subject matter is primarily a twentieth-century enterprise. Philosophers of the last century generally thought in two different ways about language. While one group took ordinary language to be in order as it is, and thus sought to free philosophy from its penchant to use language in peculiar (and degenerate) philosophical ways, another group believed that philosophical errors arose precisely because language was not in order as it is. G. E. Moore, John Austin, and the later Ludwig Wittgenstein represents the former path, Gottlob Frege, Bertrand Russell, and perhaps the early Wittgenstein the latter.[1]

It is important to understand why philosophers became so heady about language. They plausibly thought that understanding the claim that some act is good or right presupposes clarity on the meaning of "good" and "right." Similarly, grasping "Molly believes the worst about Mary" demands an understanding of "believing the worst about." Knowing that "nine is necessarily greater than seven" presumes clarity on "necessarily greater." Finally, understanding "smoking causes cancer" demands a grasp of "cause." So it was that philosophers thought that an analysis of language properly grounds ethics, philosophy of mind, philosophy of mathematics, and the philosophy of science.[2]

While giving the necessary and sufficient conditions for proper application of "philosophy of language" is not easy, a general characterization is possible: the philosophy of language concerns the compositional analysis of a working language (syntax), the relation the speaker has to this language (semantics), and the relation of this language to the world or extralinguistic reality (semantics and pragmatics).[3] Much philosophy of language optimistically believes that clarity on the nature of language leads to clarity on the nature of the world. In hopes of removing ambiguity, many linguistic philosophers make extensive use of the tools of precision: formal logic and set theory. This disposition to use mathematical tools to attack philosophical problems has been bequeathed to "analytic philosophy" generally.

While philosophers of language are interested in the form and structure of language (syntax), their ultimate concern is semantic: What does p mean? Many philosophers of language strongly link meaning and truth, that is, the meaning of proposition p is found in its *truth-conditions*. Accordingly, the meaning of sentence S is just the conditions under which S, according to its rules of reference, refers. S's meaning is just those states of affairs picked out by S were S true.[4] Moreover, a word's meaning just is the contribution it makes to the truth-conditions of the statements in which it appears.[5]

In summary, the philosophy of language employs technical means to investigate (and often reformulate) language so as to remove ambiguity and achieve precision. It is concerned with the meaning of linguistic statements as a presupposition of effective philosophizing. Many believe that headway on the question of linguistic meaning presupposes the question of truth itself and thus offers truth-conditional (or "model-theoretic") accounts of linguistic meaning.[6]

Medieval Tradition

Luther was trained in a philosophical tradition that held that the meaning of a sentence is found in its truth-conditions. This idea was presupposed in the medieval notion of *supposition*. Luther, in fact, assumed the standard medieval distinction between *signification* and *supposition*. While signification was the primary semantic notion in the Middle Ages, and while words signify objects, signification does not make true the propositions in which those words appear. For this one needs the "standing for" relation of supposition. To understand in what sense Luther can be said to be doing linguistic philosophy, it is important to look at how late medieval philosophers think about language and how it is that language means. There has been increasing appreciation over the last fifty years of the sophisticated nature of the semantic and logical contributions of medieval philosophy.[7]

While contemporary philosophers of language often offer competing accounts of linguistic meaning, in the Middle Ages the notion of *significare* was quite clear. Paul Vincent Spade points out that the notion is actually a triadic relation. Accordingly, for a word to signify x is for it to establish an understanding (*constituere intellectum*) in a person of x. Clearly the notion of signification has psychologico-causal overtones: A thing signifies that of which it makes one think. A late medieval definition runs: To signify is to represent (i) something or (ii) some things or (iii) somehow to a cognitive power.[8] A term's signification is a property of the term prior to its particular use in utterances.[9]

Medieval thinkers basically agree that written words immediately signify spoken words, and that spoken words immediately signify mental concepts, and that mental concepts immediately signify objects in the world. Signification is thus a transitive relation: just as it is true that if *a* causes *b* and *b* causes *c*, so *a* causes *c*, so, too, is it so that if *a* is a sign of *b* and *b* is a sign of *c*, so *a* is a sign of *c*.[10] Medieval thinkers tend to agree that while mental concepts *naturally* signify objects, written and spoken terms only conventionally (*ad placitum*) signify mental concepts.[11]

Medieval thinkers generally hold that written and spoken words can only *mediately* signify objects in the world. While the extralinguistic thing is the "ultimate significant," the written word is *subordinate* to the spoken word, and the spoken is *subordinate to* the mental concept.[12] Philosophers divided on whether spoken language signifies concepts or extralinguistic objects by way of subordination to concepts. Examples of the former include Aristotle, Augustine, Boethius, Jean Buridan, and sometimes Duns Scotus; representatives of the latter are William of Ockham, Walter Burley, and sometimes Scotus.[13]

As the tradition developed, *signification* was increasingly construed extensionally. Whereas earlier thinkers could hold that "man" signifies the secondary substance man, and not Plato and Socrates who instance that substance, Ockham and the subsequent nominalist tradition hold that "man" signifies all of those things of which it is truly predicated.

A word's *supposition* is its capacity to "stand for" different things. Stephen Reed writes: "Just as signification corresponds most closely—though not exactly—to contemporary ideas of meaning or sense, so supposition corresponds in some ways to modern notions of reference, denotation and extension."[14] The medieval tradition knew that the *supposition* of a word changes within various contexts. While each word has a *significatum* (or *significata*), words supposit for different objects on different occasions of use. A statement's truth-conditions are thus connected to supposition. A particular affirmative statement is true if and only if there is something that the subject and predicate both supposit for. A universal affirmative statement is true if and only if it is not the case that the subject supposits for something which the predicate does not.

Medievals distinguish three kinds of supposition: *formal or personal supposition* occurs when a word stands for an extralinguistic object; *material supposition* when the word stands for itself; and *simple supposition* when the word stands for a universal form or concept. Accordingly, "man" supposits personally when referring to a flesh-and-blood man, materially when referring to the word *man*, and simply when referring to the humanity that the man has. Personal supposition comes in two kinds: *discrete* personal supposition happens when a word stands for a particular individual; *common* personal supposition when it stands for some individual or other.[15]

The specifics of simple supposition vary among writers having differing views on universals. William of Sherwood and Walter Burley claim in simple supposition that the word supposits for what it signifies. Ockham, however, claims that simple supposition happens when a term supposits for an intention in the soul. Reed writes, "So for him, a spoken or written term has simple supposition when it stands for the mental act to which it is subordinated by the conventions of signification."[16]

In summary, the later medieval tradition held that while words might bring different concepts to mind—they might signify this or that—the proposition in which the words are ingredient is true only if the subject and predicate terms have the same *supposita*.[17] This is a truth-conditional approach to semantics. Moreover, truth is a monadic property of propositions—it is had by those that are true.

Luther's Trinitarian Semantics

Luther was trained at Erfurt in a tradition assuming the distinction between *significatio* and *suppositio,* a tradition that paid close attention to language and the precise claims made by it. Luther, in fact, was deeply interested in what a theological statement *means* and, like a good practitioner of supposition theory, he assumed that the meaning of an expression is ultimately connected to its *truth-conditions.* In his concerns and practices, Luther was, in fact, doing things not unlike what his philosophical teachers were doing, things in many ways not unlike what philosophers of language now do. Of course, Luther was always doing these things for a theological purpose, for instance, making true claims about the two natures of Christ or the relations of the persons of the Trinity. Luther knew that words used in theology often seem to behave differently semantically than words used in other contexts.[18] The trick was to get clear on that to which the terms *referred*.

The examination of Peter Hegemon on July 3, 1545, gave Luther his final public opportunity to declare his mature view on the semantics of trinitarian predication:

> If we were to take it ['God generates God'] personally, then 'God generates God' is true. But if we construe it essentially, then God does not generate Himself nor another thing. The essence does not generate, but the person does. If truly it ['God generates God'] were not to be taken personally, then it does not generate.[19]

Readers unfamiliar with Luther's disputations may not be aware of the time Luther devotes to the task of talking correctly about the Trinity.[20] Luther, in fact, had been thinking about trinitarian semantics for at least thirty-five years prior to these comments, and he discusses semantics and the role of logic in trinitarian claims in a number of disputations and other places.

In the 1539 disputation *"Verbum caro factum est,"* ("The Word Made Flesh"), Luther addresses semantic issues connected to the divine essence by providing the following example of true trinitarian premises leading to a false conclusion.

1. The Father generates within the divine.
2. The Father is the divine essence.
3. Therefore, the divine essence generates.[21]

While the syllogism is sound (*bonus*) in being valid and having true premises, the conclusion is false.[22] But how is this possible? Is there somehow a failure in logic here? A few theses later, Luther gives another example of a sound syllogism seemingly gone awry:

1. Every divine essence is the Father.
2. The Son is the divine essence.
3. Therefore, the Son is the Father.[23]

What can account for true premises and a false conclusion? Does logic not work when talking about trinitarian matters and must it thereby be simply rejected? Or should we look for a new kind of logic that would govern theological inferences and thus block the inference to the conclusion (3)?

While Luther in 1539 holds that it is false that the divine essence generates, five years later in the promotion disputation of Georg Maior and Johannes Faber, Luther claims that Lombard ought not to have denied that essence generates.[24] While Lombard had argued that the divine essence could not generate the divine essence, for if it did the same thing would have generated itself and this is impossible,[25] Luther criticizes "the Teacher" for failing to distinguish between taking a term absolutely and relatively. When taken absolutely, a term supposits for what is common to all three persons of the Trinity, but when taken relatively it supposits for each individual in which that divine essence is present. If one were to take each proposition in the first syllogism relatively, then it follows logically, of course, that the divine essence (suppositing for the Father) generates the divine essence (suppositing for the Son). Luther criticizes Lombard for not allowing this way of speaking:

> But he ought not to have denied that the essence relatively generates a person, especially when he saw, from Augustine, that God from God is generated and light from light. Therefore, when he had admitted this, it was not the case the he should have denied that argument in a similar form concerning the essence.[26]

Indeed, while in the 1539 disputation Luther recognizes what his semantics would allow, he still sides with Lombard because it is "more fitting" and "safer" for the theologian to say that "the Father generates" than to say "the essence generates."[27] However, by 1544, his semantic sense has gotten the best of him: there is simply no good reason *not* to countenance the inference to "the essence generates the essence."[28] Luther declares: "Against the Teacher (Lombard) and the pope we say, 'essence,' 'wisdom,' and 'light' are taken relatively."[29]

Graham White traces Luther's increasing doubts about whether or not one can properly say "the essence generates the essence."[30] While one might quibble with some of the details of White's account, it is true that Luther was reading Ockham, Gabriel Biel, and Pierre d'Ailly in 1509–1510, and that he was expressing some semantically inspired doubts about what could or could not properly be said about the persons of the Trinity: "If 'God' is taken relatively there, why not 'essence' as well?"[31] On a contemporary model-theoretic analysis, we might say that the statement "the essence generates the essence" is *true* if and only if the essence generates the essence. But if "essence" refers to the Father, and "essence" refers to the Son, then the "Father generates the Son" entails "divine essence generates the essence." Given the reference of "essence" and the structure of the Trinity, one might be tempted to argue that "essence generates essence" is not only true but *necessarily* so.

It is important to realize that Luther could affirm statements like "the essence generates essence" because his nominalism closely links truth and supposition. If he were a realist with respect to universals, he might have construed the syllogism as follows and thus explained why a seeming false conclusion follows from true premises:

1. The Father generates within the divine (personal supposition)
2. The Father is the divine essence (simple supposition)
3. Therefore, the divine essence generates.

Notice how this would have been similar to this well-known medieval example:

1. Man is the most dignified of creatures (simple supposition).
2. Socrates is a man (personal supposition)
3. Therefore, Socrates is the most dignified of creatures.

The problem in the second example is that there is simple supposition in (1) and personal supposition in (2). In (1) "man" supposits for the form of man, while in (2) it supposits for the concrete individual bearing that form. The explanation for the falsity of (3) is the equivocation in (1) and (2).

Luther's nominalism, however, precludes permitting simple supposition to refer to a form of divine essence apart from the persons. The nominalist move is to construe simple supposition to refer to what is common to the individuals. Just as one might say "the dog bites the dog" when it is true that "Spot bites Fido," it seems one ought to be able to say, "the divine essence generates." There is no equivocation in the first example if we understand that "divine essence" and "Father" are functioning co-referentially.

The question Luther is dealing with is complicated. Lombard had denied that essence generates essence and, because of this, Joachim of Flora believed that Lombard was committed to a quaternity in the Trinity: Father, Son, Spirit, and divine essence. Luther rejects the quaternity, suggesting that its appearance is due to not getting clear on the supposition of terms. In the 1517 disputation *"Contra scholasticam theologia"* ("Against Scholastic Theology") he decries those who would fashion a logic of faith and twenty-two years later declares "neither are the subtle inventions of the mediate and immediate supposition to be used nor to be taken advantage of in matters of faith."[32] A "logic of faith" is not a logic at all, for Luther, but one that "disunites by uniting." As Luther points out, if a distinction is made between the supposed common middle term in the major and minor premise, "the significance of the word is not the same."[33] But what was this distinction between the immediate and mediate supposition employed by d'Ailly that Luther did not like?

D'Ailly explains that "Father" immediately supposits for the person of the Father and mediately for the divine essence that person has. Alternately, "divine essence" could supposit immediately for the divine essence and mediately for the person carrying that divine essence.[34] But Luther clearly rejects "a logic of faith" that makes use of this distinction and, as Theodore Dieter points out, also the distinctions among distributing "inside the term," "outside the term," and "outside the number," distinctions employed by his Erfurt teacher, Jacobus Trutvetter.[35] Distributing "inside the term" (*distributio in termino*), "every divine essence is the Father" is true because it is entails that "there is no divine essence that is not the essence the Father has." Distributing "outside the term" (*distributio extra terminum*), there is an assertion of real identity between the Father and the essence, but this makes "every divine essence is the Father" false because neither the Son nor the Holy Spirit is the Father yet both have the divine essence. Distributing "outside the number" (*distributio extra numerum*) the statement "every divine essence is the Father" is false because the divine essence does not entail a singular person.[36]

When dealing with the Trinity, Luther clearly rejects easy equivocation, claiming that the heretic Joachim of Flora was right: "[Lombard] was rightly faulted by the abott Joachim because he asserted a quaternity in the deity."[37] Luther declares, in fact, that such equivocation is the *mater errorum* and actually suggests that retaining the Aristotelian syllogistic form in trinitarian thinking can help display the lofty nature of the trinitarian subject matter.[38] In the Trinity, "the thing itself is equivocal."[39]

Conclusion

So what are we to make of all of this? It is clear that Luther uses a pretty sophisticated batch of distinctions in order to argue on one occasion that the essence does not generate and on another instance that the essence does generate. Clearly important is what words *mean*, what conditions must obtain to *make true* various trinitarian statements. In his concern for isolating the truth-conditions of expressions—and understanding truth in terms of *suppositio* and not *significatio*—Luther's semantics is not unlike those of his teachers within the late medieval nominalist traditions. Luther in his disputations seeks to dispel ambiguity and achieve precision by getting clear on the truth-conditions of trinitarian expressions. As we have seen, a similar concern for precision by getting clear on reference animates many contemporary practitioners of the philosophy of language.

CHAPTER 8

Philipp Melanchthon

The First Lutheran Philosopher

Charles Peterson

Philipp Melanchthon was the first Lutheran philosopher.[1] Two parts of this claim—that he was a philosopher and that he was Lutheran—may require some justification. After at least gesturing toward such a justification, I will present the general contours of Melanchthon's approach to philosophy on the belief that it can be a great help to twenty-first-century Lutherans as we continue to struggle to relate *fides et ratio*.

As Timothy Wengert and others have pointed out, from the sixteenth century through the twentieth Melanchthon has been accused of betraying important aspects of Luther's thought through a late-career turn toward Scholasticism, humanism, or through pusillanimity.[2] Whether or not such charges have merit, I will here simply reject the notion that Melanchthon was not *Lutheran*. Given that at least half of the confessional material Lutheran pastors and church bodies in North America swear to uphold came from his pen, including the *Augsburg Confession* itself, Walter Bouman's claim that Melanchthon is "without question the second most important figure in the Lutheran reform movement of the sixteenth century"[3] seems undeniable.

But was Melanchthon a philosopher? While primarily dedicated to the evangelical reform of the church, Melanchthon's scholarly work is by no means limited to theology. His speeches and writings include work in classical studies and ancient philosophy, medicine, law, geometry, and mathematics and reveal a wide-ranging competence throughout the arts curriculum.[4] Even more significant are the textbooks Melanchthon wrote on rhetoric and dialectic, moral philosophy, and natural philosophy—all the major parts of philosophy as he envisioned the subject. Unfortunately, most of these remain untranslated into English.[5]

Melanchthon wrote philosophical works, he studied and critiqued the work of philosophers past, and he praised philosophy. Melanchthon did what philosophers have always done. And since Melanchthon almost literally wrote half "the book" on Lutheran*ism*, this tradition is in an important sense fundamentally "Melanchthonian." So, to conclude a long prolegomena, if ever one was poised to stand as a paragon of Lutheran philosophy, it was Philipp Melanchthon.

Initia Aristotelica

Many twentieth-century critics have accused Melanchthon of rejecting Luther's thought by way of a return to Aristotelianism.[6] And it's true that later in his career Melanchthon spoke more highly of Aristotle than of any other philosopher. In a letter to a friend he even once referred to himself as *homo peripateticus* and to his philosophy as *Aristotelica*, or *Initia Aristotelica*.[7] But Melanchthon's relationship to Aristotle the Stagirite was complex.

First, Melanchthon's appreciation for Aristotle represents neither a residual nor a revived commitment to one or another of the Scholastic medieval *viae*. Prior to coming to Wittenberg, he intended to produce a new edition of Aristotle's works, so that this philosopher's work could be read in its purity, stripped clean of so many layers of medieval commentary that had "maimed" and "mutilated" this philosopher until his true thought had "become more obscure than a sibylline oracle."[8] And even in 1558, two years before his death, he referred to Scholasticism as "that recently begotten deception which those barbarians [sic] teach in the name of philosophy."[9]

Melanchthon further broke from the medieval tradition of regarding Aristotle as "the philosopher" in that he denied that even a purified Aristotle contains the *summa* of true philosophy. In a disputation on Colossians he praises Aristotle's method as superior to that of any other philosopher, but continues, "Nevertheless, philosophy is not contained within such narrow confines that one need assume that it is all included in the books written by Aristotle."[10] And so, as he elsewhere writes, a good philosopher should not rely entirely upon Aristotle but "can now and again take something from other authors, too."[11]

Indeed, Melanchthon found other philosophers decidedly superior to the Stagirite in some ways. He regarded Plato's philosophical theology as superior to Aristotle's, and he rejected Aristotle's claim that the human mind is at birth a *tabula rasa*, advocating what has been widely taken as a Platonic notion that humans have some innate ideas. But rather than choosing between the philosophies of Aristotle and Plato, he implores the reader, "Let us love them both."[12]

Indeed, Melanchthon treats other philosophers almost as lovingly. In natural philosophy he shows great respect for Galen, claiming that the Hellenistic physician "has learnedly corrected some things and has shed light on many passages in Aristotle."[13] In dialectic he loves Cicero best, basing his own rhetoric upon that of this Roman orator.[14] And even those whom he does not treat affectionately he takes seriously. Throughout his philosophical works one can find the *Praeceptor Germaniae* arguing with utmost seriousness against ideas found among Stoics, Epicureans, and Skeptics.

Melanchthon's approach to philosophy was Aristotelian in that he promotes Aristotle's syllogistic method for searching out "what is correct, true, simple, steadfast, well-ordered and useful for life."[15] He also most highly values Aristotle's ethics—provided this discipline be regarded as treating only of civic life.[16] But given his appeal to different authorities in different areas of thought, it is not inaccurate to characterize Melanchthon's philosophy as eclectic.

The Roman Way

In this eclecticism, in the attendant relativization of the authority of Aristotle, and in his round rejection of scholasticism, Melanchthon's approach to philosophy is consistent with much of Renaissance humanism.[17] This should not be too surprising, given that on the strength of his work in rhetoric and the other *artes liberales* Melanchthon is widely regarded as an important figure by Renaissance historians.[18] But what has this Renaissance humanism to do with philosophy?

The answer to such questions depends upon what one understands by "philosophy." As Bruce Kimball points out, many contemporary readers may take it as axiomatic that the highest ideal of philosophy is pure speculative theorizing. It is in accordance with this conception that Greek metaphysics has been regarded as distinctly superior to Roman utilitarianism, focused as the latter rather was on the pragmatic concerns of statecraft, oratory, and engineering.[19]

Perhaps, however, this familiar view simply betrays a prejudice toward one understanding of philosophy and wisdom over another. Historians of philosophy have pointed out that Cicero, Quintillian, and other Romans and Greeks of the Hellenistic era held a different view, a conception of philosophy with a heritage stretching back all the way to Isocrates, the contemporary of Socrates in the fourth century B.C.E. On this alternative account, philosophy is closely associated with *ars vivendi*, and it values the whole realm of learning to the extent this is "useful" for human life in society. Philosophy does not accordingly pursue knowledge for its own sake but for the sake of enriching human life to the fullest extent possible.

This tradition, which Melanchthon refers to as "the Roman cause,"[20] portrays the ideal philosopher, the truly wise person, as the good, learned, and eloquent orator. Such an orator is to be distinguished on the one hand from the contemplative theoretician who would remain in asocial self-sufficiency and on the other hand from the sophist or the "merely eloquent" disputant-for-hire who would strive merely to be able to make the worse answer seem the better. The true orator will strive above all to put all knowledge and speech to use in society. As he wrote in 1558: "I call a philosopher one who when he has learned and knows things good and useful for mankind, takes a theory (*doctrina*) out of academic obscurity and makes it practically useful in public affairs, and instructs men about natural phenomena, or religions, or about government."[21]

To the extent that contemporary Lutherans have come to regard the speculative, abstract, and metaphysically based "Greek way" associated with Plato and
Aristotle as "real philosophy," we will have a difficult time taking this "Roman
way" seriously as philosophy. But in that case, and if Melanchthon was a propo-
nent of the "Roman way," we will be bound to mistake him. For we will either
suppose that he had nothing interesting to say philosophically, or we will suppose
that if he was a philosopher, his must be some version of "Greek" thought,
founded upon some version of Aristotelian or Platonic metaphysics. In either
case it begins to become clear why the *Praeceptor Germaniae* has remained for Lutherans, in spite of his voluminous writings and his importance for the Reformation, "The Unknown Melanchthon."[22]

Philosophy and Its Limits

Following the general practice of Cicero and other philosophers of this Roman
way,[23] Melanchthon divided philosophy into physics, ethics, and logic.[24] Among
these, "logic" enjoyed certain preeminence. As historian of philosophy Jonathan
Barnes has pointed out, for Roman philosophers such as Cicero dialectics and
rhetoric were equally important parts of *logike*,[25] which could be defined as the
overall consideration of how we think and speak. Quite consistent with this Ciceronian approach, rhetoric is in an important sense the master art in Melanchthon's thought, as some excellent and fairly recent scholarly work by Timothy
Wengert and John Schneider, and some older work by Quirinius Breen, has suggested.[26] Work remains to be done to clarify the relationships in Melanchthon's
thought between rhetoric, dialectic, and philosophy as a unity, but a few points
significant for the task at hand can be made now.

First, for some readers Melanchthon's division of philosophy into logic,
physics, and ethics may be most startling for what it leaves out, namely metaphysics. This was no accident. As Günter Frank points out, throughout his life Melanchthon uniformly rejected and never commented upon Aristotle's *Metaphysics*.
What is more, as Frank explains, "In this rejection of metaphysics—or to be precise—in refusing Aristotle's doctrine of the 'prime mover' and the world of sub-
stances presented in the twelve books of *Metaphysics*, Melanchthon completely
agreed with Luther."[27]

Second, this rejection is due to something Melanchthon learned from St.
Paul. Much of scholastic thought such as that of Aquinas was founded upon the
Aristotelian claims that the human by nature desires to know and that no natural
desire exists in vain. But Melanchthon follows Paul in insisting that while humans
may desire to know, this created desire has been subjected to futility. While humans in their original state were given clear and certain knowledge of fundamental innate ideas or *koine ennoiai*, in *hac tenebra* ("this shadow") this knowledge is

obscured, vitiated by sin. As he puts it in the *Loci communes* of 1521 with reference to our knowledge of principles of morality: "For a judgment of human comprehension is, on a whole, fallacious due to innate blindness. And accordingly even if certain patterns of morals have been engraved on our minds, they can scarcely be apprehended."[28] Furthermore, since all knowledge is based upon our apprehension of innate principles, and no *certain* knowledge can arise from principles "scarcely apprehended," Melanchthon's full account of the *koine ennoiai* forestalls the possibility of dogmatic philosophical *a priorism* for humans in our present state.

Also noteworthy in Melanchthon's account of philosophy is a turn toward the empirical. Melanchthon defines philosophy as "the teaching of human reason."[29] But philosophy is not for him merely the product of *reine Vernunft* ("pure reason"). Rather, as he put it in a disputation of Colossians, philosophy is "knowledge of natural causes and effects."[30] He writes that in warning us away from "vain philosophy," Paul "does not forbid us to count or measure bodies,"[31] which activities are indeed required for true and useful natural philosophy.

To be sure, Melanchthon is no radical empiricist. On the contrary, and as noted above, a hallmark of his psychology is his clear and repeated assertion that humans have innate ideas of numbers, of basic rules of logic, and of moral precepts.[32] Joined in a syllogism to a statement about what is observed about a particular object or case, these ideas are necessary for whatever certainty, whatever knowledge philosophy is able to provide us with.

And not only does Melanchthon's Pauline skepticism forestall any sort of Platonic metaphysical realism, but in fact Melanchthon believes that such realism had been misattributed to Plato by Origen and others like him "who do not even understand Plato." These, Melanchthon writes, were guilty of "distorting [Plato's] forms"[33] by suggesting that they are independent or even fundamental metaphysical entities instead of "images and notions which the learned conceive in their minds."[34]

Some accusations of a supposed retreat on Melanchthon's part from Luther's later in the *Praeceptor*'s career stem from what Melanchthon does take from Plato—or rather, from a misunderstanding of what he takes—namely, an account of philosophical theology. Melanchthon explicitly states that of all the useful outcomes of the study of physics or natural philosophy, the most important is that it leads the philosopher to conclude "that nature does not exist by chance, but that it is created by an eternal mind" and that "the Maker is to be worshipped with true praises."[35] And he finds that Plato demonstrates this most clearly: "For [Plato] discusses quite weightily the immortality of the human soul, and he everywhere establishes as the goal of philosophy the recognition of God, as he says in a letter: 'We philosophize correctly, if we recognize God as the father, cause, and ruler of the entire nature, and obey him by living justly' [Letters,

6, c-d]."[36] Thus, Plato's natural theology is not only legitimate according to Melanchthon; it represents the highest achievement of philosophy. What is more, as he clearly states in the *Loci communes*—both of 1521 and of 1555—philosophy thus provides knowledge of the law.

Critics of Melanchthon have long concluded from this high appraisal of Plato and of philosophy according to Plato that Melanchthon finally abandoned Scripture-based evangelical theology in favor of a Scholastic theology for which revelation is not strictly necessary. For example, in his introductory essay to Manschrek's translation of the 1555 edition of the *Loci communes*, Hans Engellund wrote: "From this naturalistic approach of Melanchthon's theology it follows that the revelation of God as attested in the Holy Scriptures can have only supplemental significance. Revelation only adds something to that which man can and ought to say about God."[37] What is more, it is on account of this supposed "fusion of reason and revelation"[38] that Melanchthon has been blamed for un-Lutheran or even anti-Lutheran developments in subsequent philosophical systems in which reason alone is able to provide all necessary or possible truth about God. So Jaroslav Pelikan would fleece Melanchthon: "Melanchthonianism, Orthodoxy, Rationalism, and Hegelianism all sought a comprehensive rational system. To that extent they all constitute a misrepresentation of Luther."[39] And Bouman fired this arrow at him: "Melanchthon bears a large share of the responsibility for the fact that after two hundred years of Lutheran theology, the result was the Enlightenment and the devastating critique of Immanuel Kant."[40]

All of this represents the great tragedy and irony of Melanchthon's legacy among Lutherans. For it was in fact the central, overriding concern of his treatment of philosophy to prevent exactly the sort of fusion Engellund and others accuse him of. As Melanchthon warns, "the most prevalent in an Iliad of ills" facing the church is "ignorant theology," which creates this sort of (con)fusion: "For it is a miscellaneous teaching, in which the great things are not explained clearly, things that should be separated are mingled together, and on the other hand those that nature claims should be pulled apart; often contradictory things are said, and things that are merely similar are seized in preference to those that are true and proper."[41]

The way to prevent such "ignorant theology," Melanchthon believed, is to take with utmost seriousness the distinction between law and gospel. Throughout his career he made and clarified this distinction, as in the 1555 *Loci* where he writes, "The Law proclaims to us the great wrath of God against our sin, and says nothing about the forgiveness of sin, out of grace, without our merit."[42] That this distinction plays a prominent role both in his Baccalaureate theses of 1519[43] and in his oration for Luther's funeral in 1546[44] indicates its enduring importance for Melanchthon.

It is true that Melanchthon believed that philosophy could reveal (though imperfectly and only in part) the law of God. And if Melanchthon maintained that the word of God consists of law and gospel, it follows that he believed that philosophy could reveal the word of God—or, rather, a part of a part of the word of God. But to suggest that for Melanchthon the revealed gospel only "supplements" the philosopher's knowledge of the word of God is to fail to understand the strict limits Melanchthon placed on philosophy. Quite contrary to Engellund, for Master Philipp it is philosophy that is of merely supplemental value for the theologian. While the theologian should regard philosophy as "a great tool," as he puts it in the *Loci* of 1555, the philosopher without Scripture and the Holy Spirit "cannot grasp" the gospel, let alone discover it.

This is the single most important word Melanchthon wished to convey about philosophy. As several of the essays in the present volume demonstrate, Lutheranism after Melanchthon has at times tended either toward fideistic rejections of philosophy or toward attempts to ground faith in some philosophical scheme or other. Rejecting both of these possibilities, Melanchthon has continually been rejected by partisans from both sides, one side claiming that, as a philosophical "intellectualist"[45] he was not really Lutheran, others finding him uninteresting philosophically.

Perhaps twenty-first-century Lutherans desiring to reject both foundationalism and fideism would find it valuable to start over from the beginning as we attempt to relate *fides et ratio*. Perhaps we would do well to pay more careful consideration to the first Lutheran philosophy, Melanchthon's "Roman way." And perhaps we could begin by letting him have the last word here and now. As Melanchthon writes in an oration praising Plato:

> True philosophy, that is, one that does not stray from reason and from demonstrations, is some notion of the divine laws: it recognizes that there is a God, it judges on civic morals, it sees that this distinction between worthy and vile acts is implanted in us by divine providence, it considers that horrid crimes are punished by God, and it also has some presentiment of immortality. It nevertheless does not see or teach what is proper to the Gospel, that is, the forgiveness of sins to be given without recompense, for the sake of the Son of God. This notion has not sprung from human minds, indeed, it is far beyond the range of human reason, but the Son of God, who is in the bosom of the Father, has made it manifest.[46]

PART II

Luther's Impact
on Continental Philosophy

CHAPTER 9

Reasoning Faithfully

Leibniz on Reason's Triumph of Faith and Love

Lea F. Schweitz

In the preliminary remarks of the *Theodicy*, Gottfried Wilhelm Leibniz (1646–1716) reminds his reader that "the question of the conformity of faith with reason has always been a great problem."[1] This essay will not solve that "great problem." However, in the face of heated disputes that claim one must choose reason or faith, science or religion, philosophy or theology, in Leibniz we find an early modern alternative. Here is a faithful, inquisitive, Lutheran thinker who proposes that faith and reason are reciprocally related. Faith and reason each have a role to play in the life of the faithful thinker, and, furthermore, each play a role in the "other's" role. For Leibniz, faith and reason need one another.

In the end, Leibniz's solution to this "great problem" may not be fully relevant, but it provides a useful mirror for critically investigating contemporary solutions to this problem and a window into constructive questions that further open up our thinking about it.[2] This essay takes up the quandary of Lutheran philosophy in the form of Leibniz's proposal on faith and reason. It argues that Leibniz sees himself standing in the Lutheran heritage when he argues that they are reciprocally related. In addition, this essay addresses two corollary views: Leibniz contends that the burden of proof for the Christian mysteries ultimately lies with the objector to the mystery rather than the believer; and he finds that the faithful thinker will be moved to acts of love. The essay concludes by suggesting that although Leibniz's views may be untenable outside of his own historical location, they raise questions to help our thinking about the "great problem" of the conformity of faith with reason.

Leibniz Reconsidered

There was a time when Leibniz would not have had a place in a book on the quandary of Lutheran philosophy. Leibniz's story begins in the Lutheran city of Leipzig at the home of Lutheran parents. His mother, Catharina Schmuch, was the daughter of a respected lawyer, and his father, Friedrich Leibniz, was the vice chairman of the faculty of philosophy and professor of moral philosophy at the University of Leipzig. They were married in 1644; two years later (and two years before the end of the Thirty Years War), Gottfried Wilhelm Leibniz was born. He was baptized at the Church of St. Nikolai, and the family chronicle reports that "at the moment of baptism, the new-born child raised his head with wide open eyes."[3] Leibniz's father interpreted this as a sign of his son's promise in furthering the work of the church and the glory of God.[4]

Despite his Lutheran origins, by the time of his death in Hanover he was called *Glaubt nichts*—"believes nothing." He earned this unfortunate and inaccurate name because of his irregular attendance at church and Holy Communion. Leibniz also had a deeply irenic spirit and an eclectic philosophical temperament; he sought out truth wherever it could be found, including in Spinoza, French Catholics, writings from China sent by Jesuit missionaries, letters and conversations with queens and princesses, Englishmen, mystics, early modern scientists, and alchemists. Depending on the audience, any one of these interlocutors might have raised some suspicion about Leibniz's confessional identity. More recently, when the scholarship on Leibniz addresses his religious or theological writings, it tends to focus on his project for church reunification or his natural theology, and these interests often minimize the confessional distinctions in his work. This might suggest that there is no quandary of Lutheran philosophy for Leibniz because he is not sufficiently Lutheran to fall into this particular quandary.

On my reading, such a view simplifies and undervalues the contributions of Lutheran heritage in Leibniz's life and thought. Take, for example, Leibniz's commitment to the Protestant principle: *Sola scriptura!* For Leibniz, revealed theology has a key role in the life of the faithful thinker. In the history of ideas, Leibniz has been handed down as a rationalist. As such, the important role of faith and religion may come as a surprise. However, Leibniz's soteriology is committed to the mystery of the Christian mysteries. Salvation itself depends on the mysteries of the Christian faith, in particular the Trinity, the incarnation, and the Eucharist, and these are not fully known by reason. Here one of the quandaries of Leibniz's Lutheran philosophy arises. Gotthold Ephraim Lessing (1729–1781) put the question this way: "In what way can it [revealed, Christian theology] exist in the head of our philosopher, how is it consonant with the principles of pure reason, what influences did it have on his life as well as on his reflections?"[5] In other words, how does the rationalist Leibniz make room for the mysteries of Christian faith without jeopardizing their status as mysteries?

Leibniz's most public and most sustained investigation into matters of faith and reason appears in the preliminary dissertation that opens his *Theodicy*.[6] Written in response to Pierre Bayle's (1647–1706) claim that faith and reason are in opposition, Leibniz takes a more moderate approach and instead claims the conformity of faith and reason. Conformity, however, is an ambiguous relation; it comes in both weak and strong varieties.

The weak sense of conformity may account simply for the "side-by-side" existence of the two conforming things. In the weak sense, faith may conform with reason simply by allowing it to operate independently, without contradiction or interference. One part of Leibniz's strategy for affirming the Christian mysteries includes a distinction between that which is within reason and that which is above reason. Reason has its jurisdiction in earthly, civic matters in the kingdom of nature, but human reason does not extend to theological matters in the kingdom of grace. Reason, law, and custom have their place in maintaining the practical concerns of everyday life for good order; all this is "within reason." Regarding the Trinity, incarnation, and Eucharist—that is, the Christian mysteries—each of these is above reason. By distinguishing these two realms, Leibniz is able to maintain the conformity of faith and reason in the weak sense.

In these moments, Leibniz's view seems to come very close to Luther's views on the two kingdoms. When Leibniz reads Luther for the purposes of his *Theodicy,* one thing he finds is a good Christian defending reason's proper use and limits. Leibniz affirms Luther's hostility to those who attempt to submit revealed truths to the "tribunal of our reason."[7] When it comes to matters of faith, and particularly the Christian mysteries, there is a sense in which reason does not have the final say. This is not because such matters are against reason or contrary to reason but because they are simply beyond reason's reach. Faith provides what is necessary in matters of salvation; reason may be self-sufficient within the created order. We see in Leibniz a Lutheran taxonomy of reason; there are some truths that are above or beyond reason. Leibniz does not take this to mean that Luther or those within the *Augsburg Confession* have dismissed reason. He writes:

> The Reformers, and especially Luther . . . spoke sometimes as if they rejected philosophy, and deemed it inimical to faith. But, properly speaking, Luther understood by philosophy only that which is in conformity with the ordinary course of Nature, or perhaps even philosophy as it was taught in the schools. . . . Aristotle was the object of his anger; and so far back as the year 1516 he contemplated purging of philosophy, when he perhaps had as yet no thought of reforming the Church. But at last he curbed his vehemence and in the *Apology for the Augsburg Confession* allowed a favorable mention of Aristotle and his *Ethics.* Melanchthon, a man of sound and moderate ideas, made little systems from the several parts of philosophy, adapted to the truths of revelation and useful in civic life, which deserve to be read even now.[8]

Both faith and reason are affirmed within their own kingdoms, and they conform in the weak sense because each is isolated in its own domain. Leibniz sees himself in the tradition of Luther, Melanchthon, and other Reformers who affirmed reason's proper place and its conformity with faith.

As we have seen, the distinction between claims that are above reason and within reason is not a denial of reason. It is neither an affirmation of the falsity of the claims above reason nor an affirmation of these claims being true in some special sense. For Leibniz, even though the mysteries are above reason, contra Pierre Bayle, they cannot be against reason: "Since reason is a gift of God, even as faith is, contention between them would cause God to contend against God."[9] It cannot be that reason is true and faith is false (or vice versa) because both come from God. This rationale goes together with Leibniz's denial of "double truth" views. Leibniz consistently denies that what may be true in philosophy might be false in theology, or vice versa, and he denies that there are multiple kinds of truth. One of Leibniz's basic assumptions is that two truths cannot contradict one another. Either what's true in philosophy is true in theology (and vice versa) or one of these is merely a "purported" truth—because truths simply cannot be contradictory. In a discussion comparing monastic vows and reason, Luther comes very close to saying something similar: "If anything is really contrary to reason, it is certainly much more against God also. For how can anything not be in conflict with heavenly truth when it is in conflict with earthly truth?"[10] With Luther, Leibniz denies that two truths can be in conflict. These denials begin to bring the "two kingdoms" closer together: faith is not against reason because both are gifts of God.

The Conformity of Faith with Reason

In what sense does Leibniz affirm a stronger sense of the conformity of faith with reason? What does Leibniz mean when he claims to have placed reason at the service of faith rather than in opposition to it?[11] How does reason's service preserve the mystery of the Christian mysteries? And what "effect" does faithful service have on reason itself? In the final section of this essay, I will argue that Leibniz employs two forms of a stronger sense of faith's conformity with reason:

- Faith strongly conforms with reason in defending the Christian mysteries; and
- Reason is strongly conformed to faith when illumined by grace.

Leibniz, like Luther, was a more occasional than systematic author; when questions or opportunities for advancing his thought arose, he responded. As such, Leibniz presents his reader with several strategies for defending the

Christian mysteries, depending on the audience and the nature of the "attack." In this essay, I want to look briefly at one such occasion.

Several times during Leibniz's long career, he addressed the Socinians, who objected to the Trinity and incarnation on the grounds that they were irrational. Take, for example, the following Socinian counterargument against the Trinity: if Jesus did not know the day of the last judgment and God does; and if Jesus is in fact God; then God would know and not know something. Since it would be irrational to believe such a contradiction, Jesus cannot be God. Leibniz argues against the counterargument by claiming that God is being used equivocally as both God the Father and Jesus, Son of God. The argument above is valid only if the ambiguity in the terms is removed, and it has been shown independently that God the Father also cannot be Jesus, Son of God, but this is precisely what is in question. Leibniz disputes the definitions and then critiques the conclusions. Ursula Goldenbaum deems Leibniz's response his "negative strategy"—negative in the sense that Leibniz's tactic is to defeat the arguments against faith claims rather than make "positive" arguments for them.[12] The negative strategy attempts to refute objections that show some irrationality in the claims of faith. Faith and reason conform in Leibniz's negative strategy because reason serves to meet the objections to the mysteries.

It is a curiously effective strategy for two reasons: it is curious because it does not attempt positive arguments for the mysteries themselves. Reason observes its proper limits. Although the Christian mysteries are mysterious, Leibniz claims that the objections to them are not. One of the tasks of the faithful thinker is to meet these objections as they arise. This strategy is effective because reason observes its limits while having a significant role to play in defending against possible refutations or objections.

It is effective because the defense relies on the mysterious nature of the mysteries. The mysteries—because they can never be articulated clearly or precisely—cannot be refuted conclusively.[13] As we saw in the Socinian case above, Leibniz defends the trinitarian nature of God by dismantling the counterargument against it. Leibniz's general strategy depends on the theological ambiguities in such counterarguments, and as in the Socinian case above, Leibniz believes that when the ambiguities are drawn out—and there will always be ambiguities because of their mysterious nature—counterarguments will be shown to be invalid. As such, Leibniz's commitment to the mysteries as mysteries guarantees a measure of certainty in the strategy of defense. This is a much stronger sense of the conformity of faith and reason: reason's success depends on the very nature of the faith claims being defended.

Leibniz's defensive strategy does not argue for the mysteries themselves. According to him, they may be presumed to be true (even though they are above reason) until they have been shown to be self-contradictory.[14] His strategy of defense assures us that reason is up to the challenge. At the same time, it reopens the question, "With whom does the burden of proof lie?" Leibniz's answer is that the believer is free to believe until such beliefs are shown to be impossible. Although his answer may not be tenable, it is a question still worth asking.

We have come a long way from seeing faith and reason as two separate kingdoms. Yet Leibniz has moments when the conformity seems even stronger and reason itself appears as a kind of theological virtue. Leibniz writes:

> And it is not to be doubted that this faith and this confidence in God, who gives us insight into his [sic] infinite goodness and prepares us for his [sic] love, in spite of the appearances of harshness that may repel us, are an admirable exercise for the virtues of Christian theology, when the divine grace in Jesus Christ arouses these motions within us. This is what Luther aptly observed. . . . One may therefore say that the triumph of true reason illumined by divine grace is at the same time the triumph of faith and love.[15]

Notice that Leibniz is careful to avoid any hint of works righteousness. Reason's work does nothing to advance the reasoner in God's eyes. Furthermore, it is not reason alone that yields a triumph of faith and love but reason illumined by grace. Like Leibniz, Brian Gerrish sees this very strong sense of conformity of faith and reason in Luther: "Reason, when regenerate, is virtually absorbed into faith, becoming faith's cognitive and intellective aspects. Because reason belongs to the natural sphere, Luther will not allow that it is competent to judge in matters of faith; and yet, because faith comes through the hearing and understanding of the Word, Luther found himself bound to concede that reason—man's [sic] rationality in the broadest sense—was, when regenerate, faith's indispensable tool."[16] For my purposes, the appearance of such a view of reason in the "rationalist" Leibniz and the explicit connection to Luther are striking. Reason has been transformed from an instrument of the devil to a theological virtue with a christological link. With God's help, it has found a place in the faith-filled life. Reasoning faithfully is no longer a quandary or paradox—even as it depends on God and maintains the mystery of the Christian mysteries.

Conclusion

I find history of philosophy is at its best when it helps us ask new questions or helps us ask old questions anew. These reflections on Leibniz's Lutheran views of the conformity of faith and reason should not be read as an implicit, nostalgic wish for a return to preenlightenment times. To my mind, Leibniz's relevance is in the questions he forces us to ask. In matters of faith and belief, where does the burden of proof lie? Where have we put our trust? And if reason is a gift of God, then how might it be of service—and even become a triumph of faith and love? Better than a solution to the question of the conformity of faith and reason, Leibniz's wrestling with this "great problem" yields questions that invite further wrestling from the various communities and contexts in which we find ourselves now.

CHAPTER 10

The Means of Revolution

Luther and Kant on the Function of the Law

Troy Dahlke

How does one become another? People episodically *do* good, but can they *become* good? "But if a man is corrupt in the very ground of his maxims," Immanuel Kant once asked, "how can he possibly bring about this revolution by his own powers and of himself become a good man?"[1] His question is not merely rhetorical; he believes that radical evil resides so deeply in human nature that it is "*inextirpable* by human powers."[2] To this point, Kant sounds Lutheran enough, but he also has faith in the necessity of freedom—how can humans be held to account if they are not free? Recognizing the rootedness of evil and a requisite freedom, Kant discerns the need for a "revolution," as opposed to a "gradual *reformation*," if one is to become another.[3]

Kant tells us *where* the revolution must take place: in the "cast of mind," as opposed to the "sensuous nature." His revolution is one of practical reason. He also describes *how* the overthrow happens: by the rule of law (as strange as that sounds for a revolutionary).[4] Here, Kant betrays his pietistic Lutheran pedigree by appropriating Martin Luther's understanding of how the law *functions*. His appropriation, however implicit, is not surprising. Although they differ widely in their religious epistemologies and, more specifically, in their grounding of the law—Kant founds it in the self-legislating reason of the autonomous self, whereas Luther locates it in the ontological reality of a revealed divine will—Kant suggests that that the "pure religion of reason" and "revealed reason" may lead to the same moral conclusions. To this end, if not to the end of moral revolution, Kant comes remarkably close to duplicating Luther's three functions of the law: the political, theological, and pedagogical.

The Political Function: Restraint and Infringement, Civil Righteousness and Legality

Luther and Kant, following Luther, describe the law as functioning in a restraining or infringing manner on sinful and evil people who are afflicted with passions and sensuous impulses. They agree that the law works negatively by fear of punishment and painful effects to hold back impulses from erupting into evil behavior. Simultaneously, the law also works positively to promote legality so that external peace generally reigns over lawlessness.

For Luther the law is the summary of God's eternal will for humanity.[5] After the fall the law remains on the heart, but its content is diffused and purpose misguided. Post-fall humanity's comprehension of the first table of the law, which commands love and trust of God and orders life for the "kingdom of God" (*regnum Dei*), is so impaired that its (mis)understanding always leads to idolatry. The second table, however, remains less obscured and orders life in the "kingdom of the world" (*regnum mundi*).[6] What remains agrees with the second half of biblical summary of the law—"love thy neighbor as thyself"—and may be apprehended, however imperfectly, by reason. From the knowable remnants of the law a "political or Gentile" function emerges over the whole of the *regnum mundi* that "restrains sins by threats and fears of punishment."[7]

Through this *restraining* function God governs and preserves the life primarily, though not exclusively, through the "different government" of the world's political and social structures.[8] Here Luther describes the law as functioning like a prison that refrains the wicked "not out of good will or out of a love for righteousness but because the prison *prevents* him."[9] It works "in the world by the rack, the gallows, and the sword . . . to *restrain* the madness" of the passionately driven.[10] Without this restraining effect life in *regnum mundi* would be "reduced to chaos."[11] For Luther, the hearts of many are so driven that altruistic instruction or the promises of reward are simply ineffective. The law, however imperfectly, prevents the wicked from following their passions without fear and impunity.[12]

While the primary purpose and effect of the political use of the law is to restrain the wicked and preserve the *regnum mundi,* it positively fosters a healthy ordering of life for those who by reason perceive and live according to the law on their hearts. By this "purely natural" endowment, people may produce an "active righteousness," which Luther calls "moral" and "civil."[13] As people actively conform to the external demands of the law, order mitigates chaos even as God rewards the civilly righteous with "the best gifts of this life."[14]

In the end, however, the political function of the law is limited. The righteousness it produces is valid only in the *regnum mundi;* it fails to create the true righteousness of the *regnum Dei.* For those who fail to see the limitations of this function of the law by presuming that a proper knowledge and keeping of the law is attainable in and for the *regnum Dei,* Luther has nothing but scorn. "The sophists are blind," he argues, "They imagine . . . that those who keep it externally are righteous in the sight of God."[15] Failing to grasp the full import of the law, they actually abuse it.[16] Because there is a need to maintain the political use and still recognize another deeper function of the law, Luther insists on a distinction between "two courtrooms," the "civil" and the "theological."[17]

Where Luther believes righteousness in the "civil courtroom" and its general concomitant of reward with "best gifts of this life" in no way signify a fulfillment of the law, so Kant recognizes that morality has nothing to do with the apparent fulfillment of the moral law and a subsequent "enjoyment of life."[18] Only when the moral law alone determines the will does true morality "from duty" arise with majesty so singular that it "has its own law and its own court."[19] Only this court is able to judge whether an action is performed "merely to fulfill the *letter* of law without containing its *spirit*."[20] By explicitly identifying a "moral court," Kant implicitly identifies a court that functions akin to Luther's civil court. In this court, the law negatively "restricts" and "infringes" through painful affects, even as it promotes a public morality that, while not being truly moral, at least conforms to the external demands of the law. Like Luther, Kant sees that there is a specific and legitimate realm—the public or civil—in which the (moral) law functions to effect mere behavior apart from the internal motive of the actor.[21]

Thus, while true morality according to Kant occurs solely when the law, for its own sake, determines a will, the same law still functions to serve the needs of the implied civil court and life in the *regnum mundi*. [22] Since humans have a "sensible existence," are affected by "inclinations" and "impulses," and are given to a "perverse heart" that places other incentives alongside or above the moral law, Kant reckons them as evil.[23] This evil manifests itself, in part, in "feelings" such as "a predominant *benevolence* toward oneself (*philautia*)."[24] Unchecked *philautia* fosters vices like animosity and envy and may even lead to the truly "diabolical."[25] By creating "disagreeable" and "pain[ful]" effects, the political function of the law causes negative affective responses in sensuous yet rational humans. Through these negative affects, whether experienced or thought *a priori*, the moral law "infringes" and "restricts" self-love and its attendant vices.[26] It checks inclinations from growing unabatedly into more diabolical vices that threaten both moral actions and ultimately the liveableness of society.

While negatively infringing upon self-love, Kant sees that the law, functioning politically, also promotes moral conduct. It restricts self-love to the "condition of agreement with this law." This condition is not yet moral, for its incentives for action are impure, but it may produce the condition of "legality."[27] A person whose conduct merely contains legality is a "man of good morals (*bene moratus*)"; he follows the "letter" of the law. Such a person appears to act no differently from "a morally good man (*moraliter bonus*)" who obeys the law's "spirit."[28] In this way, a tenuous agreement between the inclinations of self-love and the moral law is established that stabilizes life in the *regnum mundi*.

But as Luther recognizes that this is not a true fulfillment of the law, so Kant recognizes that actions done for *merely* legal reasons may lead to an abuse of the moral law, resulting in hypocritical pride and conceit. External actions may contain legality and may even appear "beautiful,"[29] but in order that hypocrisy and moral impurity do not reign, Kant, like Luther, discerns a more profound function of the law that confronts radically evil creatures; one that effects revolution.

The Theological Function:
Killing and Striking Down, Grace and Respect

For Luther and Kant, the law makes civil righteousness and moral action in the *regnum mundi* possible. The spiritual/moral creature, however, is still in need of true conversion/revolution. For this to occur, Luther and Kant respectively discern a twofold movement that begins with theological function of the law and ends in a posture of faith (Luther) or respect (Kant). For their respective purposes, each describe *how* a person can truly become another.

Chief among sins for Luther is the notion that humans can "justify" themselves and thereby merit citizenship in the *regnum Dei*. This belief puffs up creatures with the false understanding that they know God's law and can keep it.[30] They are so mistaken that they are unable even to recognize their presumption, and so they must stand in the theological courtroom and face the "chief function" of the law.[31]

Luther describes the theological function in colorful and dramatic terms. Its purposes are "to make us guilty, to humble us, to kill us, to lead us down to hell."[32] It is God's "mighty hammer" that is used "to crush that stubborn and perverse beast, presumption."[33] There is no place to hide as the law makes heaven and earth "narrower than a mouse hole" whose "narrowness [is] steadily increasing *ad infinitum.*"[34] Even the rewards of this life fail to manifest divine favor; the law's work is so "strange" that God is to be feared not only when life is difficult but also when it seems agreeable.[35]

Luther understands the theological as the chief function of the law, yet it is still God's "strange" work. As such, it is not the end of God's dealings with humanity but serves to prepare the way for God's proper work. "God does not want to trouble you in such a way that you remain in trouble," says Luther, "But . . . that you may be humbled and may acknowledge that you need the mercy of God and the blessings of Christ."[36] The chief function of the law is ultimately to direct sinners to Christ, who performs the proper work of God: rendering the guilty innocent, exalting the humbled, resurrecting the dead, and leading the damned to heaven.[37] All that properly belongs to Christ now belongs to sinners by the merely passive imputation of faith. By this imputation faith conjoins sinners to Christ who bears them anew into the *regnum Dei*.

This does not mean, however, that when justified sinners have moved into the *regnum Dei* they have moved out of sin. In and of themselves they remain sinners, but through faith they live beyond the jurisdiction and accusations of the law; they are, famously, *simul iustus et peccator*. For Luther, faith alone makes a person good. Apart from faith, all is sin. In faith, all actions, whether good or bad, are not accounted as sinful but as righteous.[38] Faith is the mark that distinguishes the truly righteous from the merely civilly righteous; it is that which, when translated into a Kantian idiom, makes one a *moraliter bonus*.

Kant also perceives a function of the law that goes beyond the political to work in a quasi-theological way. From this second use flows the twofold movement of moral revolution: the "striking down" of "self-conceit" and the awakening of "respect."

Chief among temptations for Kant is the enticement to confuse legality and morality. Those given to this temptation are filled with "self-conceit" and believe that, on the basis of mere legality, they are moral or, worse yet, they lower the moral bar by making themselves the standard of the morality. These are they who find themselves standing in morality's court, where the law "strikes down" self-conceit with such force that it "makes even the boldest evildoer tremble and forces him to hide from its sight."[39] The "innate guilt" of humanity is not only found in unintentional guilt (*culpa*) but also in deliberate guilt (*dolus*). This deliberate guilt, says Kant, displays the "insidiousness" of the heart and fosters a self-conceited moral conscience. Intoxicated with self-conceit, individuals may appear moral to themselves or even to others—the consequences of this evil disposition may or may not become apparent—and so do not even recognize the need for moral revolution.[40] This is way the law must strike forcefully. In contrast to the political courtroom that merely creates disagreeable affects, the moral courtroom downright humiliates.

But as Luther does not abstract the strange effects of the law from the broader context of God's intentions for humanity, so Kant does not abstract the negative effects of the law from the broader context of morality. Where the theological use of the law plays a vital role for Luther in the conversion, the law necessarily functions for Kant to bring about the moral revolution of even the deliberately evil. Only when subjects undergo the negative effects of the law—striking down and humiliation—are they prepared for true moral revolution: the awakening of "respect."[41]

Respect is the rational disposition that "supplies authority to the law" and opens the will to the law's determination. When the law, through the awakening of respect, becomes the "sole and supreme incentive," a revolution has occurred, and, if you will, there is an expansion of a *regnum moraliti*. Moral worth is now determined according to the law's spirit and not the basis of mere agreement with the letter or the mere enjoyment of life. Respect distinguishes the *moraliter bonus* from the person of *bene moratus*.

Those who have undergone moral revolution and reside in a *regnum moraliti* remain in *regnum mundi*. Because they are yet sensible, they are tempted to confuse morality with good morals. Until they enjoy the fruits of a practically postulated "immortality," where Kant's practically postulated "God" will effect happiness proportionate to virtue, they remain in need of the morality's court to produce humiliation and respect. But as faith is for Luther, so respect is for Kant. Sensibility aside, whatever is done in respect alone is moral; whatever is not is evil.[42]

The Pedagogical Function: Love and Duty

Luther and Kant both recognize the need for a (quasi-)theological function of the law to bring about spiritual and moral revolution, but they also know there is more to the story. For Luther, the justification of the sinner by grace through faith fosters works of love, primarily in the *regnum mundi*.[43] Similarly for Kant, the revolution in the "cast of mind" to the disposition of respect issues forth the concept of a "personality" that strives "from duty" for the law's sake. To the respective ends of love (Luther) and duty (Kant), the law functions pedagogically.[44]

Before conversion Luther holds that the law works only according to its political and theological functions. As the incarcerated hate their prison and the presumptuous hate that which humbles them, so "the whole world is hostile to the Law and hates it bitterly."[45] But when sinners are transferred into the *regnum Dei* through faith, their dispositions to the law change and a new function of the law emerges. They now "love and delight" in the law and enjoy the freedom to live, although imperfectly, according to its instruction.[46] *How* to live out this new-found love and freedom is taught most clearly and simply, according to Luther, in the Decalogue; it is the "true fountain from which all good works must spring, the true channel through which all good works must flow."[47]

Though Christians need nothing of the law itself to reap the benefits of faith, Luther holds that the first table still attends to life in the *regnum Dei* as it instructs them how, say, to use God's name rightly in prayer or worship gladly. Relieved of the burden of self-justification in the theological courtroom, the primary pedagogical function of the law is the focusing of believers *out* toward their neighbor rather than *up* toward God. Whether in response to a specific need or through general exercise of their respective vocations in the *regnum mundi*, the law so orders the thought and actions of believers that their neighbors are never means to a higher end but are ends in themselves.

Luther, however, does not forget that Christians are *simul iustus et peccator*. For this reason, the law continually serves to stir saints who are yet sinners to Christ-like activity. Believers are sometimes like balky "cattle" that need the pedagogy of the stick to rouse them. At other times, they are like children who desire to do their Father's bidding. The law serves not merely to motivate to action but to motivate certain kinds of action. It becomes the pedagogue that informs the children as to the particular intentions of their Father—they are not left to wonder what God desires of them. As such, the law, as an object of love in itself, becomes a guide for particular action according to its crystallization in Decalogue. Though believers daily fall short of fulfilling the law, daily they strive to fulfill it. This they cheerfully do, neither to gain God's affection nor to merit God's blessing but simply because this is what their Father wants.

As Luther describes spiritual conversion to faith as that which creates the conditions of loving and desiring to keep the law, Kant depicts moral revolution to a posture of respect as the necessary condition for dutifully striving to fulfill the moral law. The quasi-theological effect of the law revolutionizes the cast of mind by unmasking the dishonesty of self-conceit, thereby furthering law's determination of the will through respect. Respect *is* morality subjectively considered; yet threats to morality remain. Under the conditions of sensible existence, Kant believes that moral perfection simply is not possible. He therefore delineates a pedagogical function of the law that acts implicitly through "personality" and explicitly through "duty" to direct the moral subject in particular situations.

Respect awakens "personality"; that is, those who have undergone moral revolution discover the "sublimity" of their rational selves. "Personality" signifies the supersensible freedom of the morally converted *from* the mechanism of nature *so that* the causality of the moral law may determine the will.[48] This freedom alters the structure of incentives and who moral agents subjectively take themselves to be.[49] As the Kantian self learns to recognize the sublimity of his or her own humanity, so the self naturally considers the sublimity of others. Personality, under the tutelage of the law, orders incentives so that the self and others are never considered as means to a higher end but as ends in themselves.[50]

This awakening of personality under the pedagogy of the law opens the self to live dutifully. "The concept of duty," says Kant, "requires of the action *objective accord* with the law but requires of the maxim of the action *subjective* respect for the law."[51] Whatever actions are performed through the direction of maxims formed by any other subjective disposition may contain legality but are, in morality's court, judged to be evil. In that duty requires both objective and subjective criteria, the law functions explicitly to form maxims that govern conduct in and for the specific situations of personalities who live in two kingdoms, the sensible *regnum mundi* and the rational *regnum moraliti*.[52]

Like Luther's spiritually converted who desire to know the will of their Father, so Kantian personalities have an "interest" in the law and dutifully desire anew to form their maxims according to the law. Coupled with personality, duty informs action in such a way that it *ought* to take on universal import. Since humanity could not be sustained universally, for example, through lying, truth telling becomes a universal necessity. This universal maxim, as explicitly formed by instruction of the law, directs this particular conduct as it displays the import of personality. But here is the trick: duty, for Kant, implies not only forming and acting on maxims for the sake of the law alone but doing so *gladly*—even when pain is inevitable.

Kant knows that *gladly* following the law sets the moral bar too high for sensible creatures. He illustrates this by referencing the command, "Love God above all and your neighbor as yourself" and suggests that loving *gladly* is integral to a dutiful fulfillment. Because love is commanded it implies that it is lacking; if we loved gladly, we would not need the command. For sensible personalities, duty therefore implies not possession of a glad morality but a striving for it. The one who strives from duty may draw nearer to accordance with the law, but given the sensible conditions of the *regnum mundi* full accordance remains wanting. But under the pedagogy of the law, the morally revolutionized strive neither from coercion nor for "meritorious worth" but finally from a dutiful respect for the law as taught by the law.[53]

Conclusion

What does it mean to become another? Though ideas and idioms may overlap, Luther and Kant would answer this question in decidedly different terms. For Luther this would entail a theological realism where justification in the theological courtroom by grace through faith for Christ's sake really brings one into a real *regnum Dei*. Conversely, Kant would eschew such realism in favor of rationally and autonomously conceived "kingdom" where morality is the purpose of life. *How* does one become another? Luther and Kant see the law and how it functions as integral to true spiritual or moral revolution. In the end, it is hard not to believe that Luther would evaluate Kant's entire moral project, especially as it is inflected by Kant's epistemology and his understanding of autonomy, as somehow or another an appearance of reason the whore. This, despite the likelihood that he would recognize familiar elements in Kant's thought, especially those pertaining to the operation of the law it prepares for, effects, and carries on a revolution in the cast of mind.

CHAPTER 11

Faith, Freedom, Conscience

Luther, Fichte, and the Principle of Inwardness

Christian Lotz

As is well known, the core of Luther's doctrine can be traced back to his sharp division between the inner and the outer human being. He writes, "Man is composed of a twofold nature, a spiritual and a bodily. Regarding the spiritual nature, which they name the soul, he is called the spiritual, inward, new man; regarding the bodily nature, which they name the flesh, he is called the bodily, outward, old man."[1] According to this doctrine, the division between the world of the inner human being and the world of the fleshly outer human being must necessarily lead to the powerlessness of outer authorities, such as the state, in matters of faith and conscience. Institutions, laws, states, and authorities can only determine and regulate the outer life of human beings, but they are unable to develop any substantial force on the inner principle of faith. As Luther underlines, "We can see that to a Christian man his faith suffices for everything, and that he has no need of works for being pious. Being no longer in need of works, he is conscientiously[2] free from the law, . . . This is Christian liberty, the only faith that does not lead to laziness or malevolent works, but that we are not in need of works for reaching devoutness and salvation."[3] Although a Christian, as Luther explains in the same text, cannot be forced to do anything insofar as she is free, she is at the same time paradoxically forced to obey and subjugate herself to labor and the state. Even if the Christian encounters the gospel *in* herself, she remains as an entity outside of herself and therefore remains bound to servitude, which is best expressed as *subjectus est Christo per fidem, subjectus Caesari per corpus*. Luther puts this in the following way: "A Christian man is a willing servant and subject to every other man. Insofar as he is free, he is not forced to do anything; insofar as he is a servant, he is forced to do all sorts of things."[4] As Luther's remarks on authority, the state, and heresy further show, external (physical) punishment cannot reach the inner world of faith and the absolute inwardness of subjectivity. Faith, accordingly, can come only from the individual herself and cannot be created through outer institutions. Conscience really is just another name for this inward principle of "being-for-itself." Put still differently, conscience for Luther is, as Hoffmann puts it, the

95

"pure point" of subjectivity that remains absolutely inaccessible from the outside.[5]

It is precisely this important insight into the absolute nature of subjectivity that found its way into the epistemological and ethical doctrines of German Idealism, such as Schelling's, Fichte's, and Hegel's philosophies. So, although these successors of Kant did not always explicitly refer to Luther as one of their central influences, we can easily see how Luther's doctrines made their way into German Idealism, especially Fichte's version of it, in the following two aspects: (1) Luther's principle of conscience is displaced and transformed into a theory of moral subjectivity and "inner certainty" thereby connecting theoretical and practical reason; and (2) Luther's reflections on the relation between individuals and the state found its way into Fichte's political theories and reflections on the German nation. In this essay, however, I will exclusively deal with the first aspect, since the second aspect would require a reconstruction of the historical context to an extent that goes beyond the scope of this essay. Hence, in what follows, I will first give a brief overview of Fichte's explicit enthusiastic reaction to Luther. Second, I shall then deal in more detail with Fichte's concept of conscience by focusing on his claim that conscience is necessary for moral action.

Fichte on Luther and Protestantism

Fichte reacted enthusiastically to Luther in his earlier years and in his political writings. Many of Kant's successors, such as Schleiermacher, Hegel, Hölderlin, and Fichte, emerge out of a Protestant institutional setting. Luther, who in 1793 Fichte called the "tutelary spirit [*Schutzgeist*] of freedom,"[6] took on a central role for German Idealism inasmuch as he was taken to be the forefather of a radical philosophy of subjectivity and was celebrated as one of the central figures of the emerging German nation as well as the German educational system of the nineteenth century. In addition, Luther was important for Fichte's (and Hegel's) philosophies of history. Though Fichte acknowledged the political significance of Luther, he criticized early on the Protestant orientation toward the written text of the Bible, which, on Fichte's view, led to a loss of the "spirit" of the letters.[7] For according to Fichte, the principle of free insight and the principle of Protestant faith contradict the absolute value of the written word as something disconnected from *living* principles that are based on reason alone.[8] As Fichte remarks in his *Main Characteristics of the Present Age*, the focus on the written word led to a heightened focus on the general education of the people and, accordingly, to a loss of what was intended, namely, the *living* immediacy of the Christian message. Fichte nevertheless celebrates Protestantism as the "ultimate and greatest . . . world deed of the German people,"[9] which was guided by its fearless and enthusiastic leader.

Indeed, Luther, according to Fichte, led to the triumph of freedom over the dependency from foreign authorities.

Though Fichte's philosophy ultimately stands in extreme contrast to Luther's ontological conceptions and his two-world doctrine,[10] the central function of the principle of conscience for Fichte's practical philosophy demonstrates the deep impact that Luther, in conjunction with the general Protestant background, left in Fichte's philosophy. Hegel nicely describes this background in his *Lectures on the History of Philosophy* in the following way:

> In this new period, the principle is thinking, thinking that proceeds from itself—this inwardness which is expounded by Christianity in general and which is the Protestant principle. The universal principle is now to keep a firm hold of inwardness as such, to push back dead exteriority, authority, to regard it as unseemly. . . . The individual human being through his thoughts must have insight into what is supposed to validly prevail, to be established in the world; what is supposed to be regarded as something firm and stable must prove itself through thinking.[11]

Luther's ideas are central, according to Hegel, because they firmly establish the individual as an infinite value and self-relation—not only in theory but also in reality. And this task of further laying out what the self-relation as an *absolute* relation entails was one central task of Kant's successors; for according to Schelling, Fichte, and Hegel, Kant had not yet grasped the full scope of the newly discovered realm of subjectivity and "egoity." However, given that Fichte is less concerned with the Hegelian task of reconciling subjectivity and objectivity through a concept of absolute rationality, his project remains closer to the Kantian task of laying out the conditions for the possibility of ego, history, and state.

The Principle of Conscience in Fichte

Probably the most visible impact that Luther left in Fichte's system (though mediated by other figures such as Jacobi) can be seen in Fichte's reconstruction of the *practical* conditions of theoretical reason and knowledge. Theoretical and practical reason cannot be separated, according to Fichte, since the reality constituted by theoretical reason is ultimately founded upon practical reason. As he puts it in his *Vocation of Man*, "Faith is no knowledge, but it is a decision of the will to recognize the validity of knowledge."[12] Faith, here conceived as an epistemological principle, makes it possible that we can understand the world as something within which we are able to successfully—that is to say, freely and morally—act. Indeed, all knowledge about the reality as the world *within which* we act must be founded upon what Fichte calls "conviction," which involves the belief that I *am able* to act (even when faced with the fact that all consideration of theoretical reason remain doubtful): "my conviction," as he puts it, "is higher than all disputation."[13]

Fichte's claim that all theoretical reason must ultimately be founded upon a conviction and on faith is very similar to some of Luther's ideas, though Fichte removes the Christian core of these ideas. For example, some of Luther's revolutionary claims can be traced back to his interpretation of Romans 1:17, which Luther already referred to before 1520: "For in the gospel a righteousness from God is revealed, a righteousness that is by faith from first to last, just as it is written: 'The righteous will live by faith'" (see also Rom. 10:10: "For one believes with the heart and so is justified"). The central claim here—seen from Luther's perspective—is that the just individual must "live out of herself" and generate justice out of faith, the principle of which can no longer be found outside the human heart. In other words, only the *inner* faith of the individual can make her just, and this ultimately leads to a destruction of the difference between the gospel and the law (*lex*). As such, the tension between inner and outer falls away.[14] Here, the believer is "beyond the law" (*supra legem*), since in the believer Christ has—in the form of conscience—"taken over" the individual, which then in turn leads to good deeds without the external control of the law. The word of the gospel liberates the individual from the outer law. Consequently, what Luther outlines here is a pre-form of what Max Weber calls the "ethics of conviction" (*Gesinnungsethik*), namely, the claim that all morality goes back to the *inner* attitude and principles that the subject generates out of itself.

The relation between faith and law describes *in nuce* the moral theory of Fichte (though now translated into a mix of epistemology and practical philosophy), insofar as the *inner certainty* and *insight* into the "rightness" of an action and any external rule and law must be generated *from the inside* in order to be "right" and just. The principle that generates the goodness of actions and deeds, accordingly, must be an *immediate* principle; for even if we assume that normative rules are generated by institutions, history, society, education, and the like, these rules now have to be *posited by the subject as reasonable*. It cannot be generated through something that is outside of subjectivity. Fichte (following Kant), accordingly, must assume that human beings have access to being good on their own, which is to say, through their own reason. According to Fichte, though, and herein he differs from Kant, reason and faith are intimately interconnected. Whereas reason is able to generate the "content" of what humans morally ought to do, the inner awareness and certainty *of* what is morally right cannot be generated by reason alone. Reason, consequently, must be based on and be "backed up" by an absolute certainty of reason itself, which is (moral) faith, which is only visible in the principle of conscience. Conscience, put simply, is the inner certainty that reason must have in relation to its own force.

One central difference, however, should not be underestimated, especially as it divides Protestantism and German Idealism: the principle of faith that Fichte has in mind is no longer conceived as a Christian principle; rather, it is transformed into a necessary condition of reason in the form of *moral theology* or, put differently, into a *faith of reason unto itself* (instead of a faith that is directed toward something that differs from reason). This is the reason for Fichte's critique that Protestant theologians were "far from discovering reason as the source of truth which rests on itself."[15]

Explained more fully, "faith," according to Fichte, is identical with the agent's *conviction* that morality is not a mere illusion or inner appearance. Put still differently, faith is the condition for the possibility of understanding oneself as a practical being that is bound by morality. What he has in mind is that even the slightest act by which we transform the world presupposes the construction of oneself as an entity that *is able to realize* itself in the world. This construction is a form of faith, particularly since faith here means a special form of certainty regarding the possibility to externalize oneself in the world, which directly follows from the gap between the *present* abstract state of the agent and her *future* reality. *Faith closes this gap.* Furthermore, we should note (again) that "faith" here does not mean a mental event or a psychological act; rather, it means a specific *form* within which consciousness is related to itself.

But let us further inquire into the nature of the conviction and the required positing act that is necessary for a rational reconstruction of the concept of action. The belief in the reality of moral consciousness has a striking feature, namely, that we are unable to believe that the principle upon which we act is wrong. For as Fichte argues, if I would believe—in the very moment of a moral action—that I should not do what I am doing in this moment, I would not act. I would, so to speak, become a skeptic about my own *possibility to* act, and ultimately the impulse to act would disappear. Moral actions, therefore, presuppose that the agent is convinced in the moment of her action that she believes that her action is right and that she is free from any doubt. Put simply, the agent must believe that her action is right in the moment in which she acts. In Fichte's words, the agent's action presupposes her conviction and a basic trust in her own *as* moral consciousness. Although *after* her action, she might come to the conclusion that her action was wrong, at the moment of the act she must be convinced that there is a *real* possibility of acting in a right and, hence, moral manner. Accordingly, faith here means that we believe in the *reality* of ourselves as moral agents. Moreover, if we want to understand this structure as the necessary transcendental condition of moral actions, then we must claim, according to Fichte, that the action is ruled by a belief that cannot be doubted in the moment of an action. The nature of the conviction, therefore, is not a belief generated by theoretical reason but a *form of practical certainty*.

The reason for this is the following: if the agent would have doubts about her action when she is about to act, she would *reflect* on the rightness or wrongness of her action. Such a consciousness would then be a form of doubt, inasmuch as doubt is a reflective second order consciousness *about* one's beliefs. For example, if I *really* (and not only hypothetically) doubt in this very moment whether my writing this paper is the right thing to do, then I would ask myself in the form of a second-order consciousness whether my first-order consciousness is right or wrong. Accordingly, the certainty that we refer to in "conviction" is not a form of propositional knowledge; rather, it is, as Fichte nicely says in his *Vocation of Man*, a "necessary belief in our freedom and strength,"[16] and as such it transforms knowledge into something indubitable and allows us to act on purely subjective grounds. Conscience, thereby, is as a form of self-consciousness within which both the practical and theoretical poles are united and synthesized. Conscience is, accordingly, the "immediate consciousness of that without which there is no consciousness whatsoever: the consciousness of our higher nature and of our absolute freedom."[17]

Conclusion

To be sure, Fichte's radical reconstruction of the relation between reason and faith and Luther's revolutionary thesis about the primacy of inwardness found their way into major schools in German philosophy. However, given the sharp differences between Christian theology and philosophy, one might nevertheless wonder—with Karl Löwith—whether the ultimate reason for this compatibility should be seen in the Protestant tendency to "believe in nothing else except in pure belief itself."[18]

CHAPTER 12

Hegel and Luther
on the Finite and the Infinite

John F. Hoffmeyer

G. W. F. Hegel was an unabashedly Lutheran philosopher. He wrote that philosophy had only solidified his Lutheran identity.[1] At the same time, his understanding of the relation between philosophy and theology differs greatly from that of Martin Luther. Luther was quick to criticize philosophy for the sake of the health of theology. Hegel habitually uses the term *philosophy*, rather than *theology*, to name the best way of thinking about the content of religion. Given this difference, how could Hegel be so quick to claim a Lutheran identity as a philosopher?

A simple response is that the terms *philosophy* and *theology* mean different things for Hegel than they do for Luther. This simple claim becomes more interesting with the additional claim that Hegel's reasons for criticizing theology have much in common with Luther's reasons for criticizing philosophy. Both are criticizing forms of reason that become stuck in dichotomous thinking. More specifically, both thinkers criticize a form of rationality that treats the finite and the infinite as simple, incompatible opposites.

This essay argues that the contrast between Luther's sometimes harsh words about reason and philosophy, on the one hand, and Hegel's celebration of philosophical reason, on the other, can easily mask an underlying agreement between the two thinkers concerning the inadequacy of a simple dichotomy of the finite and the infinite for expressing spiritual truth. Building upon this underlying agreement, this essay will explore the way in which Hegel seeks to think the simultaneous unity and difference of the finite and the infinite.

Luther's Theological Critique of Philosophy

Elsewhere in this volume, more knowledgeable authors discuss Luther's approach to philosophy. Here I will make only a few simple observations. The prime referent for Luther's pronouncements on philosophy is the philosophy that he knew in his time and place. There were, of course, different philosophical schools in Luther's orbit, with complex lineages of influence. Central among those influences, particularly in philosophy's interaction with theology, was

Aristotle. A prime piece of Aristotle's influence was Aristotelian logic, in which the principle of noncontradiction plays a foundational role. According to this principle, a thing and its opposite cannot both be true.

Luther thought that this philosophy was good, even very good, as long as it did not seek to speak authoritatively about theological matters for which it lacked competence. Luther's examples of the theological incompetence of philosophy are commonly examples where philosophy can see only a contradiction, where theology sees an important truth. In other words, the overextension of philosophy's principle of noncontradiction is damaging to theology.

One important example for Luther is the philosophical insistence that the same thing cannot be both finite and infinite. Luther begins the twentieth argument of his 1540 "Disputation on the Divinity and Humanity of Christ" by noting the assumption that God and human beings cannot have any predicate in common. Underlying this assumption is the claim that there is no proportional relation between creator and creature, or between the infinite and the finite. Luther rejects this claim as a "philosophical argument." For Luther the claim makes sense as far as philosophy can see, but he insists that the Christian theologian must take a different position. If the finite and the infinite are simply incompatible opposites, the incarnation of the divine Word in Jesus of Nazareth would be impossible. There the finite and the infinite are so joined that we should say that this finite reality, this human being, is God, who is infinite. In the incarnation there is not only a proportional relation but a unity of the infinite and the finite.[2]

Hegel's Philosophical Critique of Theology

Hegel's situation is different from Luther's in ways that make it natural for Hegel to speak more positively of philosophy. He regards himself as a philosopher, and "philosophy" is one of his primary terms for describing his own work. Neither Aristotle nor any other non-Christian philosopher is the dominant figure in Hegel's conception of philosophy. Hegel elaborates his own understanding of philosophy, which is, of course, exemplified in his own philosophical production. He explicitly understands himself as a Christian philosopher, indeed, as a Lutheran one.

Hegel holds religion in high regard. For Hegel, the content of religion and philosophy is the same. Given this identity of content, Hegel can even refer to a broad sense of theology that includes philosophy. Yet when Hegel uses the word *theology*, he usually does so in a critical vein. Hegel is explicit that he is directing his critique at the dominant theologies of his day. Hegel sees two types of theology holding sway in his setting, both of which are versions of the same underlying problem. On the one hand is a "rational" theology that, in the name of reason, insists upon the existence of God but resists giving any content to the conception of who or what

God is. On the other hand is a theology that champions religious feeling but does not question the assumption that human beings cannot think positive content in the idea of God.

For Hegel, both types of theology are caught in the trap of dichotomous thinking: such thinking, like the philosophy that Luther criticized, insists upon the strict incompatibility of the finite and the infinite. The human intellect is finite, bounded. It thinks by "de-fining," by marking out boundaries (the Latin *finis* means "end," "boundary," or "limit"). The "in-finite" has no boundaries; it is by definition the "not finite." Therefore the infinite always escapes human thinking. The finite attempt to think the infinite always results in a finite impostor.

Hegel does not think that dichotomous thinking is a specifically theological problem to which philosophy is immune. Hegel is a child of the European Enlightenment and thinks that it made important contributions to the advancement of human freedom. Yet Hegel's general critique of Enlightenment rationality, whether in the work of philosophers or theologians, is that it does not move beyond fundamental dichotomies. His typical word for such dichotomous thinking is *Verstand* (usually translated into English as "understanding"). Reason only attains its full sense for Hegel in what he calls "speculative" knowing. What Hegel means by speculative knowing is the capacity to see the unity of opposites. When Hegel champions reason and philosophy, what he has in mind is this sense of speculative knowing. Hegel is not taking the other side of Luther's argument and defending a form of philosophical reason governed by the principle of noncontradiction. On the contrary, like Luther's theology, Hegelian reason in the mode of speculative knowing rejects the Aristotelian logic of noncontradiction.

Reminiscent of the fact that Luther considered the relation of the infinite and the finite to be a central place at which theology has to part ways with the principle of noncontradiction, Hegel places the relation between the infinite and the finite at the heart of his alternative to Aristotelian logic. The obvious first step in defining the infinite is to see it as the opposite of the finite. The in-finite is the "not finite." Hegel sees that this introduces a conundrum. If the infinite is the not finite, then the finite is the not infinite. The infinite is limited by the finite. Its conceptual space cannot overlap with that of the finite. But if the infinite were limited, it would not be infinite.

This conundrum leads Hegel to distinguish two understandings of the infinite. One of these understandings is inadequate because it falls victim to the conundrum. In this view, the infinite is simply the opposite of the finite. The so-called infinite turns out to be merely finite. The finite and the supposed infinite are each other's limit. Both are limited; both are finite.

The other concept of the infinite incorporates both sides of the conundrum into the infinite itself. If the infinite is the not finite, the infinite must be other than the finite, but not in such a way that the finite limits the infinite. The infinite can only be genuinely infinite if the finite is not alien to it. The infinite must be at home in the finite. The infinite must transcend the finite, but it must include the finite. Otherwise the finite will be its limit and the supposed infinite will turn out to be itself merely finite. One might say that the infinite's difference from the finite must not be a finite difference. The infinite differs infinitely from the finite.

Hegel's way of making the point is to say that what he calls the "true" infinite is the identity of the finite and the infinite. More precisely, the infinite is the identity of the identity and the difference of the infinite and the finite. Only in this way can the infinite be distinct from the finite, and distinct specifically as infinite. Were there no difference between the infinite and the finite, the opposition to the finite apparent in the very word *in-finite* would be illusory. Were there no identity between the finite and the infinite, the infinite would simply be the opposite of the finite. Limited by the finite as its opposite, the supposed infinite would actually be finite.[3]

Where understanding (*Verstand*) sees simple opposites, speculative reason sees differentiated moments of a dynamic whole. This does not mean that speculative knowing simply says that what understanding regards as opposites need to be taken together, since each side has its element of truth. The dichotomies established by understanding are not simply wrong. The "sides" that they oppose to each other are not simply illusory. But the truth of those "sides" comes to light only as we recognize that the language of "side," "dichotomy," and "opposite" is all misleading. Neither the assertion of the finite nor the assertion of the infinite is untrue, but the finite is what it is only as the finite manifestation of the infinite, and the infinite is what it is only as that which manifests itself in and through the finite.

To summarize the argument up to this point: Hegel and Luther both reject dichotomous thinking that would make adherence to the principle of noncontradiction a requirement for spiritual truth. Luther does so in the name of defending theological health against the unwarranted incursions of philosophy. Hegel does so in the name of a more spiritually adequate philosophy—that is, a philosophy more adequate to spiritual truth—in the face of both philosophy and theology settling for less adequate versions.

Hegel, Nondichotomous Thinking, and Mystical Union in Sacramental Practice

When Luther and Hegel express their concerns about philosophy and theology respectively, they are both criticizing particular, contemporary forms—not anything and everything that might go under the name of "theology" or "philosophy." Hegel is explicit about this; Luther is not. One could explain this difference, at least partially, simply by noting the greater development of historical consciousness in European intellectual life by Hegel's time as compared with Luther's. It would be important to add to this the observation that Hegel's own philosophy is both a fruit of the growth of historical consciousness and a profound contribution to that growth.

Hegel's explicit recognition that his critique of contemporary theology is not a global critique of theology is also grounded in his holistic concept of truth. This holism makes him generally allergic to dichotomous thinking. I say "generally" because Hegel is certainly not immune to resorting to dichotomies, even noxious ones, such as his spiritual dichotomy between Europe and Africa. At his best, though, Hegel resists a dichotomizing use of his own categories. (Luther, the master polemicist, has less interest in a general avoidance of dichotomizing forms.) Applied to the Hegelian categories that we have been considering, this means that "understanding" (*Verstand*) and speculative reason are not simple opposites. It would be more accurate to say that they describe zones on the trajectory of reason. "Understanding" is itself a way of thinking rationally, but it is a manner of thinking in which the dichotomizing tendency predominates, in which the capacity to see the identity of opposites is undeveloped. The further movement forward on the trajectory of reason is the growth of this capacity, the growth of what one might call the speculative habit. Along this trajectory there are, of course, differences of degree: a form of thinking can be sufficiently speculative that it no longer fits under the category of "understanding," while at the same time falling short of the most fully developed speculative forms of thought.

A deployment of this trajectory is clear in a passage that again shows Hegel's appreciation of Lutheran tradition. In comparing theological conceptions of the presence of grace in the believing community's celebration of the communion meal, Hegel does not think that any of them reach the plan of the properly "speculative." Among the theological candidates, "the Lutheran conception is without a doubt the richest in spirit." The term that Hegel uses, *geistreich*, is very high praise within his vocabulary. A German-English dictionary might translate the term as "brilliant" or "intellectually scintillating." For Hegel, the word invokes the most important concept in his philosophy: *Geist* ("spirit"). Hegel is committed to articulating a philosophy that grasps the unity of opposites—without thereby denying their opposition—because it is the very structure of spirit to recognize itself as itself only in recognizing the other as other. In other words, what Hegel calls speculative knowing is the form of reason appropriate to spirit.

By contrast with the Lutheran conception, in the Reformed view "everything speculative has disappeared." The Reformed church (the major Protestant alternative to Lutheranism in Hegel's German context) marks the point where divine truth "slips down into the prose of Enlightenment and of mere understanding." While Hegel treasures the positive work of the Enlightenment, one of his chief philosophical aims, as we have seen, is to overcome the bifurcating bent of what he calls "understanding," and what contemporary discussions frequently call

"Enlightenment rationality." For all of Hegel's praise of reason, he is not a rationalist in the way that the term is generally used. Reformed thought and Enlightenment "understanding" were mere "prose" because they had abandoned the "mystical" element, in the sense of understanding the communion meal as "mystical union." Lutheranism, by contrast, had not. Hegel specifically traces this Lutheran focus back to Luther himself, whom he praises for not having ceded to a compromise with the Reformed conception.[4]

Although Hegel does not use the terms *finite* and *infinite* in the passage just cited, the proper grasp of the relation between the two is still his basic concern. For Hegel, Roman Catholic and Reformed conceptions of the communion meal both fail to reconcile finite material substance with infinite spiritual presence. The Roman Catholic view (in Hegel's understanding) takes the correct insight that infinite spirit is manifest in finite material form but obscures this insight by separating the consecration of the material bread and wine from the spiritual act of consuming them in faith. The result is a reduction of the infinite to the finite: in this case, the elements of the communion meal. Rather than the finite material serving as the manifestation of the infinite spirit, they are the location of a "thingification" of the material presence of spirit. As always for Hegel, the improper grasp of the relation between the infinite and the finite results in structural dichotomy. Here, the bread and the wine, consecrated by the priest, are exalted as the presence of the infinite over against the worshiping community, whose own role as manifestation of the infinite is neglected.

The Reformed position (again, in Hegel's understanding) is the apparent opposite, yet shares with the Roman Catholic conception the failure to reconcile the infinite with the finite: that is, to conceive the infinite as something other than the "not finite." The Reformed position refuses to identity infinite spirit with the finite material elements of bread and wine. It is as if the infinite would lose its infinity by such identification. But by having to stay at a distance from the finite, this supposed infinite shows that it is limited by the finite. So limited, it is not infinite after all.[5]

Both the Reformed and the Roman Catholic conceptions treat the infinite as finitely other than the finite, instead of infinitely other than the finite. Contrary to their best intentions, they reduce the infinite to something finite, because they understand the infinite simply as the "not finite." The Lutheran position (once again, in Hegel's view) is also not a satisfactory account of a unity of the infinite and the finite that simultaneously preserves, indeed depends upon, their difference. Hegel thinks that it is the task of philosophy to deliver such a satisfactory account. But the Lutheran, "mystical" conception does not back away from insisting on the union of the infinite and the finite as apparent opposites. This is what makes the Lutheran conception, in Hegel's view, the "richest in spirit."

CHAPTER 13

"Faith Creates the Deity"

Luther and Feuerbach

Carter Lindberg

Ludwig Feuerbach was a rebel with a cause—to overturn philosophical idealism (Hegel) and unmask theology as anthropology: "He who clings to Hegelian philosophy also clings to theology"; "The secret of theology is anthropology."[1] The realization of this "unmasking" means that "God is nothing else than the nature of man purified from that which to the human individual appears, whether in feeling or thought, a limitation, an evil" and that "Christianity has in fact long ago vanished, not only from the reason but from the life of mankind . . . it is nothing more than a fixed idea, in flagrant contradiction to our fire and life assurance companies, our railroads . . . our scientific museums."[2]

As Luther's development led from the cloister to the world, so Feuerbach's development led from Hegel's classroom to the world; both affirmed a living faith against all forms of speculation. At the conclusion of his *Lectures on the Essence of Religion*, Feuerbach states:

> My only wish is that I have not failed in the task I set myself. . . :
> to transform the friends of God into friends of man, believers
> into thinkers, devotees of prayer into devotees of work, candi-
> dates for the hereafter into students of this world, Christians
> who, by their own profession and admission, are "*half animal, half
> angel,*" into *men*, into *whole men.*[3]

Apart from the enthusiastic embrace of his work by Marx and Engels,[4] Feuerbach has long been denounced as the "grave-digger of theology," the bourgeois atheist behind Marx and Nietzsche, the psychologizer of religion behind Freud, an early "death-of-God" theologian who twisted Luther's thought to serve his own apotheosis of man, a banal and superficial "non-knower of death" and "mis-knower of evil." Yet this "Fiery Brook" ("Feuer" "Bach"), whom Karl Barth ironically called a publican and sinner, pored through his own edition of Luther's works (the twenty-two-volume Leipzig edition, 1729–1740) to revise his *Essence of Christianity* to include a massive number of Luther citations, then wrote

The Essence of Faith according to Luther, viewed Luther as the *erste Mensch* of Christendom, and humorously referred to himself as "Luther II." In grappling with Luther, Feuerbach was a "rare bird" among post-Reformation philosophers, as Oswald Bayer points out in chapter 1 of this volume.

Feuerbach's Attraction to Luther

Why was Feuerbach so attracted to Luther? John Glasse posits two hypotheses. One is that Feuerbach was responding to an extensive criticism of his *Essence of Christianity* by the Halle theology professor, Julius Müller. Müller in a nearly one-hundred-page (!) review argues that Feuerbach's critique of Christianity depended mainly on patristic and medieval sources and thus may well apply to Roman Catholicism but not Protestantism, for which Feuerbach had provided few sources. Hence, by marshaling Luther to his side, Feuerbach could rebut Müller and other theological critics.[5] Glasse's second hypothesis is that, by his use of Luther, Feuerbach was mounting a strategic defense against state censorship and advancing his perspective that in the political context of the German *Vormärz* an appeal to Luther was a safer means to explicate political positions than direct political speech.[6] The latter point that an appeal to Luther's theology was the most effective foundation for the pre-1848 political drive in Germany toward national unity and political emancipation is painstakingly developed by Heinz-Hermann Brandhorst.[7]

Whether or not Feuerbach's polemical context was paramount in his turn to Luther studies, "Feuerbach discovered in him things that *advanced* his basic, philosophic task of the early 1840's."[8] "[I]t is now being widely recognized that Feuerbach was probably the most significant theological thinker in the nineteenth century, whose importance has finally become evident in the twentieth."[9] "Feuerbach . . . is important not merely as the pioneer of scientific empiricism, humanism and social materialism in post-Hegelian European philosophy, he is also a moral philosopher of the first rank."[10] No less a critic than Karl Barth stated: "No philosopher of his time penetrated the contemporary theological situation as effectively as he, and few spoke with such pertinence." Furthermore, Feuerbach was not a "mere skeptic and naysayer"; he affirmed the whole man, an "I-thou" ethic, and social concern; he was, as it were, a Christian realist. The downside of Feuerbach's encounter with Luther, according to Barth, was that Luther's Christology and eucharistic theology, not to mention his "extravagant" statements that faith is the "creator of deity," too easily facilitated the inversion of theology and anthropology. What Feuerbach (not to mention Luther) lacked was some good old Calvinist leaven![11]

Not surprisingly, Barth's view exercised contemporary Luther scholars. Paul Althaus bluntly states: "Barth's concern is unfounded. No line of development connects Luther with Feuerbach. For when Luther says that 'faith creates the deity,' he immediately adds 'not in (God's) person but in us.'"[12] Feuerbach himself was quite well aware of this point,[13] but Luther's famous phrase remains a flashpoint in studies of Feuerbach. In his Galatians commentary, Luther writes: "*Fides est creatrix divinitatis, non in persona, sed in nobis.*"[14] The point that where your heart is there is your God (or idol) occurs in a number of places in Luther's writings, including sermons and the exposition of the First Commandment in *The Large Catechism.*[15]

Yet it was precisely Luther's "extravagant" exposition of faith that so stimulated Feuerbach and enabled him to throw off the last remnants of idealism. In his foreword to the first volume of his *Complete Works,* Feuerbach writes: "Only there [*The Essence of Faith according to Luther*] did you fully "shake off' the philosopher to give way to the man."[16] "God-in-himself is strictly speaking only God as a metaphysical being; that is, as a pure and dispassionate being of thought. L[uther] was an enemy of metaphysics, abstraction, and dispassionateness."[17] Unlike many of the German theologians of his day, Feuerbach was not interested in repristinating Luther but rather creatively relating Luther's insights to the present context. So he wrote: "Is the work *The Essence of Faith according to Luther* for or against Luther? It is just as much for as against Luther. But is this not a contradiction rooted in the nature of the object itself?"[18]

This "for" and "against" orientation, while using Luther to explicate and substantiate his own theology, is clear in Feuerbach's interpretation of Luther's dictum, "As you believe him, so he is." For example:

> If God is such, whatever it may be, as I believe him, what else is the nature of God than the nature of faith? Is it possible for thee to believe in a God who regards thee favourably, if thou dost not regard thyself favourably, if thou despairest of man, if he is nothing to thee? . . . If thou believest that God is for thee, thou believest that nothing is or can be against thee, that nothing contradicts thee. But if thou believest that nothing is or can be against thee, thou believest—what?—nothing less than that thou art God. That God is another being is only illusion, only imagination.[19]

Feuerbach argues that this position does not make him an atheist. Rather, the negative elements of his work are only in order to emphasize and free the positive. "Certainly my work is negative, destructive; but, be it observed, only in relation to the *un*human, not to the human elements of religion."[20] "My primary concern is and always has been to illumine the obscure essence of religion with the torch of reason, in order that man may at last cease to be the victim, the play thing, of all those hostile powers which from time immemorial have employed and still are employing the darkness of religion for the oppression of mankind."[21]

The negation of the subject, Feuerbach never tires of arguing, does not entail the negation of its predicates. "Not the attribute of the divinity, but the divineness or deity of the attribute, is the first true Divine Being. . . . Hence he alone is the true atheist to whom the predicates of the Divine Being,—for example, love, wisdom, justice,—are nothing; not he to whom merely the subject of these predicates is nothing."[22] The real atheist is the person who theoretically acknowledges God and then lives as if he did not exist.

> On the ground that God is unknowable, man excuses himself to what is yet remaining of his religious conscience for his forgetfulness of God, his absorption in the world: he denies God practically by his conduct,—the world has possession of all this thoughts and inclination,—but he does not deny him theoretically, he does not attack his existence: he lets that rest. But this existence does not affect or incommode him."[23]

Talk about God as God is in himself indulges in "an unconscious, esoteric pathology, anthropology, and psychology" that removes God farther and farther away from humankind and nature.[24] To Feuerbach, Hegel's philosophy was the prime example of his day of a speculative effort to vindicate Christian theology and thereby further human self-estrangement.

> In a statement that reminds one of Kierkegaard, Feuerbach describes Hegel as the example of a self-sufficient, professional thinker whose real existence was secured by the state and consequently remained without significance for his philosophy. As such, Hegel did not know real existence and real life. Only the isolated thinker who is removed from the real, concrete world could maintain the supremacy and self-sufficiency of abstract thought. "The absolute spirit is nothing but the absolute professor."[25]

Feuerbach's point also echoes Luther: "It is through living, indeed through dying and being damned that one becomes a theologian, not through understanding, reading, or speculation."[26]

The other side of Feuerbach's attack on speculation about God as he is in himself is his emphasis on Luther's *pro me/pro nobis* understanding of faith. "Not outside us, then not in the object of faith itself, but *in us* lie the purpose and meaning of this object of faith. Not that Christ is Christ, but that he is

Christ *for you*; not that he died or that he suffered, but that he died *for you*, suffered *for you*—that is the main point."[27]

> Luther was the first to let out the secret of Christian faith. . . . The key to the mysteries of faith lies in *us*. . . . Not only did God become man for us, not only did he suffer for us, as is stated in the Nicene Creed, but he is God for us, omnipotent Creator for us, Holy Spirit for us. In short, it is for *us* that he is what he is—the "us" runs through all the articles. . . . The older faith also says, "Our Lord, Our God," but it underlines the "God"; Luther, on the other hand, underlines the "our." That is, he makes the fact that he is *ours* an essential attribute of God himself. . . . "If God sat in heaven for himself alone," says Luther, "like a block, he would not be God." God is a word the sole meaning of which is man.[28]

The Protestant faith, then, is no longer, like Catholicism, concerned with God as God is in himself, "but about what he is for man; it has, therefore, no longer a speculative or contemplative tendency. . . . It is no longer theology; it is essentially Christology, that is, religious anthropology."[29]

Humanizing God and Elevating the Person

Feuerbach's driving concern for the humanization of God and the elevation of the person leads to his emphasis on the person in community, the community of "I and thou." This "I-thou" dialectic is fundamental for fully human activity. "The true dialectic is not a monologue of a solitary thinker with himself; it is a dialogue between I and thou."[30] In this he is responding to what he perceived as the dehumanization and alienation occurring in his cultural context wherein it appeared all too often that the church provided legitimation for an absolutist and bureaucratic state (the symbiosis of throne and altar), and voiced little support for those oppressed by industrial development and capitalism.[31] "[R]eligion is man's consciousness of himself in his concrete or living totality, in which the identity of the self-consciousness exists only as the pregnant, complete unity of *I* and *thou*."[32] To be human is to be in community; the humanity of the person is not in his or her singularity but only in relation to the other, the thou. The secret of the doctrine of the Trinity is the secret of the social, communal life, the secret of I and thou.[33] The I-thou relationship is most clearly evident in the mutuality and reciprocity of human love, the love between a man and a woman.[34] Such ardent love to the other is religiously expressed by God's self-renunciation for humankind.[35]

The alienation of the modern world, Feuerbach claims, is not only interpersonal but also alienation from nature. Christian concern for salvation of the soul has devalued the world and lost sight of nature. "Only sensuous beings affect one another. I am an 'I' for myself and simultaneously a 'thou' for others. This I am, however, only as a sensuous being."[36] Faith and the sacraments are not to be spiritualized but expressed in material terms—real water, real bread and wine.[37] From his materialist perspective, Feuerbach "demythologizes" nature miracles in a way strikingly similar to Luther. "All things are subject to Christ; he is the Lord of the world, who does with it what he will; but this unlimited power over Nature is itself subject to the power of the heart;—Christ commands raging Nature to be still, but only that he may hear the sighs of the needy."[38]

Feuerbach has at times been referred to as a "materialist," but he is perhaps better designated an "existentialist" with his stress on "passion." "Love is passion, and only Abstract thought that is without feeling and without passion cancels the difference between being and nonbeing, but this difference . . . is a reality for love." "Desire not to be a philosopher, as distinct from a man; . . . Do not think as a thinker, that is, with a faculty torn from the totality of the real human being and isolated for itself; think as a living and real being . . . Think in existence."[39]

Oswald Bayer on Feuerbach and Luther

While Feuerbach uses Luther's thought to advance his own perspectives and concerns, he does not do this out of ignorance of Luther's own faith commitments. Rather, he utilizes Luther based on the conviction that this was the most faithful exegesis of the Christian faith in the philosophical and scientific context of his own day. It would take a number of yet unwritten major monographs to explore fully Feuerbach's relationship to Luther, let alone the other aspects of Feuerbach's understanding of religion.[40] The next best thing is to try to abstract some points from the work of Oswald Bayer, one of the most perceptive scholars of the relationship of Feuerbach to Luther.[41]

In his "Gegen Gott für den Menschen,"[42] Bayer affirms that Feuerbach engaged Luther as a genuine dialogue partner, exhibited "a real understanding of Luther's theology in which he comprehends its substantive relationships, the function of its individual motives and their distinctions"; specifically the problem of the *via negationis*, the particular function of Christology in relation to the doctrine of God with attention to the distinction of *Deus absconditus* and *Deus revelatus*, the distinction of Christ as *sacramentum* (*donum*) and Christ as *exemplum*, the distinction of faith and love, and the significance of the *pro me* and of the *verbum externum*.[43]

However, Feuerbach parts company with Luther in conceiving the relationship of I and thou as only the means for personal self-discovery. "The Thou of God is only the means to the goal of self formation . . . 'The *subject* of faith is only the occasion, means, image, sign, fable—*I myself* am the teaching, the sense, the goal, the subject (*Sache*)."[44] "The external Word thus has only a maieutic function. Divinity in all its perfections, that is, for Feuerbach: the person in his or her satisfied totality, the person as species (*Gattung*), under the title of (secularized!) is faith drawn into the human individual, practically consumed by it, totally appropriated by it. So there is complete identification, 'Divinity is only the *certainty of my own . . . divinity*.'"[45] So Feuerbach: "God—the object of Christian faith—is nothing but the satisfied urge toward happiness, the satisfied self-love of the Christian man." And "Thus God—or the divine being—is simply the being who expresses, promises, and objectifies human (or, rather, Christian wishes . . . God is thus nothing but the essence of the human heart—or, rather, emotion—objectified to itself as the supreme, truest, and most actual being."[46]

For Luther, however, the word of God is not merely a Socratic address that draws out who we are in terms of our species; nor the vehicle of wish fulfillment; nor the old logic that "like is known by like." Rather, the word performs what the word proclaims. To cite Bayer again: "Our thesis is that the gospel, understood as a particular speech act, is itself the ground of faith. Since the 'essence of Christianity' is a speech act, it must be illuminated, not primarily by an analysis of existence, but by an analysis of language."[47] Such analysis includes the "visible word" as well as the "audible word" of judgment and promise, law and gospel, and the human response of praise and lament.[48]

CHAPTER 14

Søren Kierkegaard

Between Skepticism and Faith's Happy Passion

David J. Gouwens

In contrast to Augustine, for whom philosophy is a lover drawing the believer to Christ, Martin Luther's famous attacks upon reason as "the Devil's mother" or "the Devil's whore" often raise a suspicion that "Lutheran philosophy" is an oxymoron. The picture is complicated by the fact that Luther's attack upon reason was itself philosophical and that Luther could also regard philosophy as a "handmaid" for his own theological reflection. Nonetheless, a quandary still appears: How may a philosopher in the Lutheran tradition negotiate the relation between philosophy and theology, reason and faith?[1]

Søren Kierkegaard provides a fascinating test case of how a philosopher within the Lutheran tradition thinks through the relations of faith and reason and how this might throw some light on the supposed quandary of the Lutheran philosopher, suggesting positive contributions from Lutheran philosophers to the future of philosophical inquiry.

To sketch out how Kierkegaard's thought addresses this quandary, I will touch briefly on three related issues: first, two caveats on how not to see Kierkegaard as a philosopher; second, Kierkegaard's appreciative yet also critical judgment of Luther on reason and faith; and third, Kierkegaard as one suggesting philosophical trajectories into the present helpful to philosophers in the Lutheran tradition, especially as Kierkegaard develops a Socratic role for philosophy.

How Not to See Kierkegaard as a Philosopher

First, two caveats should be offered at the outset concerning how not to see Kierkegaard as a philosopher. The first caveat questions the very concept of a "Lutheran philosopher." Indeed, it would be odd to characterize Kierkegaard in this way, for he never seeks to establish something called "Lutheran philosophy." Philosophy has its own wide-ranging objects of interest and concern, which may certainly include Christian and Lutheran faith, but Kierkegaard would never say that philosophy in itself becomes Lutheran. Perhaps it would be more accurate and more modest to say, as Jaroslav Pelikan put it sixty years ago, that "Kierkegaard's philosophy has much to say to Lutheran theology" and that "the work of the Christian philosopher must also be carried on *coram Deo*."[2]

The second caveat is that, just as Luther, despite his rhetorical attacks on reason, is wrongly charged with being "irrational," so, too, Kierkegaard, despite his critique of "reason," is no irrationalist. The charge often erroneously made against Kierkegaard is that while he may never have said that reason is a whore or the Devil's mother, he so celebrates the absurd, the paradox, the will, and the importance of human emotions and passions that he is in truth a philosophical irrationalist. Even some Kierkegaard scholars, as well as general readers, lodge this complaint against him.

But just as it distorts Luther to see him as an enemy of reason, so, too, it distorts Kierkegaard to see him as an irrationalist. Luther's attacks on scholastic Aristotelianism are not a rejection of reason but of illicit uses of philosophy that obscure the heart of the gospel. With regard to Kierkegaard, C. Stephen Evans rightly says that this charge of "irrationalism" is a "textbook caricature" that does not bear examination. Kierkegaard does not say, for example, that the paradox of the incarnation, "the Absolute Paradox," the "absurd," is a formal contradiction, asking a believer "to abandon the laws of logic and to embrace something which he knows is false, even impossible." Neither is the famous "leap" of faith a "blind leap" that one is urged to make for no good reasons; Kierkegaard is no volitionalist with regard to beliefs, as if beliefs could be directly willed apart from our having "reasons."[3] These characterizations fail to do justice to the sophisticated, indeed, rational way that Kierkegaard as a philosopher limns the boundaries of reason and faith. Kierkegaard's critique of reason is no more "irrationalism" than is the long history of philosophical attempts to outline the limits of reason, from ancient skepticism to Kant to Wittgenstein and others.

The center of Kierkegaard's philosophical concern is to expose the conceptual confusions that lead one to think that truth and certainty in ethics, religion, and Christian faith are achievable purely objectively, apart from passionate personal concern. This confusion takes many forms: speculative philosophy's claim to "go beyond faith" to "the System"; traditional orthodoxy's attempts to prove the truth of doctrines by Scripture or reason; Enlightenment rationalist theology's domestication of Christian faith by restricting it to the limits of reason alone. In attacking the pretensions of philosophy, Kierkegaard's target is not reason as such but inflated claims by philosophers to grasp the truth by means of disinterested reflection divorced from the interests, concerns, and passions of the person. As one of Kierkegaard's pseudonyms observes, "What philosophers say about actuality is often just as disappointing as it is when one reads on a sign in a secondhand shop: Pressing Done Here. If a person were to bring his clothes to be pressed, he would be duped, for the sign is merely for sale."[4]

Over against these objectivizing approaches in the philosophy and theology of his own day, Kierkegaard's work can be seen as a careful, judicious, circumspect philosophical exercise exploring the illusions of objective, neutral reason as the means to determine ethical and religious truth. Kierkegaard's philosophical task is a logical one, exploring meta-concepts ("objectivity," "subjectivity," "reason," "truth," "ethics," "anxiety," "despair," "faith," "passion," "emotion") and also specifically Christian theological concepts ("sin," "salvation," "incarnation," "grace," "faith and works," "works of love") in ways that highlight the context of the personal interest they entail.

Kierkegaard on Reason and Faith

Second, if Kierkegaard is neither a "Lutheran philosopher" nor an "irrationalist," we can now clarify more precisely Kierkegaard's own judgments concerning the relations of faith and reason by turning to some of Kierkegaard's journal entries on Luther himself. It is not surprising that when Kierkegaard around 1846 reads Luther intensively, especially Luther's sermons, he finds strong resonances between Luther's stress on the "for you" and his own development of the concepts of "subjectivity" and "inwardness."[5] Thus, he commends Luther for saying that the doctrine of the atonement "must be traced back to the struggle of the anguished conscience. Remove the anguished conscience, and you may as well lock the churches and convert them into dance halls."[6] Yet Kierkegaard complains, too, that "Luther is no dialectician," that sometimes Luther presents faith as "the immediate, a vitality, a kind of persevering genius with respect to this life so that one does not lose hope and confidence," in effect undialectically reducing faith to a kind of enthusiasm rather than a means of wrestling with the anguished conscience.[7] Thus, while Kierkegaard appreciates Luther's stress on subjectivity, he criticizes Luther for lacking "dialectic."

A paradigm case of dialectic, one highlighting the kinship between Kierkegaard and Luther, is to be found in *Philosophical Fragments*, for it is here that Kierkegaard dialectically develops the distinction between two teachers, Socrates and a nameless Teacher who it eventually becomes evident is Christ.[8] Striking is how Kierkegaard as philosopher and poet teases out the comparisons yet especially the contrasts between Socratic faith and Christian faith, treating each with sympathy and imagination yet not disguising the passional and conceptual contrasts between them. For example, *Fragments* explores the contrast between Socratic faith as the quest for "truth within" and faith in Christ as response to God's breaking into time with truth from "without." From this basic contrast Kierkegaard explores the attendant concepts of the paradox and the absurd and the possibility of offense; the reversal entailed in moving from Socrates's faith in the "truth within" to the follower's awareness of her or his radical sin; the awareness of one's inability to know the truth apart from the gift of faith given by the Teacher; and the essentially passional nature of Christian faith, for faith, we are told, is a "happy passion."[9] *Fragments* offers a supreme example of Kierkegaard's philosophical task of clarifying the distinctive features of Christian faith, one reflecting, too, Luther's strongly incarnational "theology of the cross" over against a "theology of glory," as Luther contrasts them in his "Heidelberg Disputation."[10] The philosophical task focusing on the distinctiveness of Christian concepts means that the goal is not to translate these concepts into intellectualist terms, or into feelings, or into moralistic categories. Neither is the task to render Christ as a Socratic teacher who elicits the truth within, reducing Christ to a "moral exemplar" of our own inherent capabilities. Kierkegaard's goal echoes Kent's words in Shakespeare's *King Lear*, "I'll teach you differences."[11] Philosophy's goal is to highlight these differences descriptively.

Kierkegaard and Lutheran Philosophers Today

Third, can we now suggest trajectories from Kierkegaard's thought into the present in a way helpful to Lutheran philosophers? If Kierkegaard would object to both a "Lutheran philosophy" and "Lutheran irrationalism," and if philosophy's task is to "teach differences," what are now the options for the Lutheran philosopher?

Kierkegaard as "dialectician" describing Christian concepts may be akin to contemporary understandings of philosophy as concept analysis, or as phenomenological investigation attempting to understand the unbelieving or believing soul from within.[12] Similarly, Kierkegaard's critique of philosophical foundationalism and the elevation of reason over faith anticipates many postmodern concerns. While Kierkegaard never wanted to found a school and while his thought stubbornly resists textbook summation, he nevertheless anticipates several contemporary philosophical approaches that Lutheran philosophers might find encouraging and helpful.

Most importantly, Kierkegaard proposes a continuing Socratic role for philosophy, one that many contemporary philosophers find attractive. Such a Socratic vision of philosophy combines ethical and religious seriousness with skepticism and irony, including an awareness of philosophy's limits. Kierkegaard's Socrates again is the model, but Socrates not as the contrast to Christ, as in *Philosophical Fragments*, but Socrates now as a model of philosophy's ongoing role. In this Socratic model of philosophy, philosophy is at once passionate and skeptical.

First, philosophy is passionate, unafraid of ethical and religious seriousness. The goal of the Lutheran philosopher is not "Lutheran philosophy" and certainly not an inflated "System." But, as Richard Rorty puts it, philosophy is not a mirror of nature but an edifying tool.[13] Rorty, of course, does not envision a specifically religious or Christian edification, but his proposal is suggestive for Lutheran philosophers, too. Here again is the point of saying with Pelikan that philosophy can be done *coram Deo*. On this account, philosophy aims not at evacuating "subjectivity" in the interests of an ever-more pure "objectivity"; the goal of philosophical inquiry, rather, is that the philosopher returns to the questions of how, in Kierkegaard's words, one becomes "an existing individual." This is why Socrates is for Kierkegaard such a powerful model for philosophical inquiry, since, as Kierkegaard's pseudonym Johannes Climacus puts it in *Concluding Unscientific Postscript*, "This is where the road swings off, and Socrates essentially emphasizes existing, whereas Plato, forgetting this, loses himself in speculative thought. Socrates' infinite merit is precisely that of being an *existing* thinker, not a speculative thinker who forgets what it means to exist."[14]

Yet, second, Socratic philosophy in Kierkegaard's hands, and for those who may learn from him, can also retain a strong sense of Socratic skepticism and irony. Despite Kierkegaard's fears that Luther was "no dialectician," in their shared concern for the centrality of faith, both willingly attacked forms of thought and living that distort faith. In this connection, Pelikan again rightly notes how Luther's stress on faith stands behind Kierkegaard's achievement of becoming "the first Christian philosopher to develop a critical philosophy in the truest and most complete sense of the word," empowering a wide-ranging, three-fold polemic against several nineteenth-century distortions of faith: intellectualism (the Hegelians), moralism (the Kantians), and aestheticism (Schleiermacher).[15] So, too, over against those who wrongly see Kierkegaard as an "individualist" with no sense of sociality and community, it is important to see how especially in the 1850s Kierkegaard's critical philosophy broadens to include a vision of philosophy as an ironic tool of cultural, religious, and social critique—now aimed at Lutheran Denmark. That for Kierkegaard this critique is a philosophical and not simply theological task is strikingly clear when one sees how Kierkegaard holds up as the model for his own critical stance none other than Socrates. In his late 1854–1855 attack upon the established Danish state Lutheran church, Kierkegaard does not envision his role to be that of a prophet, or a reformer like Luther, or a "true Christian" over against his lapsed contemporaries but simply an ironic Socratic interrogator of "Christendom." Just two months before his death, Kierkegaard writes: "The only analogy I have before me is Socrates; my task is a Socratic task, to audit the definition of what it is to be a Christian—I do not call myself a Christian (keeping the ideal free), but I can make it manifest that the others are that even less."[16]

Emerging then from Kierkegaard's pages is a Socratic vision of philosophy that unites ethical and religious seriousness with skepticism and irony. And this may serve as a model for philosophy in our own time. In a recently published book of "philosophical engagements" with Kierkegaard's thought, editor Edward

F. Mooney observes how Socrates and Kierkegaard are both skeptical *and* religious, "they pair a praise of love with privileging the care of convictions integral to *a way of life*," which in turn "undermines an easy opposition between Athens and Jerusalem, between the skeptical interrogations of Socrates and a faithful wrestling with the God of Abraham . . . or with the 'offense' of Christ."[17]

So what then of the quandary of our "Lutheran philosopher" negotiating the relation between philosophy and theology, reason and faith? One recent American Lutheran philosopher, who perhaps best captures this Kierkegaardian vision of philosophy and of the relations between reason and faith, is the late Paul L. Holmer of the University of Minnesota and Yale Divinity School, under whom I studied. Working through Holmer's posthumous papers in the Yale Divinity School library, I have been struck recently at how Holmer, one of the most insightful American students of Kierkegaard's thought, combines in his own writing, as he did in his teaching, this Kierkegaardian sense of the task of philosophy between skepticism and "the happy passion" of Christian faith.[18] Holmer appreciates deeply Kierkegaard's skeptical irony, his polemics, even his "cool" objectivity as a thinker; there is, Holmer believes, no directly evangelistic role for philosophy and certainly no illusion that analytic clarity by itself engenders Christian passions and virtues, including the gift of faith. At the same time, Holmer challenges his readers with the prospect of encountering the "happy passion" of Christian faith, an encounter that includes a profoundly philosophical and intellectual task. For Holmer, as for Kierkegaard, Christian faith is anything but anti-intellectual, for "passion" does not celebrate "experience" at the expense of reflectiveness, neither does "passion" elevate "practice" at the expense of "theory." Rather, to speak of faith as a "happy passion" allows one to see how reflection (including philosophical reflection) becomes part of a larger "sense-making" task confronting any human being. Here the passional context addresses all of us to "make sense" of our lives emotionally, morally, with one's will, but also with one's thoughts.[19]

These themes in Holmer's writings have strong resonances with both Luther and Kierkegaard. As we have seen, neither Luther nor Kierkegaard was an enemy of careful reflection, but in their critiques of philosophy, both pointed to how our habits of reflection can so easily become untethered from emotions, morals, and the will. By contrast, what Luther and Kierkegaard share, and what Holmer, too, reflects, is how Christian faith requires "the training of our thoughts."[20] Here philosophy, too, has a role to play, no longer disengaged from the struggles of the terrified conscience (Luther) or lost in a false objectivism (Kierkegaard). New prospects for philosophical reflection emerge as a truly human reflection.

If then with Augustine philosophy is a lover, and with Luther reason is sometimes a whore, perhaps for Kierkegaard and others who read and digest his pages, philosophy and theology, reason and faith, enable our passionate wrestling with our caring, loves, and commitments. In Mooney's words, again, we wrestle with our own caring, like Socrates; or we wrestle with the God of Abraham; or—with Luther and Kierkegaard—we wrestle with the offense of Christ. And perhaps, too, we wrestle with the hope of faith as a "happy passion."

CHAPTER 15

Delicious Despair and Nihilism

Luther, Nietzsche, and the Task of Living Philosophically

Gregory Johnson

What are we to make of the relationship between Luther and Nietzsche, both historically and as concerns the question, "What does it mean to live philosophically?" My hypothesis is that, in spite of seeming incommensurable differences, they, taken together, are perhaps surprisingly helpful in understanding the vocation of philosophy. Often thought to be solely the domain of theology, we will see that the question of vocation is, in both thinkers, another way of asking the perennial question, "How do we live our lives?"

To this end, I begin with Luther's notion of vocation and argue that he inaugurates a way of thinking that both reflects an understanding of the conditions that create the possibility for asking the question of vocation and opens the door for Nietzsche to pursue it in his own way. I then discuss how Nietzsche takes up similar themes in Luther but provides his own unique emphasis. I conclude by showing how Luther and Nietzsche go beyond a critical diagnosis of conditions that define lived existence and practice "radical hope." My aim is to demonstrate how both can be a resource for asking, "How do we live our lives?" in our own contexts. Let us, then, turn to Luther.

Luther's Delicious Despair

The term that best characterizes Luther's notion of vocation for my purposes is *decentralization*.[1] The question I want to keep before us is: "What does the task (vocation) of living entail once vocation has been decentralized, and what exactly transpires philosophically in Luther's move to decentralization?"[2] Decentralizing vocation entails the following. First, it removes it from a specialized assignation to a select few. If, however, this is the case, and the centralized view signifies a "saintly" standing, then twisting vocation free of its centralized position can be viewed as Luther's way of repeating the Pauline motif of the *kenosis* of God vis-à-vis humanity, only here vocation is emptied of its specialized status. Luther writes:

> How is it possible that you are not called? You have always been
> in some state or station; you have always been a husband or
> wife, or boy or girl, or servant. Picture before you the humblest
> estate. Are you a husband, and you think you have not enough
> to do in that sphere to govern your wife, children, domestics,
> and property so that all may be obedient to God and you do no
> one any harm? Yea, if you had five heads and ten hands, even
> then you would be too weak for your task, so that you would
> never dare to think of making a pilgrimage or doing any kind of
> saintly work.[3]

Second, this move entails a loss of the function of vocation thought to orient
us in ways that, when asking the question of "meaning and purpose" in life, our
anxiety could be assuaged and our endeavors both personal and collective placed
on solid footing. Vocation decentralized, then, is about *this* life, which makes it
not simply an existential choice but an example of a "spiritual discipline (or task)"
taken up in the conditions of our own existence.[4] If, however, vocation is a turn
to lived existence that provides the conditions in which we *always* ask the question
of vocation, what, then, is the condition for the possibility of vocation in Luther?
It is, I submit, *Anfechtung*, which can be understood as *delicious despair*.[5]

Anfechtung describes his experience of Mass[6] as well as his own theological
education where he tells us that this condition was "of help to me in this, for one
doesn't learn anything without practice."[7] Whether it is in terms of practicing
righteousness[8] or said to be the foundation to "wisdom beyond all wisdom,"[9]
Anfechtung is a "perennial and authentic feature of the Christian life."[10] Thus,
Anfechtung and vocation are co-constitutive, which is to say that there is not one
without the other.[11]

In light of this move away from a specialized notion of vocation, there is, in
addition to the loss of that which once functioned but no longer does, a loss of
God's presence. In other words, Luther seems to be aware that decentralizing
vocation is another way of acknowledging that "God actually and actively hides.
God hides in order not to be found where humans want to find God. But God
also hides in order to be found where God wills to be found."[12] To this end, vocation signifies the disciplined activity of looking for God, which, I am suggesting, takes place in and through *Anfechtung*. This is not to say that acknowledging
vocation as delicious despair is accepting that vocation is despair. The former is a
diagnosis that I have located as a part of Luther's move to decentralizing vocation
itself, while the latter is a way of viewing *Anfechtung* as fatalistic. Luther embraces
the former and works diligently to resist the latter.[13]

The paradigm for the co-constitutive view of vocation and *Anfechtung* is
Christ on the cross. To the degree that God is revealed, God is manifested in the

suffering work of Christ on the cross. What is this work? In the context of what I am arguing, the work on the cross is the way Christ takes up *Anfechtung*, which helps to explain Luther's fondness of faith that is "the assurance of things hoped for, the conviction of things not seen" (Heb. 11:1). Such faith, however, is "inevitably plagued by doubt and assaulted by uncertainties [*Anfechtung*]." In this way, faith "undergoes the crucible of suffering and death as the believer/theologian seeks to follow the suffering and crucified Christ."[14] There is, we can say, a structural relation between *Anfechtung*, suffering, death, and faith. As a result, we can further say that not only is vocation co-constitutive with *Anfechtung* in matters of living, but in the light of this last point we begin to see how *vocation as death* links Luther to the Socratic idea that philosophy is a practice of death. And this brings us to Nietzsche.

Nietzsche's Nihilism

At first, it might be strange to claim that Nietzsche and Luther are similar in any way. We should remember that Nietzsche, however, was familiar with Luther. For instance, he viewed Luther as a historical hero, in particular the Dionysian type of which Nietzsche approved. "So deep, courageous, and spiritual," Nietzsche writes regarding Luther and the German Reformation, "So exuberantly good and tender did this chorale of Luther sound as the first Dionysian luring call breaking forth from dense thickets at the approach of spring."[15]

To be sure, Nietzsche would offer stinging criticism of Luther, suggesting that Luther is precisely the problem with Christianity. Such an ambivalent relationship might make it strange to suggest, by way of parallel, that Nietzsche is concerned with anything like "vocation" because of the theological roots of this idea, which is a well-known target for Nietzsche.[16] Still, his appreciation of and familiarity with Luther opens the possibility for making the connections I do below. In particular, I want to demonstrate how Nietzsche engages in the kind of diagnosis we have already seen in Luther. The best place to see this is in perhaps the most famous of Nietzsche's announcements in *The Gay Science*. There we are told that the "greatest recent event—that 'God is dead;' that the belief in the Christian God has become unbelievable—is already starting to cast its first shadow over Europe."[17] Before this passage we are given the parable of the madman where Nietzsche emphasizes that not only is God dead but that "we have killed him."[18]

These passages articulate even more clearly the theme that Luther initiates with his decentralized vocation. This is the theme of loss, which is not only a diagnosis of the conditions, but here also Luther points out that we are responsible for this loss. Similarly, the loss of that which once functioned for us but now no longer does figures heavily in these passages. In section 343 this loss is described as the sun being eclipsed, whereas in section 125 it is a loss associated with the death of the Jewish and Christian form of morality. For Nietzsche, the belief in the framework that once sustained us in our endeavors of meaning, or specifically those that protect us from the onslaught of meaninglessness, are now unbelievable.[19] This is what Nietzsche summarily refers to as the "Death of God." The diagnosis is that a particular form of life has come to an end, and now we are left to ask the question, "How do we live after the loss?" In this way, the "Death of God" announcement and the move in Luther to "decentralization" parallel each other in the way that they diagnose conditions, but equally the way this opens the question of how we might live after the diagnosis.[20] Here is one way to understand the loss that connects both Luther and Nietzsche.

If God is dead, then living philosophically means the inability to grasp with *ultimate* certainty the foundations that are thought to be able to orient us to questions of our task to become a self (Christian or otherwise). This loss of ultimate certainty, however, does not necessarily exclude the possibility of either forging a notion of living a life of responsibility and commitment nor preclude the possibility of belief in God (although this was not a possibility for Nietzsche). As the contemporary interpreter of Nietzsche, Gianni Vattimo, has argued, this means, "since God can no longer be upheld as an ultimate foundation, as the absolute metaphysical structure of the real, it is possible, once again, to believe in God. True, it is not the God of metaphysics or of medieval scholasticism. But that is not the God of the Bible, of the Book that was dissolved and dismissed by modern rationalist metaphysics."[21]

The concept that Nietzsche uses to diagnose this condition is *nihilism*. In light of Nietzsche's pronouncement, *nihilism is now our vocation*.[22] This relates to the God-is-Dead parable in the following way. First, the function of the framework is thought to protect us much along the lines the way a centralized notion of vocation does by warding off *Anfechtung*. According to Nietzsche the advantage of this Christian morality hypothesis was to prevent "man from despising himself as man, from taking against life, from despairing of knowing [*Erkennen*]: it was a *means of preservation*—in sum: morality was the great antidote against practical and theoretical *nihilism*."[23] Second, and ironically, it is religion or morality in general, and Christian forms in particular, that are nihilistic. To be sure, Nietzsche is *opposed* to nihilism but uses the concept as a way both to analyze the way Christianity has itself become nihilistic. Here is one way to think about this.

Let us say that you have a form of life that functions, or is thought to function, in a way that answers the question, "What is meaning and purpose in life?" This framework is the standard of meaning. Yet we all know that no matter how much we try, we can never live up to the standard of meaning that functions to answer the question itself. As such, by definition of the standard of meaning itself, which we cannot live up to (or at least not consistently), we are, one might claim, therefore living a meaningless life. In this regard, the framework itself that functions as the standard by which we assess our lives as meaningful has meaninglessness built into its very structure. By *definition* and *function* we live a meaningless life if we cannot meet the standard of the framework that itself *defines* meaning. As a result, the framework creates nihilism. This is one way to understand Nietzsche's diagnosis that Christianity and its attending moral framework linked to the God-is-Dead parable have become nihilistic. Nietzsche rejects nihilism but, in light of his diagnosis of this condition, suggests that our task is now to learn to live nihilism. As lived, nihilism is the realization that "the highest values devaluate themselves," which calls for the invention of a new way of being in these conditions. There are two types of nihilism, active and passive.[24]

The passive nihilist "looks at the world from a certain distance, and finds it meaningless."[25] This is someone who is opposed to progress, who views those who hold to such beliefs to be the kind of dogmatism that characterizes religious fundamentalists. The passive nihilist, in short, demonstrates a "decline and recession of the *power* of spirit."[26] The passive nihilist has no interest in engaging the world in the service of something like transformation but instead turns inward and focuses on perfecting the self, whether this be in terms of perfecting one's pleasures or one's projects that define our lives. So, for instance, a passive nihilist could be one that speaks of vocation as serving the world.

The active nihilist, like the passive, still finds everything meaningless. However, unlike the passive nihilist the active nihilist refuses the inward turn to contemplation and instead "tries to destroy this world and bring another into being."[27] This characterizes everything from conventional utopian proposals to radical politics on both the right and the left. The explicit aim of the active nihilist is destruction of the world, which is why Nietzsche describes this mode of existence as "a sign of increased power of spirit."[28] In this way, nihilism reveals a condition characterized by a lack of an "action-guiding depth commitment," that is "hostile to this possibility both because of the death of God and even more because of how the news has been understood."[29]

This means that we now have to learn to "live our nihilism," which parallels living *delicious despair* in Luther. For Nietzsche, learning to live our nihilism philosophically begins with the "transvaluation of values," which as practiced by "new philosophers" means to "revalue, to reverse 'eternal values.'"[30] This, however, is too vague for understanding how we get from *Anfechtung* in Luther or nihilism in Nietzsche to what this task entails for our own context. The challenge, if we accept Luther's and Nietzsche's diagnosis, is to generate a sense of living philosophically that is rooted in a "possibility of sustaining a commitment to any such value in the current historical condition, a condition of cultural or spiritual death."[31] Such a practice that both Luther and Nietzsche employ is one that I will call, following Jonathan Lear, "radical hope."

Radical Hope

Luther and Nietzsche do not leave us paralyzed, even if their language sometimes suggests otherwise. Rather, their diagnosis of the conditions that shape the question of living (philosophically) reveal equally a possible way for living beyond a critical engagement, which I am calling radical hope.[32] What makes hope radical is that it is "directed toward a future goodness that transcends the current ability to understand what it is. Radical hope anticipates a good for which those who have the hope as yet lack the appropriate concepts with which to understand it."[33] This is the kind of work that goes on in Luther and Nietzsche in ways I suggest above. In particular, they embody radical hope in three important ways.

First, theirs is an attempt to think *after* in terms of a form of life (centralized vocation) or framework (Jewish and Christian) that once functioned in a way it no longer does. The *after* refers equally to the devastation of the loss that is revealed in the diagnosis that can be named *Anfechtung* and nihilism, and simultaneously refusing to have this be the last word. Radical hope is *not*, I want to emphasize, either Luther or Nietzsche succumbing to that which they critically engage (*Anfechtung* and nihilism) in the service of asking the question, "How do we live after the loss?" Rather, their preoccupation with things that are seen as destructive or cynical and so on is "to establish what we might legitimately hope at a time when the sense of purpose and meaning that has been bequeathed to us by our culture has collapsed."[34] In this first way, then, their thinking reflects an important trait of radical hope.

Second, both can be said to *face up to the reality of* Anfechtung *and nihilism* without being swallowed up by them. This extends the first trait in that they offer a response to these conditions by calling us to turn to the challenges that the world represents instead of stubbornly clinging to a dreamlike fantasy of something that once might have worked but no longer does "as a way of wishfully avoiding those challenges."[35] This is what, according to Lear, sets radical hope apart from optimism. The latter ultimately fails to turn toward lived existence in the way that Luther and Nietzsche do. Accordingly, we can say that neither Luther nor Nietzsche is an optimist, and this is a good thing.

Their thinking after and facing up to reality, finally, courageously employs what Lear calls "imaginative excellence," which is the capacity to "facilitate a creative and appropriate response to the world's challenges" in the service of asking the question, "How will we go on?"[36] This capacity is essential to ethical life not only because it possesses an image of what humanity might be, but, coupled with facing up to reality, it is the ability to take seriously the anxiety and vulnerability that characterizes these radically altered circumstances. Moreover, facing up to reality as an exercise of imaginative excellence means engaging the structures that once provided the resources for answering this question yet doing so at a time when traditional understandings are no longer livable. This is one way of understanding how Luther employs "priesthood of all believers" and Nietzsche the "transvaluation of values." As instances of imaginative excellence, both attempt to generate new concepts that "enabled them to go forward hopefully into a future that they would be able to grasp retrospectively, when they could remerge with concepts with which to understand themselves and their experience."[37] Thus, Luther and Nietzsche manifest the kind of courage that is a legitimate response to conditions that call for new and inventive thinking. In this light, they become for us not just windows to the past but capable guides for how we, in our own context, might take up the question, "What does it mean to live philosophically?

CHAPTER 16

Heidegger's Existential Domestication of Luther

David Vessey

By the early 1920s Heidegger was already famous among German university students, though he had published virtually nothing. Hannah Arendt recalled that "in Heidegger's case there was nothing tangible on which his fame could have been based, nothing written. . . . There was hardly more than a name, but the name traveled all over Germany like the rumor of the hidden king."[1] When in 1926 his fame led him to be considered for professorships at both the University of Berlin and Marburg University, he was pressured to publish something. Heidegger rushed into print the first two sections of *Being and Time*. The anticipated third section never appeared and, in fact, Heidegger abandoned the project, but his philosophical brilliance was confirmed. He was quickly appointed to a professorship at Marburg. Then, when his teacher Edmund Husserl retired, he was appointed to fill his position at Freiburg University. For almost fifty years *Being and Time*, one of the most important philosophical works of the twentieth century, seemed to have sprung fully formed from Heidegger's genius like Athena from Zeus's head. Only in 1975, with the beginning of the publication of 102 volumes of Heidegger's *Gesamtausgabe*, a publication process that still continues thirty-five years later, did the world start to see the contents of Heidegger's lecture notes and studies from the early 1920s. It was not until 1995 that the archives published Heidegger's 1919–1921 lectures on the phenomenology of religion; as a result, only in the last fifteen years have we come to understand how central Martin Luther's writings were for some of the key themes of *Being and Time*.

Here I will lay out some of the important ideas of *Being and Time* that can be traced back to Heidegger's study of Luther: substantially, ideas of fallenness, conscience, and being-toward-death; methodologically, the idea of *destruktion*. What we will find is that while they originally provided Heidegger with religious inspiration, he attempted to transform them entirely into philosophical categories while still preserving their existential force. More than that, he was seeking the existential, phenomenological roots for views that would take hold not just in Lutheran theology but in various ways across various theological traditions. So, even as in 1927 he could write to Rudolf Bultmann about *Being and Time* that "Augustine, Luther, and Kierkegaard are *philosophically* essential for a more radical understanding of *Da-sein*,"[2] he also could say that philosophy is essentially atheistic and all theological views need to be clarified in light of their existential origins.[3]

Luther's Influence on Heidegger

Heidegger made no attempt to contribute to Lutheran scholarship; instead, Luther appears in his writings as a source of influence for some of Heidegger's most significant views. To ask about Heidegger and Luther, then, is to see the way that Luther's views function in the background of Heidegger's views as developed in *Being and Time*.[4] I must stress *in the background*, as Heidegger does not give Luther any credit as a source for his views in *Being and Time*. *Being and Time* only mentions Luther twice.[5] Were it not for the publication of the lecture notes in the *Gesamtausgabe*, we would not know the importance of Luther for Heidegger's early thought.

Heidegger had a thoroughly theological education. He was raised Catholic and from 1909 to 1911 studied to be a priest. Influenced by his reading of Edmund Husserl, he shifted to seeking phenomenological foundations for Scholasticism; his *habilitationschrift* was a phenomenological analysis called "The Theories and Categories of Meaning in Duns Scotus." His wife was Lutheran, but they were married in 1917 in a Catholic church, in part, according to her, to help reinforce his waning Catholicism. As early as 1917 Heidegger realized that "The 'holding-to-be-true' of Catholic faith is founded entirely otherwise than the *fiducia* of the reformers."[6] By 1918 they had decided not to baptize their son in the Catholic Church, and in 1919 he had written a letter to his priest and close friend Engelbert Krebs stating that "the *system* of Catholicism" had become "problematic and unacceptable."[7] He made clear that he thought Catholicism had lost touch with the primal experience of Christianity; for example, in his 1919 winter semester course on *Basic Problems of Phenomenology* he writes, "the ancient Christian achievement was distorted and buried through the infiltration of classical science into Christianity. From time to time it reasserted itself in violent eruptions (as in Augustine, Luther, and Kierkegaard)."[8] Whatever ultimately moved him to break with Catholicism—some speculate it was his wife, some his experiences in World War I, some his reading of Paul Natorp's *Deutscher Weltberuf*—we know that Heidegger turned his close attention to Luther.

Heidegger's references to Luther appear regularly in his lecture courses between 1919 and 1923. Karl Jaspers reports visiting Heidegger in 1920 when Heidegger was steeped in studying Luther. In 1921 Heidegger acquired a full set of Luther's collected writings and in 1922, when Heidegger was seeking an appointment at the University of Marburg, Husserl writes,

> There is one major theme of [Heidegger's] studies, which are centered essentially upon the phenomenology of religion, that he, as a former 'Catholic' philosopher, understandably cannot treat here [at Freiburg] freely, namely, Luther. It would probably be of great importance for his development if he could go to Marburg. There he would be an important link between philosophy and Protestant theology (with which he is thoroughly acquainted in all of its forms and which he appreciates fully in its great unique values).[9]

In Marburg he influenced and was influenced by Bultmann and gave a number of lectures on Luther. John van Buren claims that in the early 1920s "Heidegger saw himself . . . as a kind of philosophical Luther of western metaphysics."[10] Nonetheless, by the mid-1920s as he worked toward the final draft of *Being and Time*, the references to Luther diminish. If anyone captures Heidegger's attention after 1922 it is Aristotle, and we might say for surprisingly Lutheran reasons. Aristotle was a polemical whipping boy for Luther; he took the Aristotelianism of Scholastic Christianity as the great theological confusion in the history of Christianity. Luther thought we needed to get behind the Scholastic distortion of Christianity to capture Christianity's primal meaning. Heidegger, in a parallel manner, came to see that we need to get behind the Scholastic distortion of Aristotle to capture the primal meaning of Greek thought. The great synthesis of Christianity and Aristotle in Scholasticism distorts both Christianity and Aristotle and keeps us from appreciating the lived vitality of both. One thing Heidegger discovered in his Aristotle studies in the early 1920s was the Greek sense of *ousia* as presence; with that began his exploration of what it would mean to understand being in terms of time.[11]

Fallenness, Conscience, and Being-toward-Death

Heidegger's appropriation of Luther in *Being and Time* is focused around the question of authenticity. To arrive at a new understanding of the nature of being in terms of time we need to clearly grasp ourselves as beings concerned with the question of being. But that sort of perspicuity does not come easily. Much of *Being and Time* could be seen as a diagnosis of why self-knowledge is so elusive. The two main reasons Heidegger offers are that, first, we are above all and primarily practical beings engaged with the world and defined through our engagements. Reflection on our situation comes late and typically only in response to a

breakdown of our normal practical engagement. This is not enough to fully explain why it is that we cannot achieve an authentic (*eigentlich*) self-understanding,
however. The second reason is that we are in a perpetual state of *verfallenheit*—
fallenness or falling prey.

In his lecture on Luther for Bultmann's class, Heidegger stresses the radicality
of sin in Luther. He points out,

> the idea of redemption is indeed dependent on the way original sin
> and the Fall are viewed. The sense and essence of any theology are
> to be read off in light of *iustitia originalis*. The more one fails to rec-
> ognize the radicalness of sin, the more redemption is made little
> of, and the more God's becoming man in the Incarnation loses its
> necessity. The fundamental tendency in Luther is found in this
> manner: the *corruptio* of the being of man can never be grasped
> radically enough—and he said this precisely in opposition to Scho-
> lasticism, which in speaking of *corruptio* always minimized it.[12]

It is a well-known and defining feature of Luther's theology that our sinfulness
runs so deep in our nature, and it so distorting of our understanding, that we
cannot even understand it. Reason, corrupted by sin, is incapable of realizing the
depths of its own corruption. Heidegger stresses later in the same lecture that we
should not think of sin as just something *about* us; instead, we must think of sin *as*
us. "The being of man as such is sin. . . . Thus sin is not affixing moral attributes
to man but rather his real core. In Luther, sin is a concept of existence."[13] John
van Buren suggests that Heidegger got the term *verfallenheit* directly from reading
Luther,[14] and certainly Heidegger's understanding of fallenness shares some of
Luther's understanding of sin.

For Heidegger, "Da-sein has initially always already fallen away from itself
and fallen prey to the 'world.'"[15] By being entirely absorbed in what "one" should
do, we are distracted from ourselves though "idle talk, curiosity, and ambiguity."
These three features of the world keep us in a state of "groundless floating," too
preoccupied to notice our lack of authenticity. "Inauthenticity," for Heidegger,
"does not mean anything like no-longer-being-in-the-world, but rather it constitutes precisely a distinctive kind of being-in-the-world which is completely taken
in by the world and the *Mitdasein* of the others in "the they." Not-being-its-self
functions as a *positive* possibility of beings which are absorbed in a world, essentially taking care of that world." In virtue of our fallenness in the world we are
lost in activities, which, because they are just what "one" does, by their nature
conceal from us what Heidegger will call our "ownmost potentiality"—our individuality and possible authenticity. As a result, we become part of the general
"they." This existential fallenness, as "an essential, ontological structure of

Da-sein,"[16] is the existential foundation for the kind of fallenness one finds in theological discussions. Heidegger writes,

> Our existential, ontological interpretation thus does not make any ontic statement about the "corruption of human nature," not because the necessary evidence is lacking, but because the problematic of this interpretation is *prior* to any assertion about corruption or incorruption. Falling prey is an ontological concept of motion. Ontically, we have not decided whether the human being is "drowned in sin," in the *status corruptionis*, or whether he walks in the *status integritatis* or finds himself in an interim stage, the *status gratiae*. But faith and "worldview," when they state such and such a thing and when they speak about Dasein as being-in-the-world, must come back to the existential structures set forth, provided that their statements at the same time claim to be conceptually comprehensible.[17]

Here we see the general pattern: Luther's concept of sin inspired the development of Heidegger's concept of fallenness, yet (Heidegger will claim) his secular concept of fallenness describes a primordial human phenomenon upon which Luther developed his concept of sin.

If fallenness is in any way as comprehensive for Heidegger as sin is for Luther, it is hard to see how Heidegger would be able to explain, with only secular resources, how authenticity might be possible.

> With the lostness in the they, the nearest, factical potentiality-of-being of Da-sein has always already been decided upon—tasks, rules, standards, the urgency and scope of being-in-the-world, concerned and taking care of things. The they has already taken these possibilities-of-being away from Da-sein. The they even conceals the way it as silently disburdened Da-sein of the explicit *choice* of the possibilities. It remains indefinite who is 'really' choosing. So Da-sein is taken along by the no one, without choice, and thus gets caught up in inauthenticity. This process can be reversed . . . by *making up for this not choosing*. But making up for this not choosing signifies *choosing to make this choice*—deciding for a potentiality-of-being, and making this decision from one's own self. In choosing to make this choice, Da-sein *makes possible*, first and foremost, its authentic potentiality-of-being.[18]

What being fallen prey to the "they" amounts to, above all, is the failure to rec-ognize our own agency in our actions. We simply do what one does, what "they" think is right. We don't decide to act in any particular way. By not having to take responsibility for our choices we also do not have to take responsibility for our-selves. It's not that we've made choices that are not true to ourselves, as some might think of authenticity, it's that we've failed to make choices at all—failed even to see that we should be making choices.

Fallen Da-sein, which is not only freed from the burden of choosing but blinded to its responsibility to choose, must be called to choose. It must be awoken to itself. Heidegger receives from Luther the idea that it is our conscience that calls us to ourselves.

According to Gerhard Ebeling (who consulted Heidegger in 1961 for the se-cond volume of his *Lutherstudien*),

> [Luther] is not following that idealist interpretation of con-science as an independent voice within man's heart which gives him independence, and is thus the basis for man's autonomy. What he means is that man is ultimately a hearer, someone who is seized, claimed, and subject to judgment, and for this reason his existential being depends upon which word reaches and touches his inmost being.[19]

For Luther the conscience does not function to provide reliable moral judgments; rather, it is a reminder to ourselves that we are always subject to God's judgment. It reminds us that the path of our true nature is through righteousness before God. The conscience for Luther, as an immediate awareness of our sinfulness *coram Deo*, is also the one place where we can see ourselves as a person.

For Heidegger, "the call of conscience has the character of summoning Da-sein to its ownmost potentiality-of-being-a-self."[20] One is summoned by the call of conscience to oneself or, rather, "to one's own self";[21] conscience calls one back from the "uncanniness" of (*unheimlichkeit*—our inability to be at home in) the "they." The guilt felt in the existential call of conscience is not the guilt for failing to take responsibility for ourselves; conscience calls us to become aware of the feelings of guilt for not choosing our ownmost potentiality-for-being. So the call of conscience does not call us to be one thing or another, it calls us to be-come attuned to our care for becoming authentic and the angst that accompanies that care. Heidegger says that "we shall call the eminent, authentic disclosedness attested in Da-sein itself by its conscience—the *reticent projecting oneself upon one's ownmost being-guilty which is ready for* Angst—resoluteness."[22] Resoluteness needs direction before it can point a way toward authenticity. This direction must be away from the "they" and toward something that can establish Da-sein in its own individuality; Heidegger turns toward the phenomenon of being-toward-death, another view inspired by Luther. As Luther writes, "we must turn our eyes to God, to whom the path of death leads and directs. Here we find the beginning of the narrow gate and the straight path to life."[23]

The problem of fallenness is the problem of losing ourselves in the crowd. To establish our authentic, *eigentlich* form of being-in-the-world, we need to find that perspective from which we can consider our lives independently of others. According to Heidegger our death is something we always do alone, and therefore resolutely being-toward-death provides a way of becoming authentic. Heidegger gets this idea of death straight from Luther. "The summons of death comes to us all, no one can die for another. We can shout into another's ears, but everyone must himself be prepared for the time of death, for I will not be with you then, nor you with me."[24] All the ideas we have seen are here linked together by Heidegger:

> Understanding the call of conscience reveals the lostness in 'the they.' Resoluteness brings Da-sein back to its ownmost potentiality-of-being-a-self. One's own potentiality-of-being becomes authentic and transparent in the understanding being-toward-death as the ownmost possibility. . . . The call of conscience . . . individualizes Da-sein down to its potentiality-for-being-guilty which it expects to be authentically. The unwavering trenchancy with which Da-sein is thus essentially individualized down to its ownmost potentiality-of-being discloses anticipation of death as the non-relational possibility.[25]

The nonrelationality of death is what makes projecting our life unto our death a means for escaping the pull of the they. It's not that we overcome death this way, nor live for death, as Socrates might say the philosopher lives for death, but that we live with the certainty of our death always with us and we let that certainly be the force of the call to become authentic.

Likewise, for Luther, an awareness of death should be our constant companion as righteousness can only fully be revealed in the final judgment. For example, he writes,

> The significance of baptism—the dying or drowning of sin—is not fulfilled completely in this life. Indeed this does not happen until man passes through bodily death and completely decays to dust . . . Spiritual baptism, the drowning of sin, which it signifies, lasts as long as we live and is completed only in death. . . .

> Therefore this whole life is nothing else than a spiritual baptism
> which does not cease till death.[26]

For Luther the idea of being righteous cannot be divorced from the awareness of
death; inversely, for Heidegger, the awareness of death is the key to becoming
authentic. The opening quotation to Heidegger's 1921 course on Aristotle is from
Luther: "Right from our mother's womb we begin to die."[27]

Heidegger and Luther's Theological Antropology

Heidegger's three themes—fallenness, conscience, and being-toward-death—all
have their roots in Luther's theological anthropology; they may all be summed up
under the influence of one great Lutheran theme: the replacement of the *theologia
gloriae* with *theologia crucis*. Rather than a theology based on glorifying the
knowledge of God by recognizing God in creation, Luther substitutes a theology
based on sharing in the suffering of Christ on the cross. Rather than a theology
based on redemption through knowledge of God, we have a theology based on
sinfulness and suffering unto death. Luther quotes 1 Corinthians 1:19 to the effect that we need to *destroy* the wisdom of the wise to preserve the power of the
cross. We need to *destruere*—to dismantle—what Scholasticism has constructed in
order to return to the essential experience of being Christian. Unrelated to Luther, Husserl in his phenomenological theory also argues for a kind of dismantling, an *Aufbau*, of meaning to get back to its core motivated phenomena.
Heidegger brings Luther's criticism and Husserl's phenomenology together to
argue for a *Destruktion* of the tradition of metaphysics to recapture the fundamental phenomena of Being. He writes,

> If the question of being is to achieve clarity regarding its own
> history, a loosening of the sclerotic tradition and a dissolving of
> the concealments produced by it is necessary. We understand
> this task as the destructuring [*Destruktion*] of the traditional con-
> tent of ancient ontology which is to be carried out along the
> *guidelines of the question of being*. This destructuring is based upon
> the original experiences in which the first and subsequently guid-
> ing determinations of being were gained.[28]

The *Destruktion* is not essentially negative; rather, it is positive in that it lets the
original phenomena show themselves from themselves and in themselves in a
manner suitable to phenomenological investigation, freed from the traditional
conceptualizations that have been handed down to us. Traditional theoretical interpretations of human nature tempt us to simply investigate them theoretically—

to engage in philosophical debate; they thereby distract us from the phenomena of life that give the interpretations their validity and which must be continually reaccessed and confronted anew. This is the final point, a methodological point, where Heidegger is clearly influenced by Luther.

Just as Luther seeks to free theology from its Scholastic distortions to bring us back to the primal experience of Christianity, to an experience of our sinfulness and the redemptive power of the suffering on the cross, so Heidegger seeks to free philosophy from its Scholastic distortions, to bring us back to the primal experiences of Being that inspired the Greeks to philosophize. What Heidegger tries to do with the history of philosophy—to phenomenologically get behind its traditional interpretations to uncover the existential experience that gives birth to the concepts—he tries to do with Luther, too. Although influenced by Luther, he always holds that, as a philosopher, he needs to phenomenologically get to the existential underpinnings of Luther's theological language. The cost of Heidegger's secular existentialist domestication of Luther's views is that we lose Luther's radicalness. Ironically, the attempt to find a philosophical, atheistic ground for Luther's insights diminishes their existential force. The problem is multiplied when Heidegger scholars lose track of the Lutheran roots of Heidegger's ideas; they risk producing anodyne interpretations of profoundly existential themes.[29]

PART III

The Lutheran Philosopher Today

CHAPTER 17

The Vocation of a Philosopher

William R. Russell

Student: "If Luther thought that reason was the devil's prostitute, is it wrong for me to major in philosophy?"

It happens with ironic regularity: as class nears its end, a student floats the most profound question of the day—just in time for the swell of backpack zipping, paper shuffling, jacket snapping, and cell-phone texting to swamp her query. But the wave this day could not sink the question. Her issue contains existential buoyancy—her parents wonder about the practicality of her major and her friends tease her when she notes the philosophical dimensions of TV shows and pop music. Yet she loves philosophy—the ideas, the applications, the thinkers, the history. It is as if she is called to be a philosopher.

So we try to proceed like philosophers, because we "love wisdom" (philosophy's root meaning in Greek). We define our terms and establish our method. As it turns out, she is really asking about vocation, her vocation as a philosopher—and she wants to know what Martin Luther might think about such a calling. The clarified question before us becomes, "What is the vocation of a philosopher, according to Luther?" To answer it, we distinguish between "vocation" and "philosopher." And we turn to texts by and about Luther.[1]

Student: "First, what did Luther mean by 'vocation'?"

The Reformer understands vocation in the context of God's call (*vocare*, in Latin) to serve the neighbor. In Luther's famously programmatic work, "The Freedom of the Christian," he ties his understanding of this service in the world to the indwelling of Christ in the believer: "Surely we are named after Christ, not because he is absent from us, but because he dwells in us, that is, because we believe in him and are Christs one to another and do to our neighbors as Christ does to us."[2] Broadly speaking, writes George Forell, Luther's notion of vocation emerges from his conviction that "the Christian is the means through which God works in the world."[3]

Luther developed this idea in conscious opposition to the inherited, "two-tiered" Christianity of his day. Karlfried Froehlich describes this contextual dynamic: "[The term vocation] was a polemical one, coined with a contemporary edge to protest against the concept of higher and lower callings in the Roman church, the presupposition of all forms of monasticism. Luther's 'doctrine' of vocation . . . belonged in the context of his rejection of monasticism."[4]

On one hand, Luther rejects the vocational separation between "monastics and non-monastics, perfect and less perfect, spiritual and secular Christians."[5] On the other hand, he affirms that "God uses human beings to accomplish his purpose."[6] In a Christmas sermon written at the Wartburg Castle in the early 1520s, Luther notes the shepherds' vocation as a means of service: "All works are the same to a Christian, no matter what they are. For these shepherds do not run away into the desert, they do not don monk's garb, they do not shave their heads, neither do they change their clothing, schedule, food, drink, nor any external work. They return to their place in the fields to serve God there!"[7]

Student: "How does a philosopher 'serve God'?"

According to Luther, the philosopher's ability to serve God depends on his or her ability to use reason well (that is, in modern terms, "to think critically"). As he puts it in a 1536 set of theses for his students:

> Thesis 1: Philosophy or human wisdom defines a person as an animal having reason, sensation, and body.
> Thesis 2: It is not necessary at this time to debate whether a person is properly or improperly called an animal.
> Thesis 3: But this must be known, that this definition describes a person only as a mortal and in relation to this life.
> Thesis 4: And it is certainly true that reason is the most important and the highest in rank among all things and, in comparison with other things in this life, the best and something divine.
> Thesis 5: It is the inventor and mentor of all the arts, medicines, laws, and of whatever wisdom, power, virtue, and glory humans possess in this life.
> Thesis 6: By virtue of this fact it ought to be named the essential difference by which human beings are distinguished from the animals and other things.
> Thesis 7: Holy Scripture also makes it lord over the earth, birds, fish, and cattle, saying, "Have dominion" [Gen. 1:28].
> Thesis 8: That is, that it is a sun and a kind of god appointed to administer these things in this life.
> Thesis 9: Nor did God, after the fall of Adam, take away this majesty of reason, but rather confirmed it.[8]

The key to understanding the vocation of philosophers, from Luther's perspective, is the oft-repeated phrase above, "this life." God calls philosophers to use reason to serve the common good. The world needs critical thinking, sound argument, and sustained analysis of texts and ideas. And God entrusts these kinds of abilities to philosophers. The Reformer proclaims this humorously in a sermon on John 6:

> In external and worldly matters let reason be the judge. For there you can calculate and figure out that a cow is bigger than a calf, that three spans are longer than one span, that a gulden is worth more than a groschen, that a hundred gulden are more than ten gulden, and that it is better to place a roof over the house than under it. Stay with that.
>
> You can easily figure out how to bridle a horse, for reason teaches you that. Prove yourself a master in that field. God has endowed you with reason to show you how to milk a cow, to tame a horse, and to realize that a hundred gulden are more than ten gulden. There you should demonstrate your smartness; there be a master and an adept person, and utilize your skill.[9]

Luther's humor may lapse into sarcasm, but he writes straightforwardly in *The Small Catechism* (arguably his most influential work) "I believe that God has created me together with all that exists. God has given me and still preserves my body and soul: eyes, ears, and all limbs and senses; reason and all mental faculties."[10]

Student: "If God created reason, then why did Luther say such derogatory things about it?"

When it comes to philosophy and the use of reason, Luther applies a basic set of categories that runs throughout his work: the distinction between law and gospel. For the Reformer, the gospel is God's gift of salvation offered in Jesus Christ and received by believers through the work of the Holy Spirit. The gospel is the grace of God at work to save the world. In his "theological testament," he calls this "the first and chief article":

> That Jesus Christ, our God and Lord, "was handed over to death for our trespasses and was raised for our justification" (Rom. 4[:25]); and he alone is "the Lamb of God, who takes away the sin of the world" (John 1[:29]); and "the Lord has laid on him the iniquity of us all" (Isa. 53[:6]); furthermore, "All have sinned," and "they are now justified without merit by his grace,

through the redemption that is in Christ Jesus . . . by his blood" (Rom. 3[:23-25]).

Now because this must be believed and may not be obtained or grasped otherwise with any work, law, or merit, it is clear and certain that this faith alone justifies us, as St. Paul says in Romans 3[:28, 26]: "For we hold that a person is justified by faith apart from works prescribed by the law"; and also, "that God alone is righteous and justifies the one who has faith in Jesus."

Nothing in this article can be conceded or given up, even if heaven and earth or whatever is transitory passed away. As St. Peter says in Acts 4[:12]: "There is no other name . . . given among mortals by which we must be saved." "And by his bruises we are healed" (Isa. 53[:5]).[11]

The gospel, says Luther, saves us by God's grace alone.

The law, however, has a twofold function.[12] First, the law punishes and rewards us in human affairs—so that society might flourish. This first use of the law, its "civil" or "political" use, restrains sinful people from following their natural inclinations. In this context, the law functions to maintain order.

The second use of the law is its "theological" or "accusing" function. Here the law reveals our sin and inability to live up to its demands. It convicts us of our sin. In Luther's words,

we maintain that the law was given by God, in the first place, to curb sin by means of the threat and terror of punishment and also by means of the promise and offer of grace and favor. All of this failed because of the evil that sin worked in humankind. Some, who are enemies of the law because it prohibits what they want to do and commands what they do not want to do, became worse because of it. On account of this, insofar as they are not restrained by punishment, they act against the law even more than before. These are the coarse, evil people who do evil whenever they have an opportunity. Others become blind and presumptuous, imagining that they can and do keep the law by their own powers. . . . This attitude produces hypocrites and false saints.

The foremost office or power of the law is that it reveals inherited sin and its fruits. It shows human beings into what utter depths their nature has fallen and how completely corrupt it is. The law must say to them that they neither have nor respect any god or that they worship foreign gods. This is something that they would not have believed before without the law. Thus they are terrified, humbled, despondent, and despairing. They anxiously desire help but do not know where to find it; they start to become enemies of God, to murmur, etc. This is what is meant by Romans [4:15]: "The law brings wrath," and Romans 5[:20] "Sin becomes greater through the law."[13]

David Lose aptly summarizes the Reformer at this point:

> For Luther, God's law establishes our responsibility toward our neighbor (what we should do) and, along with the gospel, establishes our identity in relation to God (who we are). What we should do is love our neighbor; who we are is sinners for whom Christ died and who, for Christ's sake, God declares righteous.[14]

The Reformer recognizes that this view of the Christian faith is fraught with philosophical problems—that at its core, the gospel is beyond the capabilities of human thought:

> I hear that Christ has one divine essence with the Father. And yet it is true that there is no more than one God. Where shall I grope or grasp, start or finish? It sounds ridiculous in my ears, and does not penetrate my reason. Yes, and it should not penetrate it. Rather, I should reply: if I hear the Word coming down from above, I believe it even though I cannot grasp it and cannot understand it. Nor do I wish to get it into my head, in the same way that I can grasp with my reason that two and five are seven,—and nobody can show me otherwise. But if He spoke from above and said, 'No, but they are eight,' I should believe it against my reason, and feel: All right!—if I want to be the judge, I won't believe! As for myself, though, I shall believe him who is the judge and arbiter. This you should do here also, even though reason cannot bear it that two persons are one God. That sounds as if I said: two are not two, but two are one. Here you have the Word and reason in direct opposition. Reason should not assume the position of master, nor act like a judge or doctor, but should doff its cap and say: two are one; I do not see it or understand it, but I believe it. Why? For the sake of him who has spoken it to us from above. If it came from me, or if reason tried to say it, no man would make me believe it. I would shove

mathematics under his nose and show him that he should accept it, that he must yield to me. But when it comes down from heaven, I will believe what he tells me, that two—yes, that all three persons are just one true God, not two or three Gods.[15]

Reason cannot fully comprehend God's saving action in Christ. And when philosophers, such as a scholastic like Thomas Aquinas or a humanist like Ulrich Zwingli, try to fit the gospel into the confines of human reason, they use God's good gift of reason as if it were a prostitute. Both Aquinas and Zwingli appeal to reason as the basis for their diametrically opposed explanations of the Lord's Supper. And then, if such thinkers (or their respective churches) would require believers to accept such philosophical analyses as a precondition for salvation, then reason is no longer simply a prostitute. It has become, in Luther's words, the "Devil's whore."

This is why Luther teaches thus in *The Small Catechism*:

> I believe that by my own reason or strength I cannot believe in Jesus Christ my Lord or come to him, but instead the Holy Spirit has called me through the gospel, enlightened me with his gifts, made me holy and kept me in the true faith, just as he calls, gathers, enlightens, and makes holy the whole Christian church on earth and keeps it with Jesus Christ in the one common, true faith.[16]

The vocation of a philosopher is indeed a God-given calling—just as the vocation of the artist or the scientist. For Luther, the risks facing the philosopher are great (that philosophy will not keep to realm of law but, forgetting the distinction between law and gospel, become a precondition for salvation). But the need for reason and philosophy in this life is significant, indeed—and the calling of the philosopher is certainly a potential vocation for faithful Christians.

Student: "Could you summarize all this for me?"

According to Martin Luther, the vocation of a philosopher is to serve the neighbor by the critical use of reason to analyze the issues of human life. This calling comes from the Creator who created creatures to wonder about the structure of reality (metaphysics), the nature of knowledge (epistemology), and the evaluation of right and wrong (ethics). It is a great and useful gift of God's for this life. When properly used, philosophy (and the vocation of a philosopher) can readily be God's work—and a life lived in service to one's neighbor and to the glory of God.

CHAPTER 18

Lutheran Environmental Philosophy

Sarah E. Fredericks

The idea of Lutheran environmental philosophy may seem odd given (1) Luther's strident comments about reason discussed elsewhere in this volume; (2) the doubts of contemporary philosophers about (a) whether environmental philosophy is "real" philosophy given its practical bent and (b) whether theological and metaphysical assumptions that pervade Lutheran thought can be a part of a philosophy; (3) the fact that most Christians in history, including Lutherans, have not explicitly thought about the environment; and (4) the claims that Christianity is at least partially to blame for the environmental crisis. And yet, if philosophy is not strictly defined as the work of the mainstream academic philosophical community or limited to the focus on humans that has characterized much Western philosophy, but is a broader category that includes ontology, the investigation of the good life, and the study of what it means to be human, then it seems there is an emerging Lutheran environmental philosophy and ethics, albeit one that is intertwined with Lutheran theology.

Nature and Environment in Luther's Thought

To understand how contemporary Lutheran environmental philosophy relates to and reinvents Lutheran thought it will be helpful to begin with an examination of Luther's thoughts about nature. Yet we must remember that nature is at the periphery of Luther's work; the relationship between God and humans is always central to him.

One of the major places Luther does discuss the relationship between humans and the world is in his commentary on Genesis. He interprets everything occurring before the creation of humanity in reference to humans. Luther believes God created the world to enable salvation, support humanity's physical bodies, and develop their faith. Humanity's creation in the image of God enables their knowledge, including an intense understanding of biota as exemplified by Adam's knowledge of the name that would best embody each animal's character.[1] Luther believes that after the fall, human relationships with God and creation were diminished because humans lost the ability (1) to understand what being made in the image of God entails and (2) to know how to use creation in a way perfectly suited to its nature.[2] After the flood these relationships were reworked yet again.[3] Animals were fearful of humans because they could, for the first time, be eaten, an "extraordinary gift" to humanity from God to reassure people of God's love and ensure they had enough food to survive.[4] Thus, we see that throughout his examination of Genesis, Luther's exegesis is focused on the God-human relationship and only peripherally on the God-world or human-world relationships.

Luther continues this trajectory in reference to nature. In numerous places Luther reflects on the marvelous nature of creation. For instance, he writes, "If we truly understand the growth of a grain of wheat . . . we would die of wonder."[5] He sees many signs of God's continuing presence in and involvement in the world: that seeds produce the same type of plant from which they come, that babies are born, that winter is followed by summer. Luther argues that people should recognize God's power in these things and let their faith be strengthened as a consequence. Similarly, Luther thinks that the world's dangers, including bedbugs, thorns, and storms, can motivate faith because they can compel a person to seek God's mercy.[6] Thus, while Luther marvels at nature in itself, he focuses on how it may aid human relations to God.

Luther also discusses the natural world in conjunction with the sacraments. Luther is adamant that the priest does not call Christ down from heaven to inhabit the bread and the wine. Rather, Luther believes that in Holy Communion God reveals Godself where God already is. Luther comes to this conclusion because he believes God is one and is the Creator and Preserver of all and assumes that to create or preserve something, the Creator/Preserver must be present. Thus, God must "be present in every single creature in its innermost and outermost being, on all sides, through and through, below and above, before and behind, so that nothing can be more truly present and within all creatures than God himself with his power."[7] Yet God is not contained in any part of creation; not "even a thousand worlds could embrace" God's majesty.[8] He recognizes the contradiction inherent in his position but is not concerned because to resolve it would be to go beyond the limits of human knowledge.[9] Luther maintains that Christ does not wish humanity to find him apart from the Word and Sacrament because to do otherwise is to tempt confusion and to focus on things not bearing on salvation.[10] He believes that only a relationship with God, dependent on and initiated through God's grace, can lead to knowledge that God cares and saves.

While many scholars were influenced by Luther's ideas, they focused on the central themes of his work rather than his peripheral claims about nature. Thus, trying to locate an explicit Lutheran environmental philosophy before the mid-twentieth century is an exercise in futility. As awareness of anthropogenic environmental damage rose, as scholars such as Lynn White Jr. began to blame religions, especially Christianity, for environmental damage, and as philosophy and theology began to focus more on bodies and the physical world, explicitly environmental thought began to emerge.

Twentieth-Century Lutheran Environmental Thought

Twentieth-century Lutheran scholars developing environmental philosophy, theology, and ethics often reworked or rejected elements of Luther's reflections of nature as they extended his core ideas to nature. For example, beginning in the 1950s Joseph Sittler expanded the ideas of grace and Christology to the entire created world. For Sittler, Christ had to have a "sphere of grace and redemption" at least as large as the whole domain of creation because humanity is of nature and thus needs its whole context to be redeemed for redemption to make sense and because all things are held in the hands of God the creator and redeemer.[11] He asserts that grace permeates and transforms all of nature and enables humanity to respond to nature out of respect and reverence.[12] Throughout Sittler's work he emphasizes that humans should relate to nature out of joy, not out of sorrow or obligation, in order to recognize the world to be what it is apart from its usefulness to a person.[13] Sittler also argues that nature is not just non-human environment but includes humanity, and all humans do and make a delightful counter to the human-nature dichotomy that is preserved in much environmental thought, even as such a dichotomy is critiqued.[14]

While Sittler influenced his many seminary students, the World Council of Churches, and other religious groups, his work is rarely cited by secular environmental thinkers. For example, he is mentioned once in the *Encyclopedia of Environmental Ethics and Philosophy,* in a history of ecotheology, and he is only briefly mentioned twice in three decades of issues of *Environmental Ethics,* the earliest and best-known journal of environmental philosophy and ethics.[15]

Paul Santmire, a Lutheran environmental theologian since the 1960s, is the most prominent Lutheran environmental thinker. Yet Santmire's audience has most often been environmentally minded Christians rather than secular philosophers. When philosophers do cite Santmire, they typically use him as an example of a trend among Christian ecotheologians or for his historical research about Christianity and nature; they do not seem to be influenced by his theological and philosophical claims.[16]

Working from the Lutheran tradition's focus on church history, and in response to claims that Christianity has been responsible for environmental crises, Santmire's works have chronicled the "ambiguous ecological promise of Christian theology."[17] He has also developed new ways of conceiving of Christian narratives and liturgy in order to uncover, highlight, and foster deep bonds with creation (including the care of creation) in Christian communities.[18] Throughout

Santmire's work we see a marked grounding in Lutheran characteristics (grace, of liturgy, of sacraments, of Scripture) even as he reworks some of Luther's notions, including his strong limitation on human-animal relationships after the flood, and develops philosophical concepts such as the I-Ens (to be discussed below).

Future Directions for Lutheran Environmental Philosophy

Scholars working to develop Lutheran environmental thought may turn to the idea of the ubiquity of Christ, the idea that Christ is in, with, and under everything and yet nowhere and not contained since these concepts could have significant implications for human interactions with biota and inorganic materials.[19] Consider Luther's statement, "Anyone who kills a man may be called a murderer of a being who belongs to God and in whom God is present."[20] Now, if all of creation is filled with God, and beings belong to God, as Luther argues elsewhere, then isn't it the case that anyone who kills a being can be called "a murderer of a being who belongs to God and in whom God is present"? This then would imply that dominion leads to death and destruction of animals, or maybe that any part of creation is not an unambiguous blessing but a situation enabled by the imperfection of the world. It implies that humans act counter to God's original intentions, that they exhibit their fallen nature when they harm the natural world, even if such acts can help humanity in the short run. This reinterpretation helps unite Luther's belief in God's love, the wonder of creation, dominion, and the ubiquity of Christ. Such a position can also enable Luther's work to ground an ethic of environmental care. One could interpret the ubiquity of Christ as a ground for the intrinsic value in each individual thing that many environmental philosophers posit. Secular philosophers, however, with their suspicion of theological and metaphysical claims are unlikely to adopt ideas of the ubiquity of Christ, no matter how well developed they become within Lutheran environmental philosophy.

Similarly, many promising ideas for Lutheran environmental thought, such as the idea of God the Creator, the cosmic Christ, and the connections of grace and nature will not have much, if any, impact on secular philosophy because they are so wedded to particular theological claims. Thus, in the remainder of this essay I will focus upon contributions Lutheran thinkers may make to the wider field of environmental philosophy regarding (1) I-Ens, (2) principles of environmental ethics, (3) ambiguity and knowledge, and (4) hope and joy.

Paul Santmire has developed new relational terminology based on the work of Martin Buber. Santmire maintains that Buber's I-It relationship, where the I objectifies the other, and the I-Thou relationship, in which parties, through language, fully and deeply experience the other, cannot describe all of the sorts of relationships that humans can have because there are encounters that are not objectifying or linguistic. Thus, Santmire posits the existence of I-Ens relationships to encompass nonobjectifying, nonlinguistic encounters, as when a person communes with the whole other, whether a tree or a person glimpsed from afar.[21] The I-Ens relationship may enable more nuanced discussions of the relationships between humans and biota. More exploration of this term is needed to explore its full potential for ethics and its ramifications for ontology and metaphysics within and outside of Lutheran thought.

A more immediately promising area of collaborative environmental endeavors among scholars and lay people alike is the application of principles of environmental ethics, including justice, participation, solidarity, sufficiency, and sustainability, that have been developed in both Christian and secular contexts.[22]

While the I-Ens terminology and the principles mentioned above are not exclusively Lutheran, some lessons of Lutheran environmental philosophy are explicitly so, yet may fill lacuna in environmental philosophy literature. For instance, the Lutheran tradition's characteristic emphasizing of education while admitting that there are theological unknowns and paradoxes may be a significant resource for environmental philosophy, which similarly engages with much knowledge about the environment and many uncertainties that arise from the complex, dynamic nature of environmental systems. Though strategies like the precautionary principle—that is, that one should not act in ways that may be destructive even if one does not know for certain that the action will be destructive—have been developed to deal with these uncertainties. Yet they are not as rich as they could be, in part because they do not deal with the full existential ramifications of uncertainty in people's everyday lives. Thus, the experience of scholars and laypeople dealing with fundamental uncertainty within the Lutheran tradition can contribute something to environmental philosophy.

Given the monumental challenges of contemporary environmental issues and the uncertainty that accompanies them, much environmental philosophy adopts a serious, worrying tone. While potentially appropriate, this outlook can provoke paralyzing feelings of guilt and despair while ignoring the joyous encounters with nature that are a part of the full scope of human engagement with nature.[23] Lutheran environmental thinkers such as Sittler, however, have a joyous approach that could bring up many new insights to environmental philosophy if fully explored. Since they ground this joy in salvation by grace through faith, which enables people to respond joyously out of faith to creation and to take up their environmental responsibilities, significant philosophical work would be needed to enable secular philosophy to embrace elements of this position.[24]

Theories of adaptive management, an environmental technique articulated in recent decades, may bridge this gap. Adaptive management entails making decisions and acting in ways that are potentially reversible as we aim for outcomes that benefit humanity and the environment simultaneously.[25] Such an approach, drawing on pragmatic philosophy, enables people to respond with hope and maybe even joy as they admit that their solutions do not have to be perfect. Rather, they can learn from their inevitable mistakes as they respond to the situation at hand.

Conclusion

Lutheran environmental thinkers can make significant contributions to academic environmental philosophy on its own terms if they choose to do so and if they more thoroughly justify their assumptions. Yet based on past trends, it seems likely that Lutheran environmental philosophers will continue to remain committed to integrating philosophy and theology as they discuss ethics, ontology, and what it means to be human in relation to environmental concerns.

CHAPTER 19

Luther and Philosophy in a Scientific Age

Gregory R. Peterson

The question I pose is this: Can Luther provide resources for thinking through philosophical issues today? That this could be so is not obvious on the face of it; after all, Luther is a theologian, not a philosopher, and his method of writing is nearly the opposite of systematic. Equally important, much has changed since the decades following the nailing of the Ninety-Five Theses, not least among them the rise of what may be called the scientific worldview. It is this intersection in particular, the idea of a Lutheran philosophy in a scientific age, that I most want to consider. Other rubrics, those of late modern/postmodern, continental, and analytic, may also be useful means of thinking through Luther's thought. But it might be immodestly argued that underlying all of these, albeit in divergent ways, is the common, often unspoken influence of the physical and biological sciences, and our awareness of the physical world into which we find ourselves thrown shapes much of our thinking. To get at some basic kernels, I will briefly consider Luther's doctrine of the bondage of the will as a test case. As will be seen, the results are not conclusive, but they are at least suggestive of the kind of moves that may be made.

The Idea of a Lutheran Philosophy

There are several reasons to think that there cannot be such a thing as a Lutheran philosophy. Not only was Luther not a philosopher, he has many unkind things to say about philosophy and about reason as a general category. With a few exceptions, such as the commentaries and the catechisms, his writings are not systematic treatises but occasional pieces, often composed in highly charged polemical contexts, and they very typically read as such. To this range of charges, there already exists a stock set of answers. Luther's famous invectives against reason and philosophy are primarily aimed at creating a space between theology and philosophy and in particular a rejection of a rigid imposition of Aristotelian modes of thinking. Correspondingly, although Luther often embraces paradoxical slogans (the philosopher might secretly desire to say, *seemingly* paradoxical), his theological writing is full of reasons and reasoning, revealing his own training influenced by nominalist currents.[1]

Such observations, however, suggest to us that it is possible to conceive of a Lutheran philosophy, not how to go about actually discovering what it might be. Here it seems we have a couple of options. One is to think of Lutheran philosophy as a set of domains of inquiry, typically following standard lines of philosophical inquiry. Thus, we might speak of "Lutheran epistemology" or "Lutheran metaphysics," both of which would be comprehensible projects to investigate. Luther's extensive reflection on and interpretation of Scripture provides ample material for reflecting on hermeneutics, and Luther's many political writings provide significant material for political philosophy as well.

Alternatively, one could examine Luther's theological commitments, and work backward to examine the grounds and reasons for these commitments in hopes of developing a more sophisticated, integral framework. An advantage to this approach is that it allows consideration of some of Luther's prominent theological claims that do not subsume easily into existing areas of philosophy. Two examples would be Luther's sacramental theology and his theology of the cross. Luther's sacramental theology, with its doctrine of divine presence, raises questions of divine action and the relation of God and nature. Luther's theology of the cross involves understandings of gift, sacrifice, and guilt that are independently sources of reflection in moral theory and continental philosophy.[2] While questions of divine action find their natural home in philosophy of religion, categories of gift, sacrifice, and guilt are of much wider application, and so we might conceive the task of individuals doing Lutheran philosophy to be one of teasing out and systematizing these concepts and their implications.

Such work can be conceived to be mainly of historical interest, but the more interesting possibility is that Luther's thought can be a resource for contemporary philosophizing. Inspiration for this may be taken from the advocates of reformed epistemology who find in the thought of John Calvin resources for their own philosophical project. Or we may point to the many philosophers of the past who continue to influence today.[3]

A Scientific Age?

Efforts to find contemporary application and insight of Luther's thought might seem to some to be stymied by an immediate roadblock, one thrown up by the historical distance between Luther's time and our own. This distance may be expressed in several ways, but one important factor is the development of modern scientific understandings of the natural world, including biological and human functioning. Luther, standing as he did between the medieval and the modern, might be understood to have a foot in both, but he was likely premodern in his cosmology. The physics of Luther's formative days was that of Aristotle and the cosmology that of Aristotle's later disciple Ptolemy. Although the late medieval

period was witnessing changing understandings of the natural world belying traditional understandings of the scientific revolution as an instantaneous event, such
considerations are not important to Luther's thought, and Luther's apparent (and
likely offhand) rejection of the new Copernican cosmology seems rather embar-
rassing now.[4] Further, Luther's several condemnations of reason and philosophy
seem to embrace a standard conflict thesis, where religion and science are understood to be attempting to explain the same phenomena, such as the origin of the
world, with one having to be the winner and one the loser. If so, this would seem
to get a Lutheran philosophy off to a very poor start; a philosophy that cannot
intelligibly reconcile itself to contemporary scientific understandings, while not
necessarily doomed at the outset, would at the least seem so unpromising as to be
not worthy of further reflection.

What I have in mind here is what is sometimes called a "scientific
worldview," with all that follows from that. This term itself is a bit problematic,
and at the least needs some unpacking. One fairly standard way to look at natural
science from the perspective of philosophy is in terms of a method or set of
methodologies, thus the "scientific method" that preoccupied much of twentieth-
century philosophy of science. Thought of in this way, science is not necessarily
of much philosophical interest except for what might be gleaned for the study of
epistemology, and as long as claims that reduce all knowledge to scientific
knowledge can be kept at bay, the relevance of the natural sciences might be understood to be minimal. Yet the natural sciences have discovered so much, it is
difficult to reflect on their results without considering the ontological and causal
claims that they produce. Indeed, the standard philosophical ontologies in some
respects seem both impoverished and unimaginative when compared to the
world that physics shows us, a cosmos of unimaginable immensity containing
both quarks and black holes and which speaks not just of space and time but
spacetime, with even this formulation perhaps being inadequate. Add to this
Darwin's account of natural selection and our growing knowledge of brain and
cognition, and a scientific worldview starts to have something of the look of
completeness to it.

Having the look of completeness, however, is not the same as being complete, and the philosopher resistant to a philosophical naturalism that reduces
ontology to what the sciences have so far discovered may find important limitations to what the sciences can and do tell us.[5] But even if one rejects the ontological completeness of the natural sciences, there would still be strong reasons for
affirming that philosophical ontologies should be broadly consistent with scientific ones. Philosophers may choose to embrace an *élan vital* that moves all life but
do so at the price of looking very ignorant indeed, and philosophers who engage
in ontological reflections without understanding the relation to scientific understandings do so with considerable risk. Luther's followers seemed to understand

this point well, albeit with caution. Osiander's anonymously written preface to Copernicus's *De Revolutionibus* eased its introduction by encouraging an instrumentalist reading of Copernicus's theory, and Melancthon's reform of the universities made possible and even encouraged the study of Copernican astronomy.[6]

The Bondage of the Will: A Test Case

This would be the challenge for a Lutheran philosophy: Can a Lutheran philosophy produce insights that are both interesting and that are intelligible when the sciences are engaged? For a test case, I suggest consideration of Luther's famous doctrine of the bondage of the will as laid out in the treatise of that title. The circumstances are well known, the treatise being a response to a work by Desiderius Erasmus, *On the Freedom of the Will*, written in 1524. In some important respects, Erasmus's treatise argues in a mode and uses categories that are quite familiar to contemporary philosophers: his understanding of the concept of freedom of the will is continuous with contemporary discussions of the topic, and his concern with the relation between freedom and divine foreknowledge is one that receives continued attention in philosophy of religion.[7] It is an important question whether the same is true of Luther's treatise, published in response to Erasmus a year later. While the question of salvation is important to Erasmus, it is central to Luther and frames the entire argument.

This centrality of soteriology potentially poses an initial problem for the philosopher, for it raises the question as to whether Luther's conceptualization of the issue is amenable to philosophical reflection. One way of interpreting Luther's thought on freedom and bondage of the will is to treat them as purely theological categories and do so in a way that makes them immune to empirical considerations. Luther's famous slogan, *simil iustus et peccator*, might be seen to take this route, since justification is purely an act of God and not in any way requiring human cooperation. Correspondingly, sin may be conceived as a kind of ontological category that is beyond the merely empirical; human beings are in a *state* of sin, and it is this state, this alienation from God, that is repaired through God's grace.

Yet divorcing the concept of sin so completely from experience is deeply dissatisfying, and while it may be argued that the *iustus* is not correlated with the empirical, it is harder to argue this with respect to the *peccator*. More than one line of interpretation may be taken to support this claim, including Luther's own biography, which includes his empirical attempts to master his sinfulness and his failure to do so. Further, Luther speaks much of "works of the law," and this and other standard locutions seem to imply strongly that bondage is very empirical indeed, visible for all to see. While sin is, theologically speaking, centrally concerned with our relation to God, its ramifications are apparent on a daily basis in the world. When Pharaoh's heart is hardened—an example Luther devotes considerable space to in "The Bondage of the Will"—the effects are plain to see.[8]

Philosophically speaking, it is worth reflecting on how Luther's conception of bondage and its relation of freedom differs from contemporary standard debates about freedom. Despite the seeming intractability of the topic and its resolution, debates about free will continue to sustain philosophical interest and even vigor, and the past two decades have seen some renewed reflection.[9] These debates have little to say about the sort of bondage Luther speaks of, and it is notable that, with the exception of "hard determinists," much of the debate is not over whether we have free will but how to conceptualize it legitimately. It may be noted that for those who embrace stronger versions of freedom—libertarian and agent-causation theorists—there exists an argumentative strategy to first establish freedom and only then consider how our freedom is limited. Arguably, Luther's strategy is the opposite, and this fact itself may shed some light on how best to think about freedom.

It would seem that Luther's doctrine of bondage would have greater traction with theories that more specifically engage moral freedom as a category. Early modern philosophers such as Thomas Hobbes and Jean-Jacques Rousseau come to mind here, with their attendant views regarding human nature. Hobbes's emphasis on human selfishness would, on the surface, seem to accord well with Luther's doctrine of bondage, but there is an important difference, for in Hobbes's case the selfishness in question is a "rational" selfishness, driven by self-interest and the need to survive, initially in the state of nature and later, by means of the social contract, in civilized society.[10] But on Luther's conception, the bondage of the will is anything but rational, and it is a limit on our ability to be what we ought to be. Closer to the concept of bondage is that of the literature on *akrasia*, weakness of will, which has roots in Aristotle and which has seen some renewed interest in recent decades.[11] Yet *akrasia* is also not quite the same concept as bondage, for it emerges when we know what we ought to do but do not in fact do it. Bondage, in contrast, includes our reasoning and justification of our actions and not only the actions themselves. If this brief analysis is correct, it would seem to be an important result and suggestive that bondage of will may be a distinct and interesting philosophical category in and of itself.

It may be asked: Why would we suppose bondage of the will to be true, especially since it runs counter to the philosopher's (often unstated) confidence in our own reasoning ability? It is here that psychology and, more broadly, cognitive science might play an interesting role, for there has developed a body of evidence over the past thirty years that casts doubt both on our reasoning ability and its relation to moral performance. Some of this material is quite well known. In the early 1960s, Stanley Milgram showed that most individuals would comply with instructions to give life-threatening electric shocks to others in an experimental context, shocks that at the highest level would have been fatal had they been really administered and their effects not faked by actors.[12] This was followed in the early 1970s by Philip Zimbardo's Stanford prison experiment in which subjects were divided into guards and prisoners and which had to be aborted after six days as the prison guards in particular lost boundaries of acceptable behavior with their use of violence and tactics of humiliation.[13] In another study, J. M. Darley and C. D. Batson asked seminarians to prepare a talk about the Good Samaritan and then had them cross campus where they passed an apparently ill individual slumped over along the route. Darley and Batson found that the primary variable in determining helping behavior was the level of hurriedness on the part of the seminarians, and the greater hurry they were in, the less inclined they were to help.[14] These three experiments are widely cited in favor of a "situationist" understanding of human motivation and have served as the basis for recent critiques of character-based ethical theories.[15]

A steady stream of experiments in recent decades seems to support the situationist thesis of these earlier efforts, and some target specifically moral judgments, leading some researchers to speak of "moral dumbfounding," a term signifying an apparent disconnect between moral explanation and actual motivation.[16] In a more recent study, even seemingly minor framing effects, such as sitting at a dirty desk, show effects on moral judgments.[17] More generally, the claim is that our moral judgments are typically the result of cognitive processes that are fast and automatic and which are formed prior to the onset of comparatively slow and deliberative conscious processing, which then is left the unlucky task of explaining why the judgment was made, often inaccurately. Jonathan Haidt, a prominent researcher in the field, has put forward a "social intuitionist" model to explain these results, arguing that our own self-reflection plays little to no role in our forming of moral judgments, although the influence of the judgments of others do.[18]

Is moral dumbfounding combined with situationism the same as bondage of the will? The idea is appealing but problematic, in part because the full import of this research material is still being assessed and there is some reason to believe that, however we understand the situationist and dumbfounding literature, it is certainly not the whole story, since we also have evidence of character traits that are stable and of conceptions of identity and self-perception that do correlate with moral action.[19] There is also a problem of systematicity: if we are systematically deceived about the nature of our motivations and moral judgments, then this would seem to hold for the researchers themselves who conduct the experiments and themselves make moral judgments. Interestingly, this emerges as a problem for the bondage thesis itself, which, if taken globally, also seems to lead to epistemic and moral skepticism.

My own intuition is that philosophers engaging the scientific literature ought to look both broader and deeper, and for this task engaging Luther's own accounts of bondage may prove fruitful, for what may be needed initially is a good phenomenology of bondage, one that will help guide reflection on the scientific results as well as possibly inspiring new scientific research as well. A fruitful turn might be made here to the already significant philosophical and scientific literature on emotion and its role in decision making, not least since some of the scientific research suggests that the will is emotional through and through.[20] When philosophers think of the will, they think of Kant's view as expressed in the *Groundwork*, and on Kant's account will and emotion are distinct. But Luther's understanding is much messier, one might say more *empirical* and correspondingly much more satisfying.

Conclusion

These are merely cursory reflections; full consideration of the bondage thesis would need considerable elaboration, let alone understanding its relation to the empirical data the cognitive sciences continue to produce. Nevertheless, they should be illustrative of some of the fruitful possibilities for considering Luther's relevance for philosophizing today. They also indicate the importance of addressing the contextual gap between Luther's day and our own and the significance of the physical and biological sciences in our own contemporary understandings. In many instances, however, this gap can be bridged profitably, and philosophers who take the time may find themselves richly rewarded. It is enough, perhaps, to see Luther with new eyes, not as philosophy's enemy but as its ally.

CHAPTER 20

Queering Kenosis

Luther and Foucault on Power and Identity

Mary Elise Lowe

If Lutheran scholars are to ensure that Luther's teachings and insights continue to inform our work, we must do more than simply apply his historic insights to contemporary questions. We should be bold enough to bring today's theological and philosophical concerns to bear on *his* theology. This essay engages the philosophy of power implicit in Luther's kenotic theology and evaluates its usefulness for emerging queer Christology. Most theologians are familiar with theologies of liberation (feminist, disabled, Latino, and so on), yet may not realize that gay, lesbian, and queer Christians are also constructing new theology, including Christology. For example, Marcella Althaus-Reid and Robert Goss critique how the story of Jesus Christ has been used to support heterosexist theology and biblical interpretation.[1] In contrast, they emphasize Jesus' humanity and embodiment and suggest that Jesus is not only in solidarity with lesbian, gay, bisexual, transgender, queer, and intersex (LGBTQI) individuals but that his humanity included all of these orientations. Although this work is commendable, these Christologies overemphasize the humanity of Jesus and lose sight of his divinity. In this essay I will argue that Luther's kenotic Christology, the self-emptying of the Son, can help queer Christology maintain both the humanity *and* divinity of Jesus Christ.

Luther's kenotic theology may provide a helpful resource for queer theology, along with his commitments to God's hiddenness, the embodiment of the Son, and service to the neighbor. However, the sovereign theory of power woven throughout Luther's kenotic Christology is problematic because it asks GLBTQI persons to give up the self, reinforces gender essentialism, and severely constrains sex. Moreover, Luther's theory of power and its subsequent applications limit one's ability to recognize and resist discriminatory practices and discourses (social power). Luther's kenotic theology could be more useful and still authentically Lutheran if we employ the relational, disciplinary, and productive view of power articulated by the French philosopher Michel Foucault. Many queer and critical theorists find Foucault's work helpful because he illuminates how power, discourses, and knowledge created the new categories and identities of prisoner, mentally ill, and homosexual. He also explores how power both constitutes and constrains individuals and identities. Supplementing Luther's kenotic Christology with Foucault's social definition of power may help LGBTQI Christians reaffirm the humanity *and* divinity of the Son, understand how homophobic discourses shape identity, and empower individuals and communities to resist these discourses. I begin with a summary of Luther's kenotic Christology and theory of power, then introduce Foucault's analytic of power and bring it into conversation with Luther's work. The essay concludes by asking, What does kenotic Christology look like when it employs a social analytic of power?

Luther's Kenotic Christology

The term *kenosis* is found in Philippians 2, "Let the same mind be in you that was in Christ Jesus, who though he was in the form of God, did not regard equality with God as something to be exploited, but emptied himself [ἑαυτὸν ἐκένωσεν], taking the form of a slave, being born in human likeness" (Phil. 2:5-7a). Luther frequently references this passage in his writings on the Bible, the Christian life, and civil authority and uses it to teach about Jesus Christ, the incarnation, the hiddenness of God, and service to the neighbor. Luther teaches that Jesus Christ fully possessed the heavenly powers of the Son but laid them aside during his earthly life,[2] writing, "[Paul] simply means that the man Christ was God, and could, even in his humanity, have borne himself as divine. But this is precisely what he did not do; he refrained; he disrobed himself of his divinity and bore himself as a mere man like others."[3] The Son laid aside the form of God, which Luther describes as "wisdom, power, righteousness, goodness—and freedom too; for Christ was a free, powerful, wise man, subject to none of the vices or sins to which all other men are subject."[4]

Paradoxically, Luther uses a text about divinity to argue for the fully embodied humanity of Jesus Christ:

> So lowly did Christ become, and with such humility did he conduct himself, that no mortal is too lowly to be his equal. . . . he followed the customs and habits of men, eating and drinking, sleeping and waking, walking and standing, hungering and thirsting . . . and having the same experience as any other man in his relation to God and the world.[5]

Luther's assertion that Jesus Christ had all the bodily experiences of other humans can be a resource for GLBTQI Christians who have been told that their bodies and desires are sinful, distorted, and polluting.

Although Jesus Christ could have exercised his divine power, Luther emphasizes the "attitude of the incarnate earthly Christ. Christ did not empty himself once for all; rather he constantly emptied himself."[6] Christians are to follow Jesus Christ and give up power and serve their neighbor. Luther preached this message to rulers, priests, and the laity, writing, "[E]ach individual Christian shall become the servant of another in accordance with the example of Christ. If one has wisdom, righteousness, or power . . . one should not keep all this to himself, but surrender it to God and become altogether as if he did not possess it."[7] Jesus Christ possessed heavenly power but did not use it; Christians are asked to give up their earthly power. Luther's emphasis on the embodied humanity and divinity of Jesus Christ is commendable, but the philosophy of power inherent in his kenotic Christology creates difficulties for many LGBTQI Christians.

Luther's Theology of Power

For Luther, power originates in God; it is infinite, and a possession that can be given or laid aside by the agent who possesses it.[8] Luther describes God's power in his reflection on the Magnificat. "'He who is mighty.' Truly, in these words she [Mary] takes away all might and power from every creature and bestows them on God alone. . . . She dares, by this one word, to make all the strong feeble, all the mighty weak, all the wise foolish, all the famous despised, and God alone the Possessor of all strength, wisdom, and glory."[9] Although God is omnipotent, it is important not to miss Luther's emphasis on the paradox that the supreme God is often hidden in weakness and foolishness. Luther calls this the wisdom of the cross, and this emphasis on paradox in both the method and content of his theology resonates with queer commitments to paradox and difference and may be a valuable insight that emerging GLBTQI theology can employ in its constructive proposals.[10] Luther also teaches that God's power could be given to all human agents and that a sovereign's power comes from God and should be modeled on the self-emptying of the Son, writing, "Behold, Christ, the supreme ruler, came to serve me. . . . I will do likewise, seeking from my subjects not my own advantage but theirs. I will use my office to serve and protect them."[11] Readers familiar with Luther know that he also writes extensively about the nonagential power of the law, gospel, sin, and death. However, I suggest that these impersonal "powers" are still agential (from Foucault's perspective) since they have their source in one agent—God.

Luther's agential theory of power also contrasts sharply with Foucault's social analytic of power with respect to civil revolt and bodies. For Luther, political resistance can be interpreted as rebellion against God's power: "Furthermore, anyone who can be proved to be a seditious person is an outlaw before God and the emperor."[12] Luther's distaste for revolt seems to contrast with his teachings regarding Christian freedom, and it is troubling to see that there seems to be little room for political resistance even if a ruler is unjust. Finally, Luther teaches that Christians should exercise power in the form of control over their bodies. He writes, "unchastity is a serious and rabid vice. It rages in all our members: in the thoughts of our heart, in the seeing of our eyes . . . in the works of our hands, our feet, and our whole body. To control all of these calls for labor and effort."[13] One can clearly see the Augustinian influence on Luther's view of bodies and sex in his assertion that they should be controlled by the self, will, or mind. In Foucault's analytic, power relates to bodies quite differently.

Foucault's Analytic of Power

Foucault rejects what he calls the sovereign/juridical model of power dominant in Western Europe until the seventeenth to eighteenth centuries, which represented power in terms of the relationship between God, the ruler, and the subject. He describes it this way: "In the case of the classical juridical theory of power, power is regarded as a right which can be possessed in the way one possesses a commodity, and which can be transferred or alienated. . . . Power is the concrete power that an individual can hold, and which he can surrender."[14] For Luther, power is a possession that can be exchanged or taken up in revolt. It is represented in terms of repression, law, contract, or control, and the effects of power are almost exclusively negative. For Foucault, power is not a possession, ability, or a right.[15] Nor does it come from a single source, agent, psychological drive, class of persons, or institution. In our era, power is disciplinary and productive, and Foucault reframes power as an event, a net, a capillary, or relationship.

> Power is 'always already there', that one is never 'outside', that there are no 'margins' in which those in rupture with the system may gambol [sic]. . . . I would suggest . . . that power is coextensive with the social body . . . that power relations are intermingled with other types of relations . . . that there are no relations of power without resistances.[16]

Elsewhere Foucault states, "Power is everywhere; not because it embraces everything, but because it comes from everywhere."[17]

Three additional clarifications demonstrate the differences between Luther (sovereign) and Foucault's (social) philosophies of power. In the new era of disciplinary power, knowledge, truth, and power are not possessed by individuals. Rather, they flow in and through discourses and disciplinary technologies to produce identities and subjects. Foucault states, "We should admit rather that power produces knowledge . . . that power and knowledge directly imply one another; that there is no power relation without the correlative constitution of a field of knowledge."[18] For example, Foucault traces the emergence of "the homosexual" and shows how laws, religious beliefs, and psychological claims colluded to create the newly discovered identity "homosexual." Second, sovereign power was primarily enacted on bodies; for example, many homosexuals were publically executed. In contrast, disciplinary power constitutes and disciplines bodies through regulation and classification, and individuals internalize the demands of power (subjection). Homosexuals are medicalized, classified, excommunicated, and punished; and Foucault argues that these disciplinary techniques are no less violent than the earlier physical punishments.

Finally, because there is space to resist and move within power relations, power is productive as well as disciplinary, constituting *and* subjecting individuals and groups. Individuals can—to a limited degree—accept or resist identities and classification and create new, subversive identities. Foucault writes, "We cannot jump *outside* the situation, and there is no point where you are free from all power relations. But you can always change it."[19] This means that stereotypes and "truths" about homosexuals can be challenged, parodied, and resisted. In contrast, Luther's philosophy of sovereign power in its feudal environment and in today's context leaves almost no room for resistance against homophobic discourses and oppressive powers.

Problems with Luther's Kenotic Christology and Philosophy of Power

Although there is much to commend in Luther's Christology, there are commitments in his kenotic theology and philosophy of power that make them difficult to incorporate into queer theology. First, Luther asks Christians to self-empty of power and give of the self to the point of suffering and death. He writes, "But Christians have no armor and weapons. They must become the victims of their enemies and allow themselves to be plagued and tortured, killed and massacred."[20] Feminist and womanist theologians argue that this call to self-empty further subjugates oppressed persons.[21] Queer theology raises an additional concern. For many LGBTQI individuals, emptying themselves can mean staying in the closet in their families, at work, or in their congregations. This hiding is a particularly destructive form of kenosis that does violence to the self and others because it involves shame, dishonesty, and a denial of one's status as a child of God.

From a queer perspective, the patriarchal trajectory of male-Father, male-Son/Jesus assumes that female and male are distinct genders with unique essences that spring from physiological differences. Luther's kenotic Christology reinforces the gender essentialism that is assumed in dominant discourses about

Jesus Christ, marriage, medicine, and law. Luther's nominalist epistemology demonstrates that he rejected the idea of fixed essences, yet his writings on sex, marriage, and family clearly evince an essentialist view of sex and gender. In addition, his kenotic Christology and philosophy of power seem to require individuals to self-empty of sex and desire. Luther emphasizes the embodiment of the Son; however, he seems to believe sexual desires and sex were also laid aside by Jesus Christ. This kenotic asexuality—combined with Mary's virginity and Paul's celibacy—has functioned to teach all persons, but especially GLBTQI persons— that bodies, desire, and sexual expression should be denied, self-emptied, or at least rigorously controlled within monogamous heterosexuality.

To be sure, Luther's theology of power was able to name and resist some of the subjugating institutional practices and oppressive beliefs of the Roman Catholic Church of his day, such as indulgences and the power of the pope. Luther successfully challenged these abuses of power in the *spiritual* realm. However, Luther is far less able than Foucault to help LBGTQI individuals because his view of power is ultimately sovereign, and Luther's claim that the world is divided into spiritual and secular realms leads him to encourage endurance over resistance.[22] This same insight hindered Luther from seeing what Foucault (and feminists) have long seen, that little separates the personal from the political, the spiritual from the secular. In addition, Luther cannot recognize how secular claims and knowledges constitute and subject individuals and groups. For example, many LGBTQI persons experience discrimination and exclusion because discourses about family, religion, psychology, and medicine have classified them as deviant. Luther's agential philosophy of power might help a GLBTQI individual recognize the *people* who discriminate against them, but since only agents possess power, Luther can't help the LGBTQI person name the legal and religious *systems* as sinful. Furthermore, Luther does not provide resources to resist discriminatory and subjugating institutions and beliefs. Since all power originates with God, resistance seems to be a sin against God. "[W]hoever, I say, despises, disobeys, or resists them is thereby despising, disobeying, and resisting the true Supreme God."[23] Luther's theology also discourages resistance because agential power can only change hands; the institutions through which power flows are not transformed. For example, after some Lutheran churches began ordaining women, some power was placed in the hands of female pastors, but the hierarchical structure and dynamics of power within the church did not change.

Kenotic Christology with a Relational Analytic of Power

Foucault's disciplinary power lessens some of these problems for GLBTQI Christians. Instead of thinking of kenosis as emptying of the self, perhaps we can develop a kenotic sensibility by combining Luther's emphasis on the divinity and kenotic attitude of Jesus Christ with Foucault's insight that power is social and productive. This would begin with an honest and critical assessment of one's location in power relations. Where do I exercise power, over whom, and in what way? How or where do social, political, or economic institutions enact power upon me? For those with privilege, this means confessing and self-emptying of the privilege they enjoy because of their race, embodiment, or education. For others, kenosis might mean identifying where they are located in capillaries of power as parents, consumers, or as able-bodied persons. Kenosis could also mean laying aside destructive powerlessness and laying hold of God's promise that we are loved and claimed by God.

Since Luther reinforces gender essentialism, perhaps one solution is to employ Foucault's contention that power, knowledge, and truth are inseparable. This allows us to recognize that the "truth" of two genders is actually constructed by the human enterprises of medicine, psychology, and religion and reinforced by social, legal, and scientific discourses. This disempowers the strength of essentialism in Luther's Christology and allows us to move toward a view of sex and gender as constructed and fluid. This also creates opportunities for resistance, including welcoming persons who identify as trans, queer, bisexual, or intersex. And self-emptying of essentialism can free all persons from sexual and gender stereotypes.

As I have indicated, Luther's kenotic theology also seems to require the self-emptying of sex, pleasure, and desire, and he believes that the self and soul exercise power in the form of control over the body.[24] For Foucault, bodies are not corrupting, and since power flows upon and through the body, soul, and self, the relationship between the three is mutually constitutive. This means that the self/mind/will does not control—in terms of power—the potentially corrupting body and its sexual desires.

Luther's sovereign model of power and its traditional interpretations make it difficult for LGBTQI persons to identify and resist exclusionary practices and homophobic discourses because social and political resistance is ultimately spiritual disobedience. In contrast, Foucault's social analytic reveals that knowledges and institutions enact power; power is everywhere, and therefore resistance is possible. This resistance could take the form of leaving one's faith community, working for greater diversity in our churches, or rethinking how power flows and is enacted in our congregations and church bodies. As a Lutheran I find it disappointing that Luther's theology seems so inadequate to the task of naming and resisting social and political powers. After all, he resisted and named the powerful institutions and sinful discourses of indulgences and works righteousness, and he surely recognized how Jesus Christ named and resisted the powerful institutions and sinful discourses of Pharisaic purity codes and the capillary power of the

Roman Empire. Ultimately, however, Luther's priority is on God's sovereignty and preserving the God-given order of creation. This leads to the ironic conclusion that Foucault's words on exposing social power may seem closer to Jesus' than previously considered and therefore more useful for LBTQI Lutherans.

Conclusion

This essay has introduced readers to Luther's kenotic Christology and shown how his philosophy of sovereign power and its interpretations can be supplemented with Foucault's analytic of productive power in order to make kenosis a fruitful concept for emerging GLBTQI Christology. I also hope that this essay—like others in this volume—has demonstrated a method or aesthetic of critically engaging Luther's thought as a resource for constructive theology and new philosophical method. This approach requires boldness as we put tough questions to Luther, and it entails creativity as we bring his rich insights to our work. It demands maturity because we must consider the limits of Luther's usefulness, and it needs a kenotic sensibility as we strive to serve the neighbor. This aesthetic of engagement with Luther's philosophy and theology will help us bring his wisdom to ever-expanding questions and newly emerging communities for many years to come.

CHAPTER 21

Philosophical Kinship

Luther, Schleiermacher, and Feminists on Reason

Mary J. Streufert

Human knowledge is not limited to the bounds of reason. This provocative and necessary criticism of reason's place in the pursuit of truth links in kinship Martin Luther, Friedrich Schleiermacher, and many postmodern feminist philosophers. This claim at first may seem unlikely. First, Schleiermacher was no Lutheran. Second, much feminist criticism of traditional philosophy also criticizes elements in Luther. But this chapter articulates the way the epistemologies of Luther, Schleiermacher, and many contemporary feminists present an important way to rethink philosophy.

Foremost, Schleiermacher was no Lutheran. In fact, he was formed by Herrnhuter Brethren, a Christian community that embraced intense personal religious experience as the central means of knowing and understanding the relationship between God and humanity. Schleiermacher's father, a Reformed military chaplain, was instrumental in ensuring the young Friedrich's early schooling at Herrnhuter Brethren schools. Although Schleiermacher eventually moved away from the Brethren schooling during seminary because of the restrictions he felt upon his knowledge and intellectual inquiry, the Brethren left an indelible mark on his religious epistemology. Human knowledge is not limited to the bounds of reason. Rather, human experience tells us about God—about what is true. What Schleiermacher had to say about human knowledge ultimately was a crucial contender in Kierkegaard's philosophical turn of arguments against Schleiermacher's contemporary, Hegel.

Of course, nearly three centuries before Schleiermacher, Luther argued vigorously against the Scholastic use of reason in philosophical theology, repeatedly bringing his readers and listeners to his conclusion that reason could make no possession of God. God is no object to be known through reason. Instead, faith is the object of theology, and humanity is the subject in the God-human relationship. Schleiermacher claimed Luther as a vital influence because of the philosophical challenges he posed to epistemology.[1]

Feminist Epistemology/Lutheran Epistemology

In the twentieth century, as increasing scores of women became educated in the Western philosophical tradition in the United States and Europe and the feminist movement for equal rights gave birth to feminist intellectual challenges to this same tradition, many feminist philosophers meted out objections to the ideals of reason and objectivity in epistemology. These objections were not unlike those same objections made by Luther and Schleiermacher. As other chapters in this volume contend, Luther's arguments that philosophy—or reason—is not the means by which one comes to full truth set a course of epistemological inquiry in Continental philosophy over the next several centuries. While one influential philosopher of religion, Jaroslov Pelikan, argued in the mid-twentieth century that Luther's provocative and necessary criticism of reason's place in the knowledge of truth did not surface again clearly until Kierkegaard,[2] it seems that Schleiermacher was an earlier champion of Luther's concerns over the place of reason in knowledge.[3] When feminist philosophical criticism of objectivity and reason in philosophical epistemology is viewed historically, both Luther and Schleiermacher surface as influences in the gradual shift in the discipline of philosophy that made possible the feminist criticism of reason and the objectifying male gaze. There is synonymy between feminist criticism of the masculine "objective" and objectifying gaze and Luther's protest against Scholastic philosophy's claim that reason is the measure of God and that reason can lay hold of God. Both critiques focus on the problem with making objects out of subjects.

This close kinship among Luther, Schleiermacher, and some feminists surfaces at least two central observations. The first is that Schleiermacher is an essential Lutheran philosophical conversation partner on epistemology because of his views on the place of reason in the search for truth. The second is that there are fruitful and interesting implications for Lutheran feminist philosophy in the secular feminist debates over reason and epistemology.

To understand Schleiermacher's kinship with Luther, we must first grasp his theological anthropology. Referring to the way humans process stimulation, he points out that we either respond to stimulation as thought or as action. What Schleiermacher wants us to see more clearly is the "moment" represented by the transition between stimulation and either thought or action. It is to the transition that he most sharply turns his attention. He refers to this human awareness before thought as "immediate awareness" or "feeling." Referring to the central importance of immediate awareness or immediate self-consciousness, Schleiermacher writes, "[I]t is the case in general that the immediate self-consciousness is always the mediating link in the transition between moments in which Knowing predominates and those in which Doing predominates."[4] In this immediate self-consciousness we are aware of that upon which we are utterly dependent. This is not a rational knowing but a human knowing that is, however, not irrational. God-consciousness occurs in that "moment" of immediate awareness; this is where God has influence and power.[5] On the other side, in thinking and acting, we have power to change. Hearkening to his Herrnhuter Brethren formation, Schleiermacher refers to the God-human relationship as "piety." Schleiermacher stipulates that no matter our diverse human forms of piety, this nonrational knowledge is the core. He writes, "The common element in all howsoever diverse expressions of piety . . . is this: the consciousness of being absolutely dependent, or which is the same thing, of being in relation with God."[6] Schleiermacher clearly shared with Luther a nonrational priority in knowledge of God.

Luther's kinship with Schleiermacher lies in his abhorrence for the use of reason to know and understand God and God's work of salvation.[7] Luther was beside himself regarding the ways in which he thought philosophical reason obscures the gospel, the knowledge of justification by grace through faith. "I certainly believe that I owe it as a matter of obedience to the Lord to bark against philosophy and speak words of encouragement to the holy scripture. . . . I have worn myself out for years at this, and can see quite clearly from my experience and from conversations with others that it is a vain and ruinous study."[8] Reason, indeed, was suspect.

When viewed from a feminist historical perspective, one question that arises is: To what extent were Luther and Schleiermacher reaching toward something quite akin to some feminist epistemological arguments in the history of philosophy? Luther and Schleiermacher both refer to reason as a means to express the certainty of experience. Reason and experience go together, which feminist philosopher Sally Haslanger ably expresses when she explores the weaknesses of a feminist philosophy that attempts to reject reason itself as inherently patriarchal.[9]

Shared Objections to the Ideal of Reason as Objective

The problem, however, is well expressed by feminist philosopher Genevieve Lloyd, who argues that the real problem is that reason is not neutral but gendered: "The supposed sexual neutrality of reason demands a male viewpoint—it coincides with the male position, which can take the female as its opposite. Woman therefore becomes the symbol of sexual difference."[10] The problem is that reason is supposedly sexless or neutral. The metaphoric maleness of reason comes from a combination of the assumed sexlessness of reason and what sexlessness supposedly is. Sexlessness is seen as an opposition to sexual difference, which, from the male perspective, is exactly what the "feminine" is, its opposite. Because of this assumed sexlessness based in oppositional sexual difference, reason "takes on an implicit but powerful maleness. It is here that the maleness of reason is most embedded and elusive."[11]

Lloyd's project gives us interesting grounds upon which to carry further Luther's and Schleiermacher's criticisms of reason from a feminist perspective. To get at the problem of reason from a feminist perspective, Lloyd points out the ways in which metaphors function philosophically and culturally. Philosophically, metaphors affect our ideals of reason. Culturally, metaphors affect our understanding of gender.[12] The question Lloyd presses is: How do symbolic maleness and symbolic femaleness work? The project to challenge the maleness of reason is not simply about getting better metaphors but about challenging what reason is understood to be vis-à-vis metaphoric maleness and femaleness—how these function symbolically.

Arguing against giants in the philosophy of religion Luce Irigaray and Jacques Derrida, Lloyd argues that there are epistemological positions that "depend upon the male-female opposition" when in fact they are claimed to be gender-neutral.[13] One central problem in Derrida, for example, is that he keeps us in the danger zone of seeing the indeterminate, the "excess" of reason, as determinately female, which simply continues what is objectionable in the maleness of reason. She argues that to understand the maleness of reason one must not interpret its "excess" as female, as Derrida leads us to think. To assume that reason is sexless, which is rooted in an ideal that is the opposite of sexual difference, is deeply rooted in the philosophical symbolic structure and "reach[es] back into the conceptualization of reason in the Western philosophical tradition."[14] Here is an important connection to Luther and Schleiermacher's arguments against the understanding and use of reason.

From a feminist perspective, reason as understood within the history of philosophy is negatively affected by the symbolic function of maleness as it has imbued Western ideals of reason. In fact, what Pelikan so long ago argued, that not until Kierkegaard did the Western philosophical tradition pick up Luther's arguments regarding the place of reason and philosophy, has interesting play here. First, I think Schleiermacher should be credited for the shift, as at least an essential forerunner to Kierkegaard's relationship with reason and philosophy. Second, if Pelikan is correct that the developments in the philosophy of religion after Luther largely embraced reason, then what many feminist theorists or philosophers argue is accurate: reason as understood in the Western philosophical tradition is problematic. Feminists not only argue that the tradition wrongly places reason as primary to experience, but that reason itself is gendered—is symbolically male—and thus continues to support a patriarchal culture while claiming neutrality.

An interesting implication for Lutheran philosophy of religion is that Luther set the course for disrupting the patriarchy of reason because of his theological arguments regarding the following: the point of theology; the relationship of humans to God (theological anthropology); and the role of reason in these relationships. In short, the point of theology for Luther, as noted above, is faith, the God-human relationship of faith. Luther's theological anthropology is marked by paradox: the person of faith is simultaneously justified and guilty, denoting the utter dependence upon God's grace that is central to Luther's understanding of humanity. Reason, therefore, does not get us closer to God or explain God; instead, humans know God through God's relationship with humanity. Schleiermacher, not Kierkegaard, is the first to pick up on the effects of a theological anthropology rooted in religious experience and the certainty of one's absolute dependence on God on epistemology: experience and reason are not oppositional but are naturally related to each other in human life. Much feminist secular philosophy, in its search to challenge male dominance in a patriarchal social and philosophical system continues an epistemology of experience and the decentering of reason therein that continued to unfold after Schleiermacher. What Lloyd, as one example in feminist discourse, makes clear is that how we think about thinking is set up in oppositional contrasts as active and passive. Symbolically male, reason stands in opposition to anything symbolically. The Western philosophical legacy stemming from Descartes, she further explains, is that the will is to reign in or order or control thinking; reason is therefore "an attainment."[15] A quick reprisal of Luther and Schleiermacher, however, allows for fruitful conversation between their criticisms of reason and objectivity and feminist criticisms on the same. Ultimately, reason is used to explain the certainty of experience for all three of these thinkers.

Basically, Luther's concern with reason and philosophy is that by them God is made into an object that the human mind can control or explain. In contrast to the Scholastic theology against which he argued, Luther understands humans to be the subjects of God; we are related to God in a dependent relationship. In so explicating the God-human relationship, however, historical theologian Brian Gerrish points out that Luther keeps the subjective and the objective together: faith is the subjective; God is the objective.[16] That is, faith is not an intellectual assent but a relationship with God.[17] Philosophy, then, for Luther, is suspect because it seeks by rational means to explain God, thus making an object out of God. As well noted in other chapters in this book, Luther thought that "the method of philosophical theology" is a theology of glory because reason leads us to understand justice as a virtue, which is quickly a slippery slope toward works righteousness.[18]

In philosophical theology, the object, Luther thought, is God. On the contrary, Luther understands the object of theology to be faith, the life of relationship with God. Schleiermacher mirrors Luther's focus on faith, not God, as the object of theology. In fact, according to Gerrish, Schleiermacher claimed Luther as a forerunner "because for Luther, too, theology arose as reflection on religious experience."[19] They share the conviction that we cannot make God our object. If we make God our object, then we objectify God, making God what we want God to be by trying to control God. This is precisely the problem that Luther and Schleiermacher argue against—objectifying God with human reason. Therefore, their related epistemologies frame human knowledge in terms of their respective theological anthropologies, which at root hold that we humans are subjects of God. Remarking on the connection between Luther and Schleiermacher, Gerrish observes, "the notion of a theology of experience does seem to forge a link between Luther and Schleiermacher—and so, a link with the existentialist theologians of our own day."[20]

Further Connections

Yet the connections from Luther to Schleiermacher to the existentialists of the last century carry even further, into contemporary liberation theologies, including feminist theology and then also feminist philosophy.[21] Feminist philosophers continue to challenge epistemological claims of objectivity and reason over experience in the Western philosophical tradition. Luther, Schleiermacher, and feminists stand as compatible yet perhaps unexpected partners in the history of philosophy.

Arguing against strands in feminist philosophy that seek a specifically "feminine" epistemology, Haslanger argues that reason in itself is not inherently patriarchal. Reason gives value to self-criticism and public debate and is therefore necessary as one means of deconstructing patriarchy.[22] Such a view reflects Luther's concern for using reason to solve the problems in ordinary human life. Haslanger seeks to deconstruct feminist philosophical arguments that reason is itself patriarchal by looking at the claims of neutrality associated with the norms of objectivity. She argues that there is an ideal of neutrality in philosophical discourse that, when satisfied, supports the objectifier and contributes to collaborating in objectification.[23] Ultimately, she argues that the ideal of neutrality is contextually gendered, meaning that reason is symbolically understood as "male."[24] Is reason itself gendered? She unravels her answer by further exploring gender.

Gendered ideals depend upon social arrangements. In other words, there will always be males and females in the world (we hope), but what it means socially to be a male or female—a boy/man or girl/woman—changes. Haslanger argues, "Ideals present themselves as standards or excellences to be valued; if we assume that the 'right' ideals are given by authority (for example, by nature or God), then it is tempting to justify a distribution of social roles by virtue of the opportunities they provide to achieve the given ideals."[25] There are also ideals of knowledge, Haslanger points out, and they have been purportedly gender-neutral, yet the ideals of knowledge are "defined by their contrast with femininity," which is how, Haslanger stipulates, "patriarchy turns one of its neatest tricks."[26] Rationality has been gendered. However, this does not mean that it is in itself to be rejected. What should be rejected is the way the gendered ideal of knowledge or reason supports patriarchy.[27] One analogy she offers is that of kindness in the slave-master ideal; kindness itself should not be rejected because of its ill-use in the slave-master ideal. Rather, the way in which it is idealized and used to support the institution of slavery should be rejected. It is the same, she argues, regarding reason in patriarchy.

Haslanger is arguing against an epistemology of objectification. "A successful objectifier attributes to something features that have been forced upon it, and he believes the object has these features 'by nature.'"[28] When objections are raised that the social arrangements are not based on nature but on social contingencies, then the objectifier strengthens his position by claiming objective distance and aperspectivity. The objectifier (in this instance) can then claim that "gender differences [are] asocial and amoral."[29] The problem is assumed objectivity. Objectification happens when some assume power over others.

Such is the case in Luther and Schleiermacher's concerns. In some sense, they, too, argue against an epistemology of objectification. The use of reason to understand God assumes that human reason has power over God, that God is the object to be known through reason. This is especially Luther's greatest concern. When we assume to be in a rational position to know God, then we objectify God, making God into what we think God should be. This is for Luther sin.

Haslanger's arguments regarding gendered objectivity and reason is an important connection. She writes, "[A]ssumed objectivity contributes to sustaining that social power, at least in contexts where its norms are broadly endorsed. . . . [A] general endorsement of the ideal of assumed objectivity reinforces the objectifier's position of power and contributes to his ongoing success."[30] This sounds radically like Luther! Luther argued that humanity cannot and should not put itself in the place of God, which he thought Scholastic philosophy did through the primacy of reason. Similarly, Schleiermacher argued against his contemporary, Hegel, who thought that God could be known through reason because both God and humanity were rational. There is an interesting connection between Scholasticism and Hegel: the critics of each argued that the assumed use of reason to know or "unmask" God masks the problem of human pride: trying to be God. Something very similar could be said along the lines of feminist philosophical criticism over gendered reason and objectivity. Feminists criticize objectivity that is claimed to be gender-neutral for masking the power relationships that maintain females in an objectified, submissive position. Although Luther's personification of reason as a whore begs feminist criticism, his criticism of reason as a tool that can be abused by placing humanity over God squares well with the feminist reading on reason that I have offered here, that reason as a tool in a philosophical system can also be abused by placing males over females. Just as one could posit along with Luther that the Scholastic and later Hegelian perspectives on reason are sinful due to the powerful positions in which they place humanity over God, so could one posit that supposedly gender-neutral epistemological objectivity is also sinful.

Conclusion

What can a Lutheran feminist philosophy do? It can claim an extra-rational epistemology along with Luther and Schleiermacher while eschewing feminist philosophical schools of thought that try to reject rationality entirely as a patriarchal problem or construction. In searching for the truth, a particularly Lutheran feminist philosophy will best be marked by the inheritance of Luther and Schleiermacher: the quest for truth is shaped by an epistemology of experience that is yet rational in its defense and expression. In other words, feminists join Luther and Schleiermacher in being distinctly experiential.

CHAPTER 22

Provocateur for the Common Good

Reflections on the Vocation of an Academic Philosopher

Pauline M. Kaurin

The philosopher cannot help but wince upon hearing Luther's references to philosophy as the "Devil's whore" and his lament that she has gone beyond her proper role: reason in the service of human governance and not as the basis of theology. In particular, Luther's venom is directed at Aristotle, whom Luther had read and taught and who had also become the foundation for the scholastic thought that dominated Christian theology. Luther refers to Aristotle as "the blind, heathen master" and decries "this damned, conceited, rascally heathen," who "has with his false words deluded and made fools of so many of the best Christians. God has sent him as a plague upon us for our sins."[1] Despite the animus toward philosophy as a mode of knowledge and toward Aristotle in particular, it seems that Luther never abandons, and in fact, reflects the *model* and *role* of the philosopher in practice. It is this role that I want to explore to reflect on the vocation of the philosopher in the contemporary context of the university steeped in Lutheran tradition. I see Luther as modeling three aspects key to the vocation of the philosopher: (1) healthy criticism of and humility toward one's own discipline and orientation toward knowledge; (2) taking seriously the role of provocateur and question asker, and (3) embodying the "pastoral" role in dealing constructively with the effects and aftermath of provocation.

Luther on Vocation

When discussing the idea of vocation, Luther typically uses the word *Beruf,* understanding this term as the Christian's earthly or spiritual work—a station or role that is helpful to the neighbor if followed.[2] Luther is well known for resisting the monastic idea of "calling" as something that makes one's work higher or holier than others. As a military ethicist, I find his discussion of the vocation of the soldier in 1526 particularly striking: "So, because it is from God that a soldier receives his fitness to do battle, he may serve therewith, serving with his skill and craft whoever desires his services; and he may accept wages for his labor. For his too is a vocation which issues from the law of love."[3] While this seems a bit counterintuitive (especially if one finds war morally and/or theologically objectionable), Luther's larger point is that the enacting of one's office is the way in which humans participate in God's care for human beings. These offices are not simply those in the public sphere but also include the private sphere; one has offices as parent, wife, son, servant, even as one also holds a public office as teacher, executioner, or prince.

In addition, vocation is temporary, since it deals with this world and not with questions of salvation and eternal life; therefore, one's vocation is ordained by God to benefit the neighbor, not the one who bears or carries out the vocation. Here the idea of the "cross of vocation" is important in that it requires that we bear it, as Christ bore his cross, not for our benefit but for the sake of the neighbor.[4] Thus, the work of vocation is to be done out of love for the neighbor, and so the labor is to be done gladly and not in expectation of reward, either material or spiritual.

Of course, since this can be challenging, Luther emphasizes the difficulty and struggles that come with the carrying out of vocation; in part this struggle is with the Devil, but Luther also acknowledges that it is a struggle with our own egos. To carry out our vocation, we need to let go, to die to this world, die to the vanity and glory that we might want from our office and do God's work *as it needs to be done.* This means that in carrying out my vocation, I cannot misuse or overstep my office, but also that I must wait and see what the neighbor needs and do just that in a particular situation.[5] This requires letting go of what I might think my vocation is and how best I might carry it out (all of which is steeped in ego and sin), and allow myself to become the instrument and mask or face of God for the good of the neighbor. This letting go is not a general principle but a way of living and being that requires this letting go and struggling against my vocation in specific situations where I am confronted with specific human need.

Vocation of a Philosopher

The stereotype of the philosopher (which unfortunately is rooted to some degree in reality) is of the isolated thinker, lost in her own reflection and on rare occasions emerging from this cocoon of thought to ask annoying questions and refusing to provide answers. The founding narratives of Western philosophy even celebrate this image: the archetypal philosopher is Socrates with his quirky personality, provoking and probing questions of the powerful sons of Athens and repeated assertions that he is but a midwife bringing forth the knowledge of others, with no knowledge of his own.[6] A recent book on *The Daily Show* celebrates host Jon Stewart as the kind of ironic provocateur, speaking truth to power, in the tradition of Socrates, so this narrative is still as much alive in the minds of philosophers themselves as it is in the popular culture.[7]

Given this stereotype and its roots (even limited ones) in reality, it is easy to see why Luther would object to philosophy as thinking too much of herself and distracting people from the true path of faith. In Luther's mind, philosophy had gotten above herself and perverted this central message; having taught Aristotle, he was well placed to mount this critique, seeing firsthand the problem and its consequences. Despite this, I think Luther's issue was largely with a certain *version* of philosophy (he had very specific content issues or criticisms relative to the Aristotelian framework, especially when it came to the question of individual human choice) and with the role it was being accorded.[8] Certainly as philosophers we spend much of our time disagreeing about content matters, great and small, as William James reflected in 1911, "I am a philosopher, and there is only one thing a philosopher can be relied on to do, and that is, to contradict other philosophers."

Beyond the content arguments about Aristotle's account of choice, in the *Nicomachean Ethics* for example, Luther's larger criticism about the role of philosophy is a fair one. I think at some point, many philosophers experience some degree of loathing for their own discipline and ways in which philosophy can and is misused. David Hume gives philosophers an important, though gentle rebuke when he says, "Be a philosopher: but, amidst all your philosophy, be still a man."[9] In practicing the office of philosopher, it is essential to keep a sense of humility about our pursuit of knowledge and to understand that pursuit as situated within, not defining, the human experience and community. We should recall that Socrates called us not just to examine others (which philosophers love to do), but also to examine *ourselves*. When the quest for knowledge becomes a competition (or "blood sport," as some have accused philosophers of practicing), it is far too easy for my ego to become invested in my version of knowledge, my own arguments at the expense of the process of pursuing knowledge as a whole. When this happens, whether in the classroom or in scholarly exchanges, we can forget that the birth process (to return to Socrates) is not about the midwife, but the baby; the midwife assists the mother in the birth process, but the baby does not belong to the midwife, despite the role the midwife had in the birth. It is easy to become tempted by the vanity and glory that comes from the attention inherent in being a public intellectual figure—publishing, promotion, making points, and succeeding in argument against others in the public and private—defining our role as philosopher according to our own vision and priorities. If this happens, we are in the danger zone that both Luther and Hume warn about and need to return to the question of how philosophy and our office as philosopher can best serve the common good, can serve the concrete and real needs of the world and our neighbor.

Philosopher in Community

In the classroom, I see my vocation of a philosopher as both provocateur and "pastor." In teaching my students both about and how to do philosophy, I ask provocative questions, spark debate, challenge assumptions and deeply held commitments. Philosophy is both the questions themselves and also a certain way of asking and dealing with the questions and their content—including logic, argument, critical analysis, and even doubt—regardless of the genre form (treatise, film, poetry, satire) this content takes. In thinking about what philosophy contributes to the common good, several things come to mind. First, philosophy and its practice strives for, and should develop, habits of clarity and precision of thought. Philosophy requires thinking about certain kinds of content, but it also requires thought in a certain disciplined and focused way. In discussing the morality and legality of the 2003 Iraq War, the distinction between preventative war (you don't wait for the mushroom cloud) and preemptive war (the threat is imminent) was critical both morally and politically. A failure to make and take seriously these distinctions can (and did) obscure critical issues and what is at stake in going to war.

Second, philosophy is rightly known (and perhaps infamous for) developing the habit of asking hard, probing, and provocative questions; philosophers examine and challenge the things that others may take for granted. Developing these habits is crucial training for citizenship and democratic accountability in the state where citizens must be willing and able to examine policy and their leaders' decisions. The recent debate in the United States over health care rightly raised questions about the role of the government and insurance companies in reproductive and end-of-life decisions that needed to be addressed in the consideration of policy. Beyond our role as citizens, asking these kinds of questions is central to our experience as humans asking questions about our own life and existence. Regardless of what government policy is about abortion or end-of-life issues, what meaning does whether and how I have children, and when and how I chose to face death, have in my own life? The impulse to examine our own existence and its meaning is a powerful one, and philosophy can provide tools, traditions, and dispositions to enhance and deepen this examination.

Third, these two habits impede the inertia of the status quo, the power of tradition and prejudice, that keeps us doing the same things unthinkingly, that keeps us on the path of least resistance. Coming from Montana, where meat eating is the norm, but for the pushing of my vegetarian and vegan friends, students, and colleagues I might not have, in any deep and systematic way, examined my reasons for eating and enjoying meat and the moral, social, political, religious, and ecological implications of those commitments. Whether in a conventional academic community, on Facebook, or in discussion with my students,

I am reenacting the life of the mind embodied by Luther when he provoked discussion (among other things) in posting his Ninety-Five Theses. Luther asked questions and provoked discussion in his and other communities by the posting of these theses, his copious writings and letters to all manner of people, and his interactions with peasant and prince alike. It would have been simpler not to challenge the practice of indulgences, not to take issue with the elitism of the clergy and the church, but Luther demonstrated the role and office of a philosopher (even if he might not have thought of himself as such and, in fact, probably would have resisted the description "philosopher") in asking hard questions and challenging the status quo.

While philosophers usually enjoy this provocateur role a great deal, we may overlook the implications and effects of this process of asking questions, developing and tearing apart arguments. As a philosopher, I know the liberation and excitement that comes with tearing down and questioning all that one had thought before, but as a scholar and a human on my own existential path I know the disorientation, fear, anxiety, and stress that these questions and arguments can wreak on one's life. This is why I think philosophers have to cultivate a role that may seem unnatural and uncomfortable given the founding narratives and actual practice of philosophy: that of the "pastor," the shepherd caring for the sheep, that of the guide to reconstruction.

This returns us directly to Luther's argument that our vocation is not about and for us but about and for the service and good of the neighbor. Clearly the questioning and provocation can serve the common good and the neighbor as elucidated above, but it also creates concrete needs and after-effects for which philosophers must also be responsible. The student who comes to my office wrestling with the implications for his faith life raised by questions about the problem of evil we discussed in class that day is depending upon and needs my skills of construction as much as he needs my critical and analytical skills. It might be tempting for me to say that philosophers just ask questions and let others clean up the mess and figure out how to put things back together, but this is ignoring the need of the neighbor and allowing me to hide from the difficulty and challenges of my office. I cannot simply be a philosopher as I want to be one; I must be a philosopher as the neighbor needs me to be a philosopher.

This means that part of my office, my vocation as a philosopher, involves revelation about how one tries to put the pieces back together, a sense of being a companion on the journey together, which involves engagement not just of the rational arguments, evidence (which philosophers are good at and enjoy), but also engagement with the emotive, existential, and practical pieces that come with, in, and through the practice of philosophy. Part of my office is to model for others how to do this in a way that is consistent with my office as a philosopher, an ethicist, a person of faith, a mother, a wife, a sister, a daughter, and a friend. This role is at least as important as the role of provocateur and is a responsibility that comes with that role.

Beyond the classroom, in the broader university community and as a citizen of a globally oriented world, I view my vocation in terms of bringing the questions and arguments (and the critical and analytical skills that enable that activity) to the broader discussions of our community and society. One might think that in a university community rooted in a particular faith perspective, the philosopher practices her or his office in a somewhat hostile environment, but my experience does not necessarily bear this out. The philosopher in this context can occupy both an internal and external position, just as in the classroom I occupy both the roles of provocateur and "pastor." I can provoke with hard questions, help clarify ideas, challenge assumptions from an external perspective, but I can also function as a bridge to assist in the work of construction, of building community identity from an internal perspective and commitment to the mission and values of Lutheran higher education and my particular institution.

Recently there has been a fair amount of discussion and hand wringing about the future of institutions of this sort; they are viewed as under siege in an increasingly secular, multicultural world where education is driven by results-oriented, commercial orientations. Philosophers like Martha Nussbaum see their role as challenging these moves in higher education, protecting academic freedom, and advocating for the humanities and the liberal arts.[10] This is an important role for philosophers, but we should not overlook our possible role in constructing new worlds and dealing with the effects of radical change (technological, political, social, ecological, as well as educational) in the world and in the humans around us. While the model of Socrates is important, we should also return occasionally to the model of Luther: provoking but also delivering pastoral "care" and advice to deal with the after-effects of his provocation; delivering rebuke *and* counsel to the rebelling peasants; offering up support *as well as* warnings to princes and leaders; giving reassurance to the abused wife, to the soldier, and to the executioner. Our vocation calls us to serve in the world, among and amid the human community with all its challenges, joys, and messiness.

Philosophers from Socrates to Husserl (and nearly everyone in between) have wrestled with the role of philosophy and the philosopher in society. Some advocate a sort of monastic separateness, aloofness from society so that the philosopher can be a clear-eyed critic; others have insisted the philosopher can only better society from the inside, as a member embedded in the messiness and complexity of human community. Both of these impulses have merit and, I believe, generate a useful and productive tension, perhaps even to the point of paradox (which Lutherans love). The orientation toward the concrete needs of the neighbor and the common good is what resonates with my experience at Lutheran institutions of higher education and requires an ability to be in human community but also to see how human community can harm and how it might need to change to better serve the neighbor. As philosophers, we can use Luther as a touchstone to remind ourselves to have a sense of humility and skepticism toward our own discipline while we enact the roles of provocateur and pastor, of gadfly and guide.

CHAPTER 23

Luther and the Vocation of Public Philosophy

Martin E. Marty

American philosopher Mortimer Adler, co-inventor and promoter of the "Great Books of the Western World" program and author of many books, none of them great, aspired to be America's foremost public philosopher. His friend, admirer, and editor of *The Great Ideas Today*, John Van Doren, commented a few years after his death: "You won't find his name in a dictionary of philosophers. . . . There is not a single mention of him. . . . He doesn't exist. I think it's a great pity."[1]

German theologian Martin Luther, professor of Old Testament at Wittenberg five centuries ago who did not aspire to be any kind of philosopher and is often (mis)cast simply as an antiphilosopher, enjoyed a different fate. You will find his name in many dictionaries of philosophers—there *are* many mentions of him, he *does* exist. Of course, no one, from Wittenberg times until now, would cast him as a philosopher and give him tenure in a philosophy department. He would belong in scriptural studies within a theology department and could only be smuggled in elsewhere in philosophical theology, wherever that subdiscipline exists.

Luther did not tout Aristotle but instead made a career-long case against him. If Professor—he preferred "Doctor"—Luther shows up in formal philosophical history it is for his anti-Aristotelianism, anti-Scholasticism, and, ambiguously, his nominalism. For the rest, historians of philosophy and theology trace his strong but indirect influences on many aspects of philosophy into our time, including in America. Insofar as Luther is cast as a philosopher of any sort, the question arises—again, over against the model of Adler—Was he and is he a *public* philosopher? Mention that and questions follow: What is a public philosopher? If he was one, what kind of public philosopher was he? Why should anyone care? Partial answers to such questions can help scholars trace and account for some influences of Luther in contemporary America and might aid those responsible for setting and pursuing agendas for Lutheran scholarship in the years ahead. (It is not necessary to get into debates about whether Luther was a

"public intellectual," a term laden with meanings and productive of controversies that do not need rehearsal here.)

Luther as Public Philosopher

In the usual framing of the subject, the word *public*, as in "public philosopher,"
appears in contrast not so much to the word *private* as to *academic* or as specialist
in technical, arcane philosophy—valid though it be—which cannot easily be
communicated to or grasped by a variety of broader publics. On one level, Luther
is certainly of the public sort. Very little of what he wrote or said was designed to
be constrained by academic boundaries and practices. He aspired to reach large
and diverse audiences and readerships and developed rhetorical skills that helped
him persuade princes and, in the popular mythology, paupers alike. (He favored
Cicero the rhetorician among the classics.) His employment of the relatively new
invention of the printing press and publishers' exploitation of him assured a following unmatched in size and influence in his time. He was equipped to make use
of academic forums such as disputations but then to break convention by aiming
for publics far beyond those in the classroom. He derided academics who had
little interest in or ability to reach the citizenry. Luther conceived of his calling as
that of teacher in Saxony and environs, but he also always had his eye on his fa-
voring princes and his disfavoring enemies in Rome, the Holy Roman Empire,
and their cohorts. Yes, he was public.

Discourse about public philosophy in the past is sharpened in debates about
what it means today. Whoever would deal with Luther in such contexts has to
exemplify conceptual propriety. One convenient definer of one option among
many appears in reports of the American Philosophical Association's Committee
on Public Philosophy. In a conversation in April, 2010, its participants advocated
three positions that can frame talk about Luther in the public role. First, philosophical practice is a public good and should therefore be practiced in and with
various publics. Second, it is philosophy that has the explicit aim of benefiting
public life. Third, it should be "liberatory," that is, it should assist and empower
those who are most vulnerable and suffer injustice, particularly through a critical
analysis of power structures. We will return to these after having approached
Luther.

To begin to assess his approach, one does well to turn to a typical dictionary
of philosophy, in this case, *The Encyclopedia of Philosophy*, to see how this topic is
treated and how it informs the topic of his publicness as a thinker and writer. The
case is exemplary because its author is Brian A. Gerrish, author of a norm-setting
book on the subject of *Grace and Reason*, "reason" being at issue in most discussions of philosophies that related to faith in Luther's time. He does justice,
briskly, to the overfamiliar references in Luther to reason as "the Devil's whore"

but then shows how regularly Luther appeals to reason, especially in public circumstances in the political order. Gerrish deals with "apparent ambiguities" in this bifocal approach to reason and thus to philosophy. The fundamental distinction to be kept in mind here is Luther's separating the two realms of human existence, the heavenly kingdom and the earthly kingdom. In the former, reason has no formal role and can devilishly and whorishly delude the human into contending that rational inquiry can help make one right with God—as Luther saw the inherited, Rome-centered Catholic church doing. There is no way to stretch this concept into the sphere of public philosophy. Reason certainly may help clarify theological assertions. He could speak of "regenerated reason," useful in certain spiritual pursuits, but these by definition were confined to particular believers and were also by definition and intent not public. Luther not only had nothing against its use in matters philological, linguistic, grammatical, or propositional, but those were the limits.

As for the former, Luther voices an often underappreciated regard for the place of reason and the work of philosophy in that earthly kingdom. In Gerrish's summary, they were adequate instruments for dealing with "physical subsistence" (*oeconomia*) and the regulation of life in society (*politia*). One could add that reason and philosophy could play their part in aesthetics, a field that interested music-minded Luther, and in judgments in many cultural areas. It is in these zones of the "earthly kingdom" that Doctor Luther attracts interest and offers possibilities.[2]

This assignment of differing functions to reason has led many to speak of Luther's "double-truth" approach in philosophy. In one disputation, according to Gerrish in his book that expands the subject, Luther did come close to the "double-truth" position of Robert Holcot, a nominalist thinker: "A proposition may be false in theology and true in philosophy, and *vice versa.*" Gerrish writes: "Although," for Luther, "it is to be held that two truths never contradict each other (*Omne verum vero consonat*), yet the same proposition is not true in different disciplines (*idem non est verum in diversis professionibus*)." Luther saw no *contradiction* between the deliverances of philosophy and of theology, but "philosophical categories and techniques are not *applicable* in theological matters."[3]

The difficulty Lutherans often have in defining and applying the approach to the two kingdoms (that is, realms, regiments, spheres) can confuse publics, just as the "not true" approach to different disciplines or "professions" can create confusion among many American publics. To take an informative illustration from a line of Luther that has entered folklore: "Better be ruled by a smart Turk than a dumb Christian." I have not found any Luther scholar, even one now equipped with word-search instruments on computers, who has located this precise and condensed phrase, although in a more rambling and expanded form Luther says something like it and it is consistent with his philosophy of the *politia*. Yet in theology he can and did vehemently condemn the infidel "Turk," who, lacking grace, could not be called "good" or anything else positive.

Almost five centuries later some of Luther's heirs mystify those who want to discern or invent a "Christian America" over against the infidels of our time. They will often invoke as secular minded some quoted founders of the nation and secularist-heirs today on matters of *politia*. They may then, in their theological discipline, profession, or mode, speak very critically of non-God approaches to life. Their duality in such a case can be written off by some as the result of their foolish inconsistency, betrayal, confusion, guile, or strategy. No, they *mean* it, and they have theological and philosophical justifications for speaking in these two sets of terms. H. Richard Niebuhr, in his classic *Christ and Culture*, captures some of this approach in his category "Christ and Culture in Paradox."[4] It is a minority voice, often unheard, often confusing, in a nation where what Niebuhr calls a "Christ Transforming Culture" and other nondialectical approaches command more political power and popular support.

Two Kingdoms/Modes of Experience: Resisting Category Mistakes

The helpful distinction among "diverse professions" or "disciplines" is not un-heard of in secular philosophy in our time. One example that has captured my attention in recent years offers the concept of "modes of experience," which can here be analogous to the two kinds of reason found in Luther's writings. These are best developed by British idealist philosopher Michael Oakeshott. He defines "modality" as "human experience recognized as a variety of independent, self-consistent worlds of discourse, each the invention of human intelligence, but each also to be understood as abstract and an arrest in human experience." The philosopher distinguishes between the practical (which includes the religious), the historical, the poetic, and the scientific modes of understanding. Experience is "whole," but is necessarily broken up "through 'modification' and those 'arrests in experience.'"

We seem to be far from the drastic distinctions between the earthly king-dom and the heavenly kingdom. Here all that is at issue is the different modes—in Luther's term, "professions," or in Gerrish's "disciplines"—such as history, poetry, science, and the practical. Yet "there is no direct relation between any two of these," for "each abstract world of ideas is a specific organization of the whole of experience, exclusive of every other organization." So one cannot "pass in argument from any one of these worlds of ideas to any other without involv-ing ourselves in a confusion." Oakeshott calls such *ignoratio elenchi* a category mis-take. Thus, when in a TV show Basil Fawlty's motor-car breaks down, he grabs a branch of a tree and starts hitting it on the hood. A cruel category mistake it is, from the viewpoint of the auto. Away from metaphor: I as a historian have "the past" as my disciplinary differentia, while the scientist has "measurement," the poetic artist has "imagination," and the practical mode calls for "changing" the world.[5]

In Luther's world and philosophy, it is a profound, decisive category mistake to try to use "reason" or "the law" to find favor with God. Here, in the terms of the Lutheran Confessions, *lex semper accusat,* the law always and only accuses. Yet apart from the teaching and experience of being justified (*in loco iustificationis*), the law is also the power of God, never "unto salvation" but always for the care of the neighbor. Luther blasted the Catholic theologians and anyone else who thought that through contemplative aspiration one could become right with God. Even pursuit of that aspiration, which would to him have been a moral and theological category mistake, was shattering to the person, calling forth condemnation from God. Yet God honors what Luther called "civil righteousness." It does not avail in one category, salvation. It is a carrying out of divine purpose among humans in their economic, political, and social worlds.

No doubt analogies among Luther's putative "double-truth" or dialectical approach and other contemporary philosophies, such as pragmatism and aspects of language analyses, could be worked out. The concern over "category mistakes" among the "modes of experience" strikes me as being particularly congenial and illuminating as a bridge toward understanding how the scholarly Doctor Luther relates to public philosophy in a world vastly different from the one he addressed in sixteenth-century Saxony, the Holy Roman Empire, and elsewhere in a reality we call "Christendom." Christendom assured the presence of a public, with certain presumed common understandings, because they were backed by the civil sword.

Applying Luther to Public Philosophy for the Twenty-First Century

It is here in place to return to three contemporary elements in public philosophy, using American Philosophical Association criteria. First, we recall that philosophical practice is a public good and should be practiced in and with various publics. For Luther, as mentioned, the publics he could reach were within Christendom, so there was little bridging in him to other religious publics. Scholars do find that the sixteenth-century world was full of religious publics, particularly those given to the world of witches and relics. Some even contend that the Lutheran and Protestant Reformations, viewed from certain angles, were Christianizing movements that countered these folk religions. Luther's preaching regularly dealt with all this, but always theologically.

That left Islamic and Jewish publics. Islam was remote, though Luther and the Holy Roman Empire leaders were aware that Muslim troops were at their borders. He took pains to learn something about Islam and even purchased and studied a (bad) translation of the Qur'an. He studied Jewish texts early in his career and made some linguistic and conciliatory efforts. But he rarely addressed Jews or Muslims as fellow members of life in the earthly kingdom, who brought approaches of their own. His approach was theological and polemical, and it worked toward the "public good" only on grounds satisfactory to those who shared his philosophy. It is hard to find precedent in him for approaching these other publics in any positive way.

Second, it is philosophy that has the explicit aim of benefiting public life. Here it is possible to begin to work out a Luther-an philosophy of the public good. The basics are there in his explanations to the first article of the Creed, in his Catechisms, where creation and preservation are the issues. Here the recipient of good ordering and care may *interpret* the blessings of the divine order without recognizing the source of its benefits, and can bracket and leave behind theological and "saving" intentions and explanations.

Third, "public philosophy should be liberatory." Some will see this to be modern academe's loading of the case by referring to what inhibits liberation as being the forces of conservatism. But the public philosopher here can relate to progressives and conservatives alike. Theologically, Luther is engrossed with the language of liberation, but almost always it is of a theological cast, and his attempts to provide a philosophy of liberation in the political order are slight. At the same time, the anthropological assumptions in Luther's public life reveal him to be proclaiming liberation in forms that allowed him to benefit from and to enhance alliances that do promote human good. This occurred without his changing the category into the search for salvation, and what liberation means in that sphere or realm or "kingdom." In public life he was inconsistent and situational, as can be seen by his condemnation of the peasants in the Peasants' War of 1525 and his attempt to judge the princes as they had gone way over the line in violence to put down rebellion. Most of what Luther had to say about liberation was theological, the result of his preaching, pastoral care, and domestic concern for those deprived. One can discern much of his public philosophy in the language and activities he used on this front.

Public philosophy in Luther's day and our own more often than not deals with *oeconomia* and *politia*, the economic and political realms, where the Reformer had more interest and competence than in what we might call more purely theoretical inquiries and statements. For example, as always, he was not very interested in the "giver" or "doer"—the one tempted to make claims on God for her or his good works—but he cared greatly about the receiver of justice and mercy. In that consideration he was truly "public," nondiscriminatory, seeking no sectarian tag to label the one in need.

Samuel Torvend, in *Luther and the Hungry Poor: Gathered Fragments*, illustrated this with reference to the "common good." Christians who are "antigovernment" today or any day would find little support in Luther, who readily tied "the state" to support of the common good. Torvend reminds readers that Luther had no interest in theocracy, as many "common-good" Christians through the centuries have.

> While he clearly rejected the notion promoted by some reformers that the state should be governed by "Christian" laws and, in effect, become a theocracy, he nonetheless argued vociferously that Christians must labor with persuasion and genuine love for the abolition of unjust practices or laws that caused or maintained human suffering. In the service of one's neighbor and the common good, a Christian could not stand by in the presence of manifold evil and say or do nothing. . . . Thus, Christians should urge the passage of laws and practices that supported the common good.[6]

In such declarations Luther was showing that he would address the whole society, from the government in the state, to the leadership and members of the church, and also, without religious or other description, "the hungry poor."

Conclusion

Doctor Martin Luther, in his witness to and work within two kingdoms and with his concern for what he called both "proper righteousness," which meant saving knowledge or action, and "alien" righteousness, which meant attention to the needs and interests of the neighbor, the "other," provided the rudiments of a public philosophy voiced by Christians through what we have called cautiously the "double-truth" approach, of Christ and culture in paradox. For many Lutherans that concept is more acted upon than understood, but understanding *and* acting, most agree, is today more urgent than ever before. Luther, not a "philosopher's philosopher," could serve the common good in new ways as a "public scholar."

Epilogue

The Quandary of Lutheran Philosophy

Jennifer Hockenbery Dragseth

One could argue that just as no scholar would study a medieval philosopher without studying Augustine, no historian of ideas should study a modern (or postmodern) philosopher without first reading Luther. This volume has presented connections between Luther and many later Lutheran philosophers. This makes sociological and historical sense. Certainly the worldviews taught on father's knee, overheard at the family dinner table, memorized for confirmation classes, and lectured in the college classroom would profoundly influence the way one sees the world, one's self, and one's God. But Luther's influence as a thinker has had an impact on many philosophers who were not Lutheran as well. After all, Luther radically changed the way modern Western people think about individuality, ecclesiology, social justice, politics, education, literacy, and significantly about the relationship between philosophy and theology.

Indeed, his influence concerning the relationship between philosophy and theology, between reason and faith, is exactly why the conversation about Lutheran philosophy is so problematic (even oxymoronic). How can a Lutheran both affirm Lutheran theology and do philosophy when Luther himself firmly held a skeptical position toward reason and the philosophical discipline?

Lover, Handmaid, Whore: The Problem of Christian Philosophy

The apostle Paul, in the letter to the Colossians that is attributed to him, writes that Christians must beware lest anyone take them "captive through vain philosophy and empty deceit." (Col. 2:8). What Paul means by this has been reinterpreted throughout the ages by the major authorities in the Western Christian church.

The fourth-century African bishop Augustine, like many early Christians, insists the emphasis is on vain philosophy. Augustine writes emphatically to a friend he wishes to convert to philosophical study:

195

> Now philosophy nourishes and sustains me in that retirement we
> have so much hoped for. It has freed me completely from the
> superstitions into which I had thrown you headlong with myself.
> Philosophy teaches and teaches truly, that nothing whatsoever
> that is discerned by mortal eyes, or that any of the senses comes
> into contact with should be worshipped. Instead, everything of
> the sort must be despised. Philosophy promises that it will dis-
> play the true and hidden God, and now and again deigns to
> show us a glimpse of Him through the bright clouds as it were.
> . . . No age has any reason to complain that it is excluded from
> the breasts of philosophy! Though I'm well acquainted with your
> thirst for philosophy, I wanted to send along a foretaste to incite
> you to cling to it and suckle the more eagerly.[1]

For Augustine, Christian philosophy is no paradox. He claims in the *Confessions*
that his heart would be restless until it rests with God who is the Truth. More
boldly, in the *Soliloquies*, he renounces sex, claiming that he wishes only to lie na-
ked under the bedclothes with Wisdom. As seen above, he declares that philosophy is the woman whose breasts comfort every age. For Augustine, philosophy is
not a simple handmaid, she is the lover for whom he left his concubine. Philosophy is often identified with Christ in feminine form, a lover or a mother who
pulls the seeker into her lap, strokes his hair, and gives him peace. While the el-
derly Augustine, in his *Retractions*, does lament how much weight he gave the liberal arts and academic philosophy in his early years, Augustine's lifelong account
of philosophy is the account of a lover enthralled by his beloved.

In the thirteenth century, Thomas Aquinas demoted philosophy from lover
to handmaid. Thomas's view of philosophy is that she is very helpful within certain realms. Even in theology, her use of reason is helpful in clarifying understanding. Philosophy is no longer Christ in feminine form, the woman who offers
salvation and beatitude, but she is still worth pursuing.

In contrast to both Augustine and Aquinas, the former Augustinian monk
Luther uses fierce rhetoric not to promote philosophy but to warn the faithful
against her. He writes in the "Disputation on the Word Made Flesh,"

> This is the proposition of this disputation, that the same thing is
> not true in theology and philosophy. For we know that it is one
> thing to understand, another thing to believe. Therefore, philos-
> ophy and theology are to be differentiated; it is the task of phi-
> losophy to understand by the use of reason; it is the task of
> theology truly to believe what is above all reason. Faith is not

bound by, or subject to, the rules or words of philosophy, but it is on that account free. And just as God has created many spheres in heaven, so too there are distinct domains among these faculties.[2]

Luther says even more firmly in the "Disputation concerning Man," "We say that philosophy knows nothing at all about man. . . . In short, philosophers know nothing about God the creator and man made of a lump of earth."[3]

Martin Luther bears the mark of Augustine in many of his teachings, and there is an argument to be made that he is not as different philosophically from Thomas as he polemically claims. But philosophy's allegory certainly points to a divide between Luther and the two masters of theology that preceded him. In Luther, reason is called the Devil's mother, the Devil's grandmother, and, of course, the Devil's whore. Thus, philosophy with reason as its main tool is limited in scope. Philosophy, indeed, is the woman who should be quiet in church.[4] While philosophy may be useful in certain domains, ultimately philosophy cannot help us know our true nature, God's true nature, or our true relationship with the loving divine. Moreover, when philosophy tries to go beyond her limitations, the result is not merely fruitless but dangerous.

Yet, the quandary is not solved by a simple divorce between theology and philosophy for Luther or his followers. The relationship is much more interesting, as this volume has demonstrated.

Philosophy and Luther

The first essays in this volume put Luther's radical rhetoric against philosophy into the context of his actual understanding of philosophy and his own philosophical work. Thus, these essays demonstrate that even in Luther's own work good thinking is not divorced from philosophical thinking. As Oswald Bayer rhetorically asks, "'Philosophical modes of thought'! Are there also other than 'philosophical' modes of thought?" Indeed, the essays reveal that Luther's own disputations are philosophically argued, his own knowledge and understanding of the philosophers before him is broad and deep, his own views are philosophically articulate, and his first friends and supporters see philosophy's use and value. As in all the sections, there is more work to be done. Luther's vast amount of writing, not to mention Melanchthon's, has much to offer a historian or a philosopher who wishes to understand Luther more deeply. But in these essays, the important foundation has been laid. Clearly, Luther makes powerful and important arguments about the potential abuse of lady philosophy, and certainly he draws thick boundaries around the areas where she is allowed free reign; but equally clearly Luther is thinking philosophically and meta-philosophically in ways that would influence the practitioners of philosophy after him.

Lutheran Continental Philosophers

The second section of this book demonstrates that Luther's impact on philosophy is enormous and widespread. Philosophy may be a whore, but Lutherans have continued to study her, albeit paying attention to appropriate boundaries depending on the philosophical current of their times. Each essay takes a specific philosopher who was informed by Lutheran teachings and discusses a single point of the philosopher's work. Some essays take a single idea of a specific philosopher and present revealing comparisons between the later thinker and Luther. The other essays address the vocations of philosophy and reason in the various Lutheran philosophers.

The careful scholarship in each of these pieces exposes only one specific point for each thinker. The hope for the future of the history of ideas is that these philosophers be reread with an eye to their Lutheran heritage in order to understand the context and the ideas more fully. Certainly, the list of continental thinkers influenced by Luther is not complete. Hamann and Herder both demonstrate uniquely Lutheran ways of doing philosophy. Schelling not only was raised Lutheran, like his college roommate Hegel, but studied Lutheran theology before going into philosophy. And there is much work to be done on the influence of Luther on Wittgenstein, whose father's work on the Lutheran church council may have caused Ludwig to complete his only published book on philosophy with the line, "What we cannot speak about we must pass over in silence."[5]

The Future of Lutheran Philosophy

Many Lutherans might argue that Wittgenstein's firm admonition that philosophy not go beyond herself might be Luther's best recommendation to twenty-first-century philosophy. Many twenty-first-century philosophers, Lutheran or not, might be satisfied with this. Contemporary postmodernity is ever more skeptical of the rational quest. Like the fourth-century's academics, most contemporary philosophers see their vocation as only to critique the hubristic claims of the other sciences, reminding all that we are hopelessly caught in abusive discourses beyond which lies no transcendent truth. But simultaneously, in religion and theology, many believers claim that philosophy has no vocation at all and certainly not as critic, since faith must stand alone. Lutheran philosophers may have something unique to put forward at this juncture if they assert that, like humans themselves, human discourse is broken indeed but also justified. Aware of the limits of analysis but hopeful in God's grace, Lutheran thinkers can assert that philosophy, while limited in scope, is possible and useful within certain domains, especially in helping us to live together well. The third section is the bare beginning of where such Lutheran philosophy might go in the twenty-first century.

Bill Russell begins the section by framing Luther's own understanding of the vocation of a philosopher as a set of answers to a contemporary undergraduate philosophy major. In so doing, Russell describes not only Luther's view of the limits of reason but also Luther's view of the responsibilities of the philosopher. Taking these responsibilities seriously, the other essays tackle specific philosophical issues from environmental ethics to philosophy of mind, from feminist epistemology to queer identity and philosophy of power. Most importantly, perhaps, is the question of philosophy itself. At the turn of the millennium, many philosophers, certainly not only Lutheran ones, are considering the possibility of the end of philosophy, both as an academic discipline and as a pursuit of greater understanding. The last two essays of the third section discuss the importance of philosophy in the academy and in the public. Pauline Kaurin focuses on the role of the academic philosopher as teacher and colleague, while Martin Marty explains the importance of the philosopher as a public intellectual. Both essays present to the reader a path for the philosopher with a Lutheran heritage.

Conclusion

This book is but a starting place. It serves as a vehicle for scholars of Luther and scholars of philosophy to come together to discuss the quandary of Lutheran philosophy. It argues that Lutheran philosophy, quandary though it may be, is a deep and rich vein of thinking. As such the book has presented its research and now stands as a call for more new research in the history of Luther's own ideas, in the understanding of continental philosophy, and in the future of ideas. Perhaps the Lutheran hour is yet to come. Let us be up to the task.

NOTES

Introduction

1. A version of this paper was presented at the American Academy of Religion Annual Meeting in Chicago, November 2008. A shortened version of this paper was published in *Lutheran Forum* 43/1 (Spring 2009): 57–64.

2. Heinrich Heine, *Religion and Philosophy in Germany: A Fragment*, trans. John Snodgrass (Boston: Beacon, 1959).

3. Jaroslav Pelikan, *From Luther to Kierkegaard: A Study in the History of Theology* (St. Louis: Concordia, 1950), 1.

4. Erik H. Erikson, *Young Man Luther: A Study in Psychoanalysis and History* (New York: Norton, 1950).

5. Roland H. Bainton, *Here I Stand: The Life of Martin Luther* (New York/Nashville: Abingdon, 1950).

6. Luther published a second version with a new preface to the work in 1518. LW 31:73–76.

7. There remains no better exposition of this than George W. Forell's *Faith Active in Love: An Investigation of the Principles Underlying Luther's Social Ethics* (Minneapolis: Augsburg, 1954).

8. Gerhard Ebeling, *Luther: An Introduction to His Thought*, trans. R. A. Wilson (Philadelphia: Fortress Press, 1970 [1964]), 77.

9. The Luther-Erasmus debate on the freedom of the will, in 1525, represented a fundamental division between Luther and the humanists, a division that also affected the position of Philipp Melanchthon.

10. Heine, *Religion and Philosophy in Germany*, 60.

11. Ibid., 64.

12. Ibid., 69. "The protestant pietists are mystics without imagination, and the protestant orthodox are dogmatists without intelligence."

13. Ebeling, *Luther*, 28.

14. Pelikan, *From Luther to Kierkegaard*, 108.

15. Heine's rumination on the fate of not just deism but Jehovah after the publication of the *Critique of Pure Reason* more than anticipates Nietzsche: "Here ye not the bells resounding? Kneel down. They are bringing the sacraments to a dying god!" *Religion and Philosophy in Germany*, 103.

16. Gerhard Ebeling, from his lectures to all faculties of the University of Zurich, Winter Term, 1962/1963.

17. Presentation at Capital University, Columbus, Ohio, 1983, during a celebration of the five hundredth anniversary of Luther's birth.

Chapter 1: Philosophical Modes of Thought of Luther's Theology

1. This lecture was given on October 21, 1999, at the Institute for European History, Mainz. It was first published in *Lutherforschung im 20. Jahrhundert. Rückblick—Bilanz— Ausblick*, ed. Rainer Vinke (Mainz 2004), 135–49.

2. Erwin Metzke, "Lutherforschung und deutsche Philosophiegeschichte," *Blätter für Deutsche Philosophie: Zeitschrift der Deutschen Philosophischen Gesellschaft* (Berlin 1934/35), 355. See the later judgment in Heinrich Bornkamm, *Luther im Spiegel der deutschen Geistesgeschichte: Mit ausgewählten Texten von Lessing bis zur Gegenwart*, 2d ed. (Göttingen 1970), 154: "Besides the question of Luther's relation to Kant [see below, n.6], philosophical engagement with him over the last half century has otherwise all but petered out." Bornkamm's assessment of the importance of Metzke for the topic of this lecture is worth noting: "From the philosophical standpoint, only one new attempt was made to understand Luther's significance for the history of philosophy and for philosophical thinking generally, and that is the two essays by Erwin Metzke" (156; see also 157 for the mention of Metzke's "planned work on the 'general problem of Luther's philosophical significance'").

3. Erwin Metzke, "Sakrament und Metaphysik: Eine Lutherstudie über das Verhältnis des christlichen Denkens zum Leiblich-Materiellen" (1948), in *Coincidentia Oppositorum: Gesammelte Studien zur Philosophiegeschichte*, ed. Karlfried Gründer (Witten 1961), 159.

4. Gottfried Wilhelm Leibniz, *Die Theodizee*, 2d ed. (Hamburg 1968), 25, 43, 65–94, 314, 352, 428; the majority of the passages refer to *De servo arbitrio* ("The Bound Will"). Eng. trans.: *Theodicy: Essays on the Goodness of God, the Freedom of Man, and the Origin of Evil*, ed. Austin M. Farrer, trans. E. M. Muggard from C. J. Gerhardt's edition of the collected philosophical works 1875–90 (London: Routledge, 1952).

5. Friedrich Wilhelm Joseph Schelling, *Philosophische Untersuchungen über das Wesen der menschlichen Freiheit und die damit zusammenhängenden Gegenstände* (1809), stw 138 (Frankfurt/M. 1975), 111 n.27; Eng. trans.: *Philosophical Inquiries into the Essence of Human Freedom* (Albany: SUNY Press, 2006).

6. On the concrete mediation of the heritage: Martin Brecht and Jörg Sandberger, "Hegels Begegnung mit der Theologie im Tübinger Stift: Eine neue Quelle für die Studienzeit Hegels," *Hegel–Studien* 5 (1969): 47–81. See further: Jörg Baur, *Luther und seine klassischen Erben: Theologische Aufsätze und Forschungen* (Tübingen 1993), 206f., 302.

7. Friedrich Paulsen, "Kant—der Philosoph des Protestantismus," *Kantstudien* 4 (1899): 1–31; Bruno Bauch, *Luther und Kant* (Berlin 1904). See Bornkamm, *Luther im Spiegel*, 103–5.

8. See Emanuel Hirsch, *Die idealistische Philosophie und das Christentum* (Gütersloh 1926); idem, "Fichtes, Schleiermachers und Hegels Verhältnis zur Reformation" (1930), reprinted in his *Lutherstudien* II (Gütersloh 1954), 121–68.

9. See Bornkamm, *Luther im Spiegel*. Further: Walter Mostert, "Luther III. Wirkungsgeschichte," in *Theologische Realenzyklopedie* 21 (1991): 567–94.

10. See Ernst-Wilhelm Kohls, "Das Bild der Reformation bei Wilhelm Dilthey, Adolf v. Harnack und Ernst Troeltsch," *Neue Zeitschrift für Systematische Theologie und Religionsphilosophie* 11 (1969): 269–78.

11. Schopenhauer provides detailed quotations not only from *De servo arbitrio* (see his *The Two Fundamental Problems of Ethics* [1840; Eng. trans. 2009, 2010], in Arthur

Schopenhauer, *Sämtliche Werke* [hereafter *SW*], ed. Wolfgang v. Löhneysen, vol. III [Darmstadt 1977], 584, 590), but also from Luther's Galatians commentary (*The World as Will and Representation*, suppl. to IV, chap. 46 in *SW* II [Darmstadt 1976; Eng. trans. 1966], 743f.) and from *The Large Catechism* (*The World as Will and Representation*, suppl. to IV, chap. 46 in *SW* II, 805). Furthermore, when he wants to stress the fact that good works proceed from faith, an idea that is very important to him, he invariably refers to *De libertate christiana* ("The Freedom of the Christian") (see *The World as Will and Representation*, IV §70 in *SW* I [Darmstadt 1974], 553; "Criticism of Kantian Philosophy," in *The World as Will and Representation*, *SW* I, 702).

12. Ludwig Feuerbach, *The Essence of Faith according to Martin Luther* (1844; Eng. trans. 1967). On that, see Oswald Bayer, *Leibliches Wort. Reformation und Neuzeit im Konflikt* (Tübingen 1992), 205–41. Arve Brunvoll, *"Gott ist Mensch": Die Luther-Rezeption Ludwig Feuerbachs und die Entwicklung seiner Religionskritik*, Europäische Studien zur Ideen- und Wissenschaftsgeschichte 3 (Frankfurt/M. 1996).

13. See Bornkamm, *Luther im Spiegel*, 95–100, and Mostert, "Luther III. Wirkungsgeschichte," 576 and 590 (Literatur).

14. "The philosophical reserve over against Luther has certainly been strengthened by the fact that recent theological movements, especially dialectical theology, have made a sharp in-principle distinction between biblical-reformational and philosophical thought and have tried to think of Luther's opposition to the Catholic tradition in precisely this way" (Bornkamm, *Luther im Spiegel*, 154f.). Dialectical theology, of a Bultmannian character, was strengthened here by the thesis, as put forward by Heidegger, that it is necessary to draw a sharp boundary between theology and philosophy (see below, n.14).

15. Martin Heidegger, *Being and Time* (1927; Eng. trans. 1962 and 1996), §3. Further: idem, *The Phenomenology of Religious Life* (Bloomington: Indiana University Press, 2004): "The aim of the object of theology is not attained," as Heidegger asserts with reference to thesis 19 of the Heidelberg Disputation (1518), "by way of a metaphysical consideration of the world" (213, trans. alt.). See Otto Pöggeler, *Martin Heidegger's Path of Thinking*, trans. Daniel Magurshak and Sigmund Barber (Atlantic Highlands, N.J.: Humanities Press International, 1987), 24–31 on Luther, esp. 26f. Pöggeler sums up Heidegger this way (p. 31): "The factical life-experience of the Christian faith has not been able to wrest itself away from inadequate metaphysical conceptualization. Thus Augustine, Luther, Kierkegaard offer more an 'ontic' than an 'ontological' explanation; they saw decisive matters in an 'ontic' manner, but they would not have been able to arrive at an adequate 'ontological' concept. They therefore 'edify all the more compellingly' where they speak with 'the least degree of conceptualization' (*Sein und Zeit*, 190 note). Since 'ontologically' they are dominated by ancient philosophy, there is often more to be learned from their 'edifying' writings than their 'theoretical' ones (235 note)" (trans. alt.). See the fine account of Heidegger's relation to Luther in Bornkamm, *Luther im Spiegel*, 160–64. In the 1920s Heidegger captured the imagination of theology because he advocated the separation, if not the diastasis, of theology and philosophy. He set this out programmatically in *Phänomenologie und Theologie* (1927; Frankfurt/M. 1970) where he refers to theses 19 and 20 of the Heidelberg Disputation. But he failed to recognize the metaphysical character of the pre-Reformation *theologia crucis* as a *via negationis*, which is also lived wholly existentially. He is interested only in the distinction between a "facticity of Dasein" (Heidegger, *The*

Phenomenology of Religious Life, 212, trans. alt.)—to that extent the young Luther is approved—and a "metaphysical" safeguard that amounts to an ontological oblivion of Being and that he claims to find in the later Luther and in orthodox Lutheranism. Furthermore, Heidegger reproaches Luther, as well as Augustine and Kierkegaard, for only speaking and writing in an "existential" (*existentiell*) manner and for never having worked out the "existentials" (*existentialen*) (except for Kierkegaard's "concept of dread"; on that, see the equally splendid remarks of Bornkamm, *Luther im Spiegel*, 161–64).

16. Friedrich Brunstäd, *Gesammelte Aufsätze und kleinere Schriften*, ed. Eugen Gerstenmaier and Carl Gunther Schweitzer (Berlin 1957). See Joachim Ringleben, "Über die Anfänge von Friedrich Brunstäd: Eine theologiegeschichtliche Erinnerung," *Neue Zeitschrift für Systematische Theologie und Religionsphilosophie* 24 (1982): 71–93.

17. Rudolf Malter, *Das reformatorische Denken und die Philosophie: Luthers Entwurf einer transzendental-praktischen Metaphysik* (Bonn 1980); see Malter, "Luther und die Geschichte der Metaphysik," in Tuomo Mannermaa, et al., eds., *Thesaurus Lutheri: Auf der Suche nach neuen Paradigmen der Luther-Forschung* (Helsinki 1987), 37–52.

18. See, e.g., WA 10/II:295, 16–296, 11 = LW 45:39 ("The Estate of Marriage," 1522): "When that clever harlot, our natural reason . . ." and the *probatio* to the second of the philosophical theses of the Heidelberg Disputation (WA 59:409, 20f. = LW 31:41). On that, see Oswald Bayer, *Gott als Autor: Zu einer poietologischen Theologie* (Tübingen 1999), 256, as well as Wolfgang Janke, *Kritik der präzisierten Welt* (Freiburg/Munich 1999), 43 n.11. Reason is a "harlot" when it misuses this divine gift, for even after the fall reason is "something divine" (*divinum quiddam*) (WA 39/I:175, 10 = LW 34:137, "Disputation Concerning Man," 1536). Thus, Luther could even write a little book on dialectics for his son Hans (WA 60:140–62; see WA TR 4:647–49). For the broader context, see Karl-Heinz zur Mühlen, *Reformatorische Vernunftkritik und neuzeitliches Denken: Dargestellt am Werk M. Luthers und Fr. Gogartens* (Tübingen 1980).

19. Karl Jaspers, *Einführung in die Philosophie* [12 radio talks] (Munich 1949, 1953), 155. Eng. trans.: *Way to Wisdom: An Introduction to Philosophy* (1960). (See Bornkamm, *Luther im Spiegel*, 160f.). See also Jaspers, "Die nichtchristlichen Religionen und das Abendland," in *Die großen nichtchristlichen Religionen unserer Zeit* (no editor) (Stuttgart 1954), 115–26 (on Luther: 122f.)

20. WA 18 (625,25–626,24):626, 9 = LW 33:52.

21. Erasmus of Rotterdam, *The Complaint of Peace* (1917/2010). The place where Popper takes exception to Luther is instructive: Popper argues that, for moral reasons, scientific theories must be able to be falsified so that theories die instead of people. He takes Luther's thesis—that the world cannot endure God's word and that therefore where that word becomes known in its purity the result is and must be a "state of tumult" (see above, n.19), to mean the approval of bloody civil wars and wars of religions. In his moralism, Popper misses Luther's point.

22. See Herbert Marcuse, "Studie über Autorität und Familie" (1936), in Marcuse, *Ideen zu einer kritischen Theorie der Gesellschaft* (Frankfurt/Main 1969), 55–156. Eng. trans.: "Studies about Authority and Family," in *Reason and Revolution: Hegel and the Rise of Social Theory*, 2d ed. (London: Routledge & Kegan Paul, 1968). See further: Oswald Bayer, "Marcuses Kritik an Luthers Freiheitsbegriff," in Bayer, *Leibliches Wort* (see above, n.11), 151–75.

23. "He who has hatred toward all the sciences, and who pretends that wisdom alone is to be esteemed, is called a misologist": Immanuel Kant, *Lectures on Logic*, The Cambridge Edition of the Works of Immanuel Kant in Translation, ed. J. Michael Young (Cambridge: Cambridge University Press, 1992), 260. See Plato's *Laches* 188c 6; *Phaedo* 89d 1-4; *Republic* 456a 4.

24. Thomas Mann, "Die drei Gewaltigen" (1949), in Mann, *Gesammelte Werke* (12 vols); vol. 10: *Reden und Aufsätze* 2, (374–83) 376. On that, see Mostert, "Luther III," 581: "Luther, the bull-necked, godly barbarian, whose genius is contaminated by the demonic features of *Doctor Faustus*, is the embodiment of the anti-human, anti-democratic German clergy, irascible and rude, stout and gentle, sensuous and thoughtful, an advocate of the individual, his immediacy to God and his subjectivity, over against the objective, over against the church's educational authority and its humane education, and over against critical reason." Mann's judgment here is dependent on Nietzsche: Mostert, "Luther III," 581. On the relation between Luther and Nietzsche, see the bibliography in Mostert, "Luther III," 590.

25. Kurt Wuchterl, *Analyse und Kritik der religiösen Vernunft: Grundzüge einer paradigmenbezogenen Religionsphilosophie* (Bern/Stuttgart 1989), 177.

26. Bornkamm, *Luther im Spiegel*, 168. This observation comes at the end of his brilliant account, which is both sober and informed, of the philosophical struggles over Luther in the twentieth century (150–68).

27. Gerhard Ebeling appears to affirm this. See his "Luthers Wirklichkeitsverständnis," in *Theologie in den Gegensätzen des Lebens: Wort und Glaube* IV (Tübingen 1995), 460–75.

28. H. G. Meier, Art. "Denkform," in *Historischen Wörterbuch der Philosophie* 2, 107.

29. Bruno Bauch ("Unser philosophisches Interesse an Luther," *Zeitschrift für Philosophie und philosophische Kritik* 164 [Halle 1917], 128–48) emphasizes the importance of Luther not only as an "object of philosophy" but also as a "philosophical subject," because "without his achievement, even the greatest achievements of the whole of modern philosophy, the achievements of German Idealism, are unthinkable historically" (129).

30. See Oswald Bayer, *Theology the Lutheran Way*, trans. Jeffrey G. Silcock and Mark C. Mattes (Grand Rapids: Eerdmans, 2007), 12, 16, but esp. 80–82; Bayer, *Gott als Autor*, 278f.

31. See Gerhard Ebeling, *Disputatio de homine* (*Lutherstudien* II), 3 vols. (Tübingen 1977, 1982, 1989).

32. For the passionate agreement of the pre-Reformation Luther with the neo-Platonic *via negationis*, see only WA 56:393, 1-3 = LW 25:383 (on Rom. 9:3, 1515/16).

33. We see this in the ninth of the philosophical theses to the Heidelberg Disputation. On that, see Theodor Dieter, *Der junge Luther und Aristoteles: Eine historisch-systematische Untersuchung zum Verhältnis von Theologie und Philosophie* (Berlin/New York 2001), 619–27.

34. See above, n.32.

35. Dieter (*Der junge Luther und Aristoteles*, 217–28) shows that Petrus Johannes Olivi developed his understanding of freedom in sharp rejection of Aristotelian views. Duns Scotus completed this development and described his understanding as an interpretation of Aristotle, even though it contradicted Aristotle in substance. Then, to come full circle, Luther could find the traditional Christian concept of freedom attributed to Aristotle in the commentary of Johannes Buridanus which, in Luther's day, was in wide circulation.

36. Dieter, *Der junge Luther und Aristoteles*, 633.

37. Traditionally, this is followed by the "Topics" and the "Sophistical Refutations." More recent scholarship puts the Topics first.

38. See below, n.52.

39. Graham White, *Luther as Nominalist: A Study of the Logical Methods Used in Martin Luther's Disputations in the Light of Their Medieval Background* (Helsinki 1994). Further: idem, "Theology and Logic: The Case of Ebeling," *Modern Theology* 4 (1987): 17–34; idem, "Luther on Ecclesiastes and the Limits of Human Ability," *Neue Zeitschrift für Systematische Theologie und Religionsphilosophie* 29 (1987): 180–94.

40. Heikki Kirjavainen, "Die Paradoxie des Simul-Prinzips," *Neue Zeitschrift für Systematische Theologie und Religionsphilosophie* 28 (1986): 29-50; Kirjavainen, "Luther und Aristoteles: Die Frage der zweifachen Gerechtigkeit im Lichte der transitiven vs. intransitiven Willentheorie," in Miikka Ruokanen, ed., *Luther in Finnland* (Helsinki 1986), 111–29.

41. Simo Knuuttila, "Luther's View of Logic and the Revelation," *Medioevo: Rivista di Storia della filosofia medievale* 24 (1998): 219–34.

42. Reijo Työrinoja, "*Nova vocabula et nova lingua*. Luther's Conception of Doctrinal Formulas" in Tuomo Mannermaa u.a., eds., *Thesaurus Lutheri*, 221–36. Idem, "*Proprietas Verbi*. Luther's Conception of Philosophical and Theological Language in the Disputation: *Verbum caro factum est* (Joh. 1:14), 1539," in Heikki Kirjavainen, ed., *Faith, Will, and Grammar: Some Themes of Intensional Logic and Semantics in Medieval and Reformation Thought* (Helsinki 1986), 141–78. Idem, "*Opus theologicum*. Luther and Medieval Theories of action," *Neue Zeitschrift für Systematische Theologie und Religionsphilosophie* 44 (2002): 119–53.

43. See, e.g., WA 7:336, 30-36 = LW 32:24 ("Defense and Explanation of All the Articles of Dr. Martin Luther Which Were Unjustly Condemned by the Roman Bull," 1521): "This life, therefore, is not righteousness but a becoming righteous, not health but a becoming healthy, not being but becoming, not rest but exercise. We are not yet what we shall be, but we are on the way. The process is not yet finished, but it is continuing. This is not the end but the journey. Everything does not yet gleam and sparkle, but all is being purified" (trans. alt.).

44. See below, III.4 and III.5.

45. It has become customary to speak of "relational ontology" since Wilfried Joest, *Ontologie der Person bei Luther* (Göttingen 1967), esp. 14, 37, 362, and Gerhard Ebeling, *Dogmatik des christlichen Glaubens*, 3 vols. (Tübingen 1979), esp. I:215, 219–24, 233; II:102, 330, 335, 346, 500; III:91, 142). On the abiding necessity to distinguish between "relational ontology" and "substance ontology," see Bayer, *Theology the Lutheran Way*, 79 nn.420f. For further observations on relational ontology, see Theodor Dieter, "'Du mußt den Geist haben': Anthropologie und Pneumatologie bei Luther," in *Der Heilige Geist: Ökumenische und reformatorische Untersuchungen* (Erlangen 1996), 65–88. The question of Luther's ontology is a topic of particular interest to Finnish Luther research. See the paradigmatic work: *Luther und Ontologie: Das Sein Christi im Glauben als strukturierendes Prinzip der Theologie Luthers*, ed. Anja Ghiselli, Kari Kopperi, and Rainer Vinke (Erlangen 1993).

46. John D. Zizioulas, *Being as Communion: Studies in Personhood and the Church* (New York: St. Vladimirs Seminary Press, 1997).

47. WA 40/II:354, 3f. (on Ps. 51:4, 1532); see 40/II:421, 6f. (as well as 421, 22-26): "Dilectio versatur in praedicamento relationis" ("Love operates in the category of relation") (on Ps. 51:12). Further: WA 4/III:334, 8, 21-27 (on Ps. 129:8, 1532/33). For the

connection with trinitarian theology, see especially the doctoral disputation of Petrus Hegemon (1545): WA 39/II:337–401, particularly the theses 11–17 (39/II:339f.).

48. Jörg Baur, "Luther und die Philosophie," *Neue Zeitschrift für Systematische Theologie und Religionsphilosophie* 26 (1984): 13–28 (= Baur, *Luther und seine klassischen Erben*, 13–28). See above, n.37.

49. Bayer, *Theology the Lutheran Way*, 82, 193–98.

50. Oswald Bayer, "Tod Gottes und Herrenmahl" (1971), in Bayer, *Leibliches Wort*, 289–305. Bayer, "Poetological [sic] Doctrine of the Trinity," trans. Christine Helmer, *Lutheran Quarterly* 15 (2001): 45–58.

51. Stefano Leoni, "'Fides creatrix divinitatis': La fede come esistenza di Dio in Lutero," *Archivio di Filosofia* 59 (1991): 13–35; Leoni, "Motus essentia Dei, Deus essentia beatorum. Ontologia e teologia in una predica giovanile di Lutero," *Protestantesimo* 51 (1996): 219–46 (= "Trinitarische und christologische Ontologie bei Luther. Wesen als Bewegung in Luthers Weihnachtspredigt von 1514," *Luther-Jahrbuch* 65 [1998]: 53–84); Leoni, "Nicht Nachwort, sondern Machtwort. Die Grammatik des Geistes in Luthers 'Vom Abendmahl Christi. Bekenntnis,'" *Neue Zeitschrift für Systematische Theologie und Religionsphilosophie* 42 (2000): 246–66.

52. Enrico De Negri, *La teologia di Lutero. Rivelazione e dialettica* (Florence 1967); Ger. Trans.: *Offenbarung und Dialektik. Luthers Realtheologie* (Darmstadt 1973). De Negri sees in Luther a "logic of becoming" (Ger. 215): Luther eliminated "irrevocably the static copula of the verb 'to be' and put in its place a verb of motion with all its energy, namely, that of 'becoming.' The two different natures of Christ exist in unity, for in him "they become one thing . . . ; the bread for its part has become one essence with the body of Christ" (Ger. 215).

53. Here I follow Baur (see above, n.47).

54. Luther's anthropology and ethics is defined by an analogical union: husband and wife, parents and children, authorities and subjects are united through God's word. See Oswald Bayer, "Nature and Institution: Luther's Doctrine of the Three Estates," in *Freedom in Response—Lutheran Ethics: Sources and Controversies*, trans. Jeffrey Cayzer (New York: Oxford University Press, 2007), 90–118.

55. On "*extremorum composition*," see WA 6:510, 25–30; 511, 34–38 = LW 36:33–35 ("The Babylonian Captivity of the Church," 1520). Luther cites the passage, "An affirmative sentence requires *extremorum compositio*, the agreement of the subject and the predicate" (trans. alt.), and supports this with a reference to Aristotle's *Metaphysics* VI. However, this reference is incorrect, as Rudolph Mau shows: Martin Luther, *Studienausgabe* 2 (Berlin 1982), 190 n.119. On this reference to Aristotle, see Reinhard Schwarz, "Gott ist Mensch: Zur Lehre von der Person Christi bei den Ockhamisten und bei Luther," *Zeitschrift für Theologie und Kirche* 63 (1966): 289–351, esp. 339–45. See Oswald Bayer, *Promissio: Geschichte der reformatorischen Wende in Luthers Theologie* (1971; 2d ed., 1989), 315f.

56. See Günther Wohlfart, *Der spekulative Satz* (Berlin/New York 1981).

57. Following Erich Seeberg, the idea of the "concrete spirit" plays an important role in Erwin Metzke's reception of Luther, Hamann, and Hegel. See Karlfried Gründer, "Die philosophiegeschichtlichen Forschungen Erwin Metzkes," in Metzke, *Coincidentia oppositorum*, 355, 362, and 364. Hegel reception that has been decidedly influenced by

Lebensphilosophie is characterized completely by the perspective of the "concrete spirit": Franz Hildebrandt, *Est. Das lutherische Prinzip* (Göttingen 1931).

58. See further Risto Saarinen, "Metapher und biblische Redefiguren als Elemente der Sprachphilosophie Luthers," *Neue Zeitschrift für Systematische Theologie und Religionsphilosophie* 30 (1988): 18–39.

59. On this, see Thomas Wabel, *Sprache als Grenze in Luthers theologischer Hermeneutik und Wittgensteins Sprachphilosophie* (Berlin/New York 1998).

60. Aristotle, Περὶ ἑρμηνείας (*De interpretatione*) 17a (chap. 4): "Not every [sentence] declares something, but only those containing truth or falsity. But that is not universally the case. A request, for instance, is a sentence but it is neither true nor false. But let us pass over the other types of sentence, as a discussion of these belongs rather to rhetoric or poetics. Here we are dealing only with a sentence in the sense of the proposition," Aristotle, Book I: The *Categories, On Interpretation, Prior Analytics* (Loeb Classical Library 1973), 121 (trans. alt.).

61. In the sentence, "This is my body for you (sinners)," the bread and the body are united and, at the same time, sinners and the justified are united so that in, with, and under this sentence sinners *are* the justified.

62. Aristotle, on the other hand, shifts εὐχή (request and prayer) into the section on rhetoric and poetics, for this is an example of another sentence that is incapable of bearing truth. See above, n.59.

63. On the differentiation of this judgment: Bayer, *Promissio*, 315 n.112.

64. Bayer, *Promissio*, 315f. is cited in the following two paragraphs.

65. WA TR 4:666, 8f. (No. 5106); 1540.

66. The following conjecture seems compelling: "Luther discovers the positive spiritual importance of all worldly reality after his new conception of word and sacrament has made him aware of how worldly reality mediates spiritual reality, not only negatively but positively" (Bayer, "Nature and Institution," in *Freedom in Response*, 98.

67. N II,198,29 (*Aesthetica in nuce*, 1762). For an explanation: Oswald Bayer, *Schöpfung als Anrede: Zur einer Hermeneutik der Schöpfung* (Tübingen, 2nd. ed. 1990), 9–32.

68. It is not by accident that the philosopher who could most appreciate Luther as a philosopher, namely Erwin Metzke, first of all thoroughly acquainted himself with Hamann.

69. See the literature cited in nn. 38–41.

70. On *semper in motu* as a theme in Luther's theology: Bayer, *Promissio*, 30f., 33–36, 41, 66, 120f., 134f., 137, 139, 202, 221, 270, 340, 348. For a comprehensive and thorough treatment, see Dieter, *Der junge Luther und Aristoteles*, 276-377 (chap. 4: "The Aristotelian Concept of Motion in Luther's Theology"). The following is a summary of this chapter. See also De Negri, *La teologia di Lutero*.

71. The following is a summary of Dieter, *Der junge Luther und Aristoteles*, 257–75 (chap. 3: "Aristotelian Epistemology in Luther's Theology").

72. Since Bayer wrote this article before Dieter's book had been published, the translation of the last sentence has been adjusted to take this into account.

Chapter 2: Does Luther Have a "Waxen Nose"?

1. In his work on Luther, Volker Leppin demonstrates connections between Luther and late-medieval spirituality and mysticism. See specifically his biography, *Martin Luther, Gestalten des Mittelalters und der Renaissance* (Darmstadt: Wissenschaftliche Buchgesellschaft, 2006).

2. The bulk of Luther's disputations, not including the early disputations from the 15-teens, are collected in WA 39/I and WA 39/II.

3. Graham White, *Luther as Nominalist: A Study of the Logical Methods used in Martin Luther's Disputations in the Light of Their Medieval Background*, Schriften der Luther-Agricola-Gesellschaft 30 (Helsinki: Luther-Argicola-Society, 1994); Christine Helmer, *The Trinity and Martin Luther: A Study of the Relationship between Genre, Language, and the Trinity in Luther's Works (1523–1546)*, Veröffentlichungen des Instituts für Europäische Geschichte/Abteilung Abendländische Religionsgeschichte 174 (Mainz: Zabern, 1999); Theodor Dieter, *Der junge Luther und Aristoteles: Eine historisch-systematische Untersuchung zum Verhältnis von Theologie und Philosophie*, Theologische Bibliothek Töpelmann 105 (Berlin: de Gruyter, 2001).

4. This reference is to his repeated injunctions against speculating on predestination that would result in "breaking one's neck," or at the very least serious spiritual distress. See Table Talk no. 5070, entitled (in LW) "Predestination Cannot Be Searched Out" and dated to June 11 and 19, 1540: "But we are fools who neglect the revealed Word and the will of the Father in Christ and, instead, investigate mysteries which ought only to be worshiped. As a result many break their necks" (LW 54:385).

5. On this debate between Ockham and Scotus as staged in one of Luther's trinitarian disputations, see Helmer, *The Trinity and Martin Luther*, 98–107; see Luther's doctoral disputation of Georg Major and Johannes Faber (Dec. 12, 1544) in WA 39/II: 287–320; on Ockham's doctrine of the Trinity, see Marilyn McCord Adams, *William Ockham*, vol. 2, Publications in Medieval Studies/The Medieval Institute of Notre Dame 27 (Notre Dame: University of Notre Dame Press, 1987), 997–1007.

6. See Albrecht Ritschl, "Theology and Metaphysics," in *Three Essays*, trans. Philip Hefner (Philadelphia: Fortress Press, 1972; reprint: Eugene: Wipf & Stock, 2005), 149–218.

7. Albrecht Ritschl, *A Critical History of the Christian Doctrine of Justification and Reconciliation*, trans. (of the 1st ed. of vol. 1 from 1870) John S. Black (Edinburgh: Edmonston & Douglas, 1872), 199.

8. Oswald Bayer, *Martin Luther's Theology: A Contemporary Interpretation*, trans. Thomas H. Trapp (Grand Rapids: Eerdmans, 2008), 337–40, here 338 (emphasis in original).

9. Ibid., 339. Bayer's designation is issued from a conceptual distinction used first by Theodosius Harnack to interpret Luther's doctrine of God, the distinction between a God outside of Christ and a God in Christ. I find it very unfortunate in an age of religious pluralism to map this distinction onto non-Christians and Christians.

10. Ibid., 220.

11. Ibid., 339.

Chapter 3: "Putting on the Neighbor"

1. Martin Luther, "The Freedom of a Christian," LW 31:371.

2. LW 54:171, No. 2808b (1532)

3. Paul Hinlicky, *Paths Not Taken: Fates of Theology from Luther through Leibnitz* (Grand Rapids: Eerdmans, 2009), 216. Heiko Oberman has summed it up nicely, "Luther owed his love for the classical writers, especially for Virgil and Cicero, to the Erfurt humanists; through his contact with them he acquired a feeling for rhetoric and rhetorical figures, which he later considered crucial prerequisites for a proper scriptural exegesis" (*Luther: Man between God and the Devil* [New Haven: Yale University Press, 1989]). Indeed, many in Luther's time, and before, read Cicero studiously (see Paul MacKendrick, *The Philosophical Books of Cicero* [New York: St. Martin's, 1989], 258–65; also see Cary J. Nederman, "The Union of Wisdom and Eloquence before the Renaissance: The Ciceronian Orator in Medieval Thought," *Journal of Medieval History* 18 (1992): 75–95; and idem, "Nature, Sin, and the Origins of Society: The Ciceronian Tradition in Medieval Political Thought," *Journal of the History of Ideas* 49 (January–March 1988): 3–26; also idem, "Cicero," in *Political Thinkers*, ed. D. Boucher and P. Kelly (New York: Oxford University Press, 2009), 100–113; also see Jean Porter's significant interpretation of Cicero's influence on Thomas Aquinas's approach to natural law and virtue (*Nature as Reason: A Thomistic Theory of the Natural Law* (Grand Rapids: Eerdmans, 2005), 8–19, 266–68). Augustine, whom Luther of course pondered diligently, confessed that he converted to Christianity by reading Cicero's *Hortensius* and subsequently cited Cicero 130 times in *City of God* alone.

4. Heiko A. Oberman, *Forerunners of the Reformation: The Shape of Late Medieval Thought* (New York: Holt, Rinehart and Winston, 1966), 123–31.

5. I will use the term "practical reason," which is the traditional term for moral reason or for what Luther sometimes called "natural reason." Christopher Toner's brief definition is helpful: "Practical reason is the employment of reason in service of living a good life, and the great medieval thinkers all gave accounts of it. Practical reason is reasoning about, or better toward, an action, and an action always has a goal or end, this end being understood to be in some sense good" ("Medieval Theories of Practical Reason," *The Internet Encyclopedia of Philosophy*, http://www.iep.utm.edu/prac-med/). For Luther, as we will see, living a good life is always good relationally, that is, relative to the good of one's neighbors.

6. Brian A. Gerrish's *Grace and Reason: A Study in the Theology of Luther* (Chicago: University of Chicago Press, 1962) still remains the best English-language account of Luther's view of reason, though he did not account for Luther's particular notion of practical reason or for the Ciceronian impulse in Luther.

7. LW 31:376; also 26:189–97.

8. LW 31:372–73.

9. LW 31:376.

10. Martin Luther, "Sermon on Epiphany (Isaiah 60:1-6)" (1522), in John Lenker, ed., *Sermons of Martin Luther: The Church Postils*, vol. 6 (Grand Rapids: Baker, 1995), 319.

11. LW 26:10; also 31:297–306

12. LW 51:374; 40:175.

13. LW 31:12.

14. LW 26:161, 167, 255–56, 262–67.

15. LW 26:284, 291–92.

16. LW 26:168.

17. LW 26:262.

18. LW 31:371.

19. LW 26:129–30, 430–31.

20. LW 31:361. Already in "The Blessed Sacrament of the Holy and True Body of Christ, and the Brotherhoods" (1519) (LW 35:49–73) Luther had traced the phenomenology of ecclesial sociality of bodied love, which is assumed in "The Freedom of a Christian" though not specified. A fuller treatment would need to articulate the entwinement of ecclesial communion and neighbor sociality.

21. LW 31:343.

22. LW 31:9, 361; also 26:169.

23. LW 31:371. In this way Luther argued biblically that love is formed by, and hence perfected by, faith, thus reversing Thomas's maxim that faith is formed by, and hence completed or perfected by, love (LW 26:161; also 26:88, 90, 146). This is the heart of Luther's commitment to the *sola fide* of justification, the Reformation's "most embattled *sola* of all" (see Robert W. Bertram, "Recent Lutheran Theologies of Justification by Faith: A Sampling," in H. George Anderson, T. Austin Murphy, and Joseph A. Burgess, eds., *Justification by Faith: Lutherans and Catholics in Dialogue VII* [Minneapolis: Augsburg, 1985], 252).

24. LW 31:371.

25. LW 31:367.

26. See Gary M. Simpson, "'Written on Their Hearts': Thinking with Luther about Scripture, Natural Law, and the Moral Life," *Word & World* 30 (Fall 2010): 419–28; and idem, "'You Shall Bear Witness to Me': Thinking with Luther about Christ and the Scriptures," *Word & World* 29 (Fall 2009): 380–88.

27. LW 31:371; also 26:279, 283–84, 288.

28. LW 35:53–59; 31:155–60.

29. LW 31:371.

30. LW 31:367–68.

31. LW 13:199.

32. LW 2:160.

33. LW 13:198.

34. LW 2:159.

35. LW 54:171, No. 2808b (1532); *WA, Br* 1:17 (Nr5) (1509). See also Walther von Loewenich, *Martin Luther: The Man and His Work* (Minneapolis: Augsburg, 1986), 46–65; also Martin Brecht, *Martin Luther*, vol.1, *His Road to Reformation 1483–1521* (Philadelphia: Fortress Press, 1985), 32–38, 90–93, 120–21.

36. LW 54:243, No. 3608e.

37. LW 54:476, No. 5677 (1546).

38. Marcus Tullius Cicero, *De inventione* I.1.1 (Cambridge: Harvard University Press, 1968). Cicero confirmed the bond of wisdom and eloquence at the heart of human nature and society in his mature *On Oratory* (*De oratore* II.2.6; II.1.5; II.11.48) (Cambridge: Harvard University Press, 1942). I am indebted to Nederman's (see n.3, above) and MacKendrick's

(*The Philosophical Books of Cicero,* 13–16, 254–56) accounts of Cicero's oratorical innovation of the Greek rhetorical and philosophical traditions.

39. Cicero, *De officiis* I.16.50 (Cambridge: Harvard University Press, 1961).

40. LW 54:171, No. 2808b.

41. LW 33:19.

42. LW 13:55.

43. LW 12:209–13.

44. Augustine, *The City of God* (New York: Fathers of the Church, 1952), 12.28.

45. Aristotle, *Politics,* 1253a9-10 (Cambridge: Harvard University Press, 1967); and idem, *Physics,* 192b9-193b21 (Cambridge: Harvard University Press, 1963).

46. Reinhold Niebuhr's view of Luther's "pure pessimism" has influenced many (*The Children of Light and the Children of Darkness* [New York: Scribner, 1941], 44–45).

47. See Nederman for the important Ciceronian influence on numerous medieval conciliar theologians ("Nature, Sin and the Origins of Society").

48. Cicero, *De inventione* I.2.2; also *De officiis* I.4.11-13; I.16.50-52.

49. LW 40:319.

50. LW 13:46–47; 14:112–17; 20:171–73; 26:94–98; 45:311–37. In his Table Talks Luther confesses that Cicero's argument for God's existence and continuing providence has "often moved me deeply" (LW 54:423–24, No 5440 (1542); also see 54:474–75, No. 5671 (1544).

51. Cicero, *De optimo genere oratorum* I.3.4 (Cambridge: Harvard University Press, 1968).

52. Nederman, "Cicero," 104.

53. The English translator decimated Luther's eloquent and evocative metaphor, "to look the other in the mouth"—my translation (*WA* 30/II:637)—and translated Luther's German, "be guided by their language" (LW 35:189). A true desecration!

54. This is Charles Taylor's poignant phrase (*Source of the Self* [Cambridge: Harvard University Press, 1989], 211–18).

55. Nederman, "Cicero," 104.

56. LW 35:45–73; 39:305–14; 40:31–35.

57. LW 27:93.

58. LW 54:325, No. 4178 (1538); also 54:241, No. 3604A; and 46:100.

Chapter 4: Luther and Augustine—Revisited

1. This article is an abbreviated and revised English translation of my German: "Produktives Mißverständnis: Zur Rezeption der Theologie des lateinischen Kirchenvaters Augustinus im Werk Martin Luthers (1483–1546)," in *Augustinus: Supren und Psiegelungen seines Denkens,* vol. I, ed. Norbert Fischer (Hamburg 2009), 59–80.

2. Cf. Karl Heinz, "Zur Mühlen: Zur Erforschung des „jungen Luther" seit 1876," *Lutherjahrbuch* 50 (1983): 48–125; Otto Hermann Pesch, "Zwanzig Jahre katholische Lutherforschung," *Lutherische Rundschau* 16 (1966): 392–406; ed. Rainer Vinke, *Lutherforschung im 20. Jahrhundert.* Rückblick – Bilanz—Ausblick (Mainz 2004).

3. See Vinzenz Pfnür, Einig in der Rechtfertigungslehre? Die Rechtfertigungslehre der Confessio Augustana (1530) und die Stellungnahme der katholischen Kontro-

verstheologie zwischen 1530 und 1535 in Bd. 60. Abt. Abendländische Religionsgeschichte; Veröffentlichungen des Instituts für Europäische Geschichte, Mainz, Bd. 60 (Wiesbaden 1970). See also the series edited by Karl Kardinal Lehmann and Wolfhart Pannenberg. Dialog der Kirchen, Freiburg im Breisgan; Herder; Göttingen: Vandenhoeck & Ruprecht © 1986.

4. For the following see Markus Wriedt, "Via Augustini—Ausprägungen des spätmittelalterlichen Augustinismus in der observanten Kongregation der Augustinerermiten," in *Luther und das monastische Erbe,* ed. Christoph Bultmann, Volker Leppin, and Andreas Lindner (Tübingen 2007), 9–38; also see "Augustin, Augustinismus," in *Handbuch der Rhetorik* (Tübingen 2011).

5. See WA 63:52–84; WAB 15:21–23; WAT 6:525f., and a very brief survey by Albrecht Beutel in *Augustin Handbuch,* ed. Volker Henning Drecoll (Tübingen 2007), 615–22. See also Hans Ulrich Delius, *Augustin als Quelle Luthers: Eine Materialsammlung* (Berlin 1984); cf. Peter Meier, *Zeitschrift für Kirchngeschichte* 98 (1987): 117–23.

6. WA 9:5–25.

7. WA 9:29–94.

8. Bernhard Lohse, "Die Bedeutung Augustins für den jungen Luther (1965)," in idem, *Evangelium in der Geschichte.* Studien zu Luther und der Reformation. Zum 60. Geburtstag des Autors herausgegeben von Leif Grane, Bernd Moeller, und Otto Hermann Pesch, (Göttingen 1988), 11–30; Leif Grane, *Modus loquendi theologicus: Luthers Kampf um die Erneuerung der Theologie 1515–1518* (Leiden 1975).

9. Bernhard Lohse, ed., *Luthers reformatorischer Durchbruch I* (Darmstadt 1968) and *Luthers reformatorischer Durchbruch II* (Stuttgart 1988).

10. "That place in Paul was for me truly the gate to paradise. Later I read Augustine's *On the Spirit and the Letter,* where contrary to hope I found that he, too, interpreted God's righteousness in a similar way, as the righteousness with which God clothes us when he justifies us. Although this was heretofore said imperfectly and he did not explain all things concerning imputation clearly, it nevertheless was pleasing that God's righteousness with which we are justified was taught." LW 34:337.

11. Cf. Gabriele Schmidt-Lauber, *Luthers Vorlesung über den Römerbrief 1515/1516: Ein Vergleich zwischen Luthers Manuskript und den studentischen Nachschriften* (Köln 1994).

12. WA 51:10.

13. WA 50:539, 21-23.

Chapter 5: Whore or Handmaid?

1. LW 40:175; 51:374.

2. *Summa Theologicae* (hereafter *ST*) 1a, q.1, a.5 *sed contra* (L 4, 16). In this essay I use the standard abbreviations for referring to Thomas's works. All references are to the critical edition, *Sancti Thomae Aquinatis doctoris angelici Opera omnia iussu Leonis XIII. O.M. edita,* cura et studio fratrum praedicatorum (Romae, 1882–), hereafter "L."

3. For a more comprehensive discussion of this evidence, see my essay, "Syllogism or Paradox: Aquinas and Luther on Theological Method," in *Theological Studies* 59 (1998): 3–21. For Luther in particular, see the essays on "Reason" and "Theology" in my *The*

Westminster Handbook to Martin Luther (Louisville: Westminster John Knox, 2010), 112–16 and 128–32.

4. G. K. Chesterton, *St. Thomas Aquinas* (New York: Sheed & Ward, 1933), 21.

5. WA 42:93, 37; cf. LW 1:124.

6. LW 1:63.

7. LW 1:112.

8. LW 34:137.

9. Ibid.

10. WA 10/I-1:531, 6-11.

11. LW 41:60.

12. LW 52:84; 22:150–51.

13. LW 19:53; cf. WA 56:176, 15-32.

14. LW 26:399.

15. LW 19:54.

16. WA 22:108, 12-15.

17. LW 44:336.

18. LW 32:112.

19. LW 19:54.

20. LW 19:55–56.

21. WA 10/I-1:532, 1-12.

22. LW 31:38.

23. WA 39:II:13, 10-12.

24. WA 30/II:300, 21-27.

25. WA 15:184, 32-33. On the question of what precisely Luther knew about Thomas Aquinas, opinions differ. On the one hand, see my own investigation outlined in *Luther and Thomas Aquinas: The Angelic Doctor in the Thought of the Reformer,* (Stuttgart: Steiner, 1989), strongly supported by Otto Herman Pesch, *Martin Luther, Thomas von Aquin und die reformatorische Kritik an der Scholastik: Zur Geschichte und Wirkungsgeschichte eines Missverstantnisses mit weltgeschichtlichen Folgen,* (Hamburg: J. Jungius-Gesellschaft, 1994). On the other hand, see Stefan Gradl, "Inspektor Columbo irrt: Kriminalistische Uberlegungen zur Frage 'Kannte Luther Thomas?'" in *Luther: Zeitschrift der Luther-Gesellschaft* 2 (2006): 83–99.

26. For orientation on this larger issue, the following studies are indispensable: Marie-Dominique Chenu, *Toward Understanding Saint Thomas* (Chicago: Regnery, 1964); Otto Herman Pesch, *Thomas von Aquin: Grenze und Grösse mittelalterliche Theologie* (Mainz: Matthias-Grünewald, 1988); and Jean-Pierre Torrell, *Saint Thomas Aquinas: His Person and His Work* (Washington: Catholic University Press, 1996).

27. *De veritate,* q.15, a.1 *corpus* (L 22:2, 478–80); cf. Chenu, *Toward Understanding Saint Thomas,* 177.

28. *S.T.* 1a, q.32, a.1 ad 2 (L 4, 350).

29. *Summa contra gentiles* (hereafter *SCG*) 1, chap. 8.1 (L 13, 21).

30. *SCG* I, chap. 9.2 (L 13, 22).

31. *ST* 1a, q.1, a.8 (L 4, 21–22).

32. *ST* 1a, q.1, a.8 ad 2 (L 4, 22).

33. *Super Boetium de Trinitate* q.2, a.1 ad 5 (L 50, 94).

34. *Super Boetium de Trinitate* q.3, a.1, c (L 50, 107–8).
35. *SCG* I, chap. 9.2 (L 13, 22).
36. *ST* 1a, q.32, a.1 (L 4, 350).
37. Chenu, *Toward Understanding Saint Thomas*, 179; Torrell, *Saint Thomas Aquinas*, 266.
38. *ST* 1a, q.2, a.3 (L 4, 31–32).
39. Pesch, *Thomas von Aquin*, 132.
40. Ibid., 127.

Chapter 6: Luther's "Atheism"

1 Walter von Loewenich, *Luther's Theology of the Cross,* trans. H. J. A. Bouman (Minneapolis: Augsburg, 1976), 27–49.

2. For the seminal analysis, see Martin Heidegger, *The Phenomenology of Religious Life,* trans. M. Fritsch and J. A. Gosetti-Ferencei (Bloomington: Indiana University Press, 2004). On Heidegger's engagement with Luther, see Paul R. Hinlicky, "Luther and Heidegger: A Review Essay of Benjamin D. Crowe, *Heidegger's Religious Origins: Destruction and Authenticity*" *Lutheran Quarterly* 22/1 (Spring 2008): 78–86.

3. Paul Tillich, *Systematic Theology*, 3 vols. (Chicago: University of Chicago Press, 1967), II:116–17.

4. See Part III, Chapter 4, "Die Unbegreiflichkeit Gottes in der Spannung zwischen verborgenem und offensbarem Gott," in Thomas Reinhuber, *Kämpfender Glaube: Studien zu Luthers Bekenntnis am Ende von* De servo arbitrio (Berlin: Walter de Gruyter, 2000), 102–49. While Luther sharply rejects any "Theodizee der Vernunft" (183–85), Luther's entire argument builds to what might be called a "theodicy of faith" (following Romans 8; 186, 197 n.564). Here "struggling" faith is not irrationalism, but cleaving to God in Christ as the promised future in the teeth of a present, Christless experience of God. Just so, the question of theodicy must be asked but cannot (yet) satisfactorily be answered (200); the eschatological reserve, the "not yet" of faith, must be maintained (225–26). The light of glory is not yet (227): thus "bleibt die Spannung in der Erfahrung Gottes und in Gott selbst" (228). The cost of this interpretation is that Reinhuber must repeatedly assert that Luther's arguments are unsystematic and self-contradictory (e.g., 199, 201). This is not sound method. Especially damaging is Reinhuber's crucial concession that it is possible to see a "progression" in the course of the three lights of nature, grace, and glory (206ff.) with which Luther concluded *De servo arbitrio*. What is really at issue (not merely in Luther interpretation!) is whether the "inconceivability" of God is to be taken as an (unargued) essential attribute of God, which would make of God a nominalist *deus exlex,* or whether divine incomprehensibility is taken as the mysterious unity of the Trinity, not yet visible as the reign, yet never in all eternity to be comprehended. Compare the treatment of *De servo abitrio* in Paul R. Hinlicky, *Luther and the Beloved Community: A Path for Christian Theology after Christendom* (Grand Rapids: Eerdmans, 2010), 139–78.

5. Oswald Bayer, *Martin Luther's Theology: A Contemporary Interpretation,* trans. Thomas H. Trapp (Grand Rapids: Eerdmans, 2007), 215.

6. Christine Helmer, *The Trinity and Martin Luther: A Study on the Relationship between Genre, Language and the Trinity in Luther's Works (1523–1546)* (Mainz: Philipp von Zabern, 1999), 146–53.

7. For the full argument, see Hinlicky, *Beloved Community*, 105–38.

8. Tillich, *Systematic Theology*, I:22.

9. Leonard S. Smith, *Religion and the Rise of History: Martin Luther and the Cultural Revolution in Germany, 1760–1810* (Eugene, Ore.: Cascade, 2009). As I am explicating Luther's way of contrasting philosophy and theology in this essay, I won't say anything about the possibility of "Christian philosophy," even though, contra Heidegger, I concluded my book *Paths Not Taken* with a definite summons to such a vocation (Paul R. Hinlicky, *Paths Not Taken: Theology from Luther through Leibniz* [Grand Rapids: Eerdmans, 2009], 293–94).

10. Martin Luther, *The Bondage of the Will*, trans. J. I. Packer & O. R. Johnston (Grand Rapids: Revell, 2000), 315–16.

11. Frederick C. Beiser, "Jacobi and the Pantheism Controversy," in Beiser, *The Fate of Reason: German Philosophy from Kant to Fichte* (Cambridge: Harvard University Press, 1987), 44–91.

12. "Toward the Critique of Hegel's Philosophy of Law," in *Writings of the Young Marx on Philosophy and Society,* trans. Loyd D. Easton and Kurt H. Guddat (Garden City, N.Y.: Anchor, 1967), 259.

13. Karl Marx, *On Religion,* trans. Saul K. Padover (New York: McGraw-Hill, 1974), 35–37.

14. Further on Marx, see Hinlicky, *Beloved Community,* 301–31.

15. In Ludwig Feuerbach, *The Essence of Christianity,* trans. G. Eliot (New York: Harper Torchbooks, 1957), xxii.

16. Ibid., xxii–xxiii.

17. Slavoj Žižek, "The Fear of Four Words: A Modest Plea for the Hegelian Reading of Christianity," in Slavoj Žižek and John Milbank, *The Monstrosity of Christ: Paradox or Dialectic?* ed. Creston Davis (Cambridge: MIT Press, 2009), 24–109.

18. Georg W. F. Hegel, *Lectures on the Philosophy of Religion,* ed. P. C. Hodgson (Berkeley: University of California Press, 1988), 417–18.

19. Lewis Ayres, *Nicea and Its Legacy: An Approach to Fourth-Century Trinitarian Theology* (New York: Oxford University Press, 2006), 406.

20. Adam Drozdek, *Greek Philosophers as Theologians: The Divine Arche* (Burlington, Vt.: Ashgate, 2007).

21. For the full case, see Paul R. Hinlicky, *Divine Complexity: The Rise of Creedal Christianity* (Minneapolis: Fortress Press, 2010).

22. Hinlicky, *Paths*, 150–76.

23. Eberhard Jüngel, *God as the Mystery of the World: On the Foundation of the Theology of the Crucified One in the Dispute between Theism and Atheism,* trans. D. L. Guder (Grand Rapids: Eerdmans, 1983). For more rigorously historical argumentation, see O. Bayer and B. Gleede, eds., *Creator est creatura: Luthers Christologie als Lehre von der Idiomenkommunikation* (Berlin: De Gruyter, 2007).

24. Robert W. Jenson, *Systematic Theology,* 2 vols. (New York: Oxford University Press, 1997), 1:207–23.

25. Robert W. Jenson, "An Ontology of Freedom in the *De Servo Arbitrio* of Luther," *Modern Theology* 10/3 (July 1994): 247–52.

26. This is quite unlike Hegel's point of departure, which is a speculative notion of God as essentially creative; see the important critique of Cyril O'Regan, *The Heterodox Hegel* (Albany: SUNY Press, 1994).

27. J. F. Keating and T. J. White, O.P., eds., *Divine Impassibility and the Mystery of Human Suffering* (Grand Rapids: Eerdmans, 2009).

28. Alexandre Kojeve, *Introduction to the Reading of Hegel: Lectures on the Phenomenology of Spirit,* trans. James H. Nichols Jr. (Ithaca: Cornell University Press, 1996).

29. LW 37:366.

30. LW 37:61.

31. "If God has the finite only over against himself, then he himself is finite and limited." Hegel, *Philosophy of Religion*, 406.

32. Ibid.

33. In the same treatise, on the same page, Luther can axiomatically assert divine simplicity, taken as a rule of reverent speech about the unique being of the Creator of all that is other than Himself, *not* as any kind of metaphysical insight. "We know, however, that God's power, arm, hand, nature, face, Spirit, wisdom, etc., are all one thing; for apart from the creation there is nothing but the one simple Deity" LW 37:61.

34. E.g., John Dillon, *The Middle Platonists: 80 B.C. to A.D. 220*, rev. ed. (Ithaca: Cornell University Press, 1996).

35. "Disputation against Scholastic Theology," LW 31:3–16.

36. Heiko Oberman, *The Dawn of the Reformation: Essays in Late Medieval and Early Reformation Thought* (Edinburgh: T & T Clark, 1986); idem, *The Harvest of Medieval Theology: Gabriel Biel and Late Medieval Nominalism* (Grand Rapids: Baker Academic, 2000).

37. LW 31:41–42.

38. David Bentley Hart, *The Beauty of the Infinite: The Aesthetics of Christian Truth* (Grand Rapids: Eerdmans, 2003), 133.

39. This representative sample of Luther's preaching on the spiritual suffering of Christ, originally preached in Wittenberg by Luther on All Saints, Nov. 1, 1537, was published a generation later by Andreas Poach (1515–1585): *The Eighth Psalm of David preached and explained by Dr. Martin Luther,* as Poach titled it in 1572 (WA 45:205–50; trans. LW 12:95–136). I will confine my remarks, however, to the 1537 *Nachschrift* (stenographic record), not Poach's expanded edition (which is what appears in LW 12), as reconstructed from the WA.

40. E.g., Luther's commentary on "The Binding of Isaac" as Abraham's trial of faith, e.g, LW 4:95.

41. For a survey of the issues involved and an intriguing comparison of Luther and Thomas Aquinas, see Bruce D. Marshall, "The Dereliction of Christ and the Impassibility of God," in Keating and White, eds., *Divine Impassibility,* 246–98.

42. The First Apology of Justin," *The Ante-Nicene Fathers,* ed. A. Roberts and J. Donaldson (Grand Rapids: Erdmans, 1975), 1:163–87.

43. LW 4:355.

44. I.a., LW 4:320–21.

45. See Paul R. Hinlicky, "The New Language of the Spirit: Critical Dogmatics in the Tradition of Luther," chap. 3, Dennis Bielfeldt, Paul Hinlicky, and Mickey Mattox, *The Substance of the Faith: Luther's Doctrinal Theology for Today* (Minneapolis: Fortress Press, 2008), 131–90.

46. WA 45:239: "The Divinity has thus hidden itself, so that it is possible to say that there is no deity here. Only devil, hell, eternal fire and eternal dead."

47. Ibid., 240: "The Diety has withdrawn."

48. On the comparison of the Christologies of Luther and Schweitzer, see Hinlicky, *Beloved Community*, 31–65.

49. Toward the end of the sermon, Luther remembered to say: "Ideo verus deus et homo, secundem humanitatem gestorben, gelitten und verlassen et resurrexit, et tamen crucifixus est dominus supra omnes creaturas. Ideo angeli eum adorant etiam hominem, quia unica persona, non zertrennt Gott und mensch" (WA 45:240–41). Thus, Poach was justified to recur to the doctrine of the one person and the communication of idioms in his theologically corrected 1572 edition of Luther's sermon at the point where Luther speaks of the deity withdrawing in Christ's spiritual suffering: "And in fact he was forsaken by God." Poach adds immediately, "This does not mean that the deity was separated from the humanity—for in this person who is Christ, the Son of God and of Mary, deity and humanity are so united that they can never be separated or divided," LW 12:126. It can only mean, then, that the separation occurred within the divine Life.

50. "Confession concerning Christ's Supper," in LW 37:202.

51. Friedrich Nietzsche, *Genealogy of Morals*, trans. Walter Kaufmann and R. J. Haufmann (New York: Random House, 1967), II.23, 92.

52. On the relation of Luther to Zwingli, see Hinlicky, *Beloved Community*, 139–78. On the *Wirkungsgeschichte* of this relationship, which I see repeated in the Leibniz-Spinoza engagement, see Hinlicky, *Paths*, 43–86.

53. LW 37:72.

54. Ibid., 253.

Chapter 7: Luther's Philosophy of Language

1. See Richard Rorty's introduction in *The Linguistic Turn* (Chicago: University of Chicago Press, 1967).

2. See Christopher Peacocke, "The Philosophy of Language," in A. C. Grayling, *Philosophy 2: Further Through the Subject* (New York: Oxford University Press, 1998), 72–121.

3. While syntax concerns relations among linguistic symbols, and pragmatics the relations of uttering, using, responding, etc., to extralinguistic entities where the intention of the speaker, her linguistic ability, belief, audience and context of use are crucial, semantics deals with the relations of referring, denoting, and of connoting extralinguistic objects. Semantic theories divide among theories of meaning (connoting and intensions), theories of reference (denoting and extensions), theories combining both, and pragmatic theories taking meaning to be the use made of an expression by interactive participants.

4. One can distinguish *metaphysical* and *semantic* approaches to truth—especially in the medieval tradition. The first construes truth relationally and focuses on properties and states making truth bearers true. The second understands truth to be a nonrelational property of the linguistic entity itself. The first claims that proposition p is true if and only if things are as p signifies them to be; the second that p is true if and only if p signifies things as they are. See Catarina Dutilh Novaes, "Medieval Theories of Truth," http://staff.science.uva.nl/~dutilh/articles/truth.pdf.

5. One can contrast the *truth-conditional semantics* of Davidson with the *proof-theoretic* semantics of Dummett. The first bases meaning on *truth*, the second bases on *assertibility*.

The first locates meaning in terms of the *interpretations* or *extensions* of the language (its reference), the second finds the meaning of an expression in the *role* that it plays within an inferential system. While truth-conditional (called "model-theoretic") semantics is denotational in spirit, proof-theoretic semantics tries to formalize Wittgenstein's insight that "meaning is *use*." Accordingly, a sentence's meaning is the *rule* for its correct utterance. For a proof-theoretic account see Peter Schroeder-Heister, "Validity Concepts in Proof-Theoretic Semantics," *Synthese* 148 (2006): 525–71.

6. "Model-theoretic" accounts assign an interpretation via a naming function. The sentence or group of sentences is given a "model" in terms of set-theoretic inclusion, intersection and union. Thus, for some x, "Px & Rx" is interpreted as "there is at least one element of domain D, such that it has the property P and the property R." The thing for which x stands is accordingly included in the intersection of things having P and R.

7. See William Kneale and Martha Kneale, *The Development of Logic* (Oxford: Clarendon, 1962); and Norman Kretzmann, Anthony Kenny, and Jan Pinborg, eds., *The Cambridge History of Later Medieval Philosophy* (Cambridge: Cambridge University Press, 1982).

8. Ibid., 64.

9. Stephen Reed, "Medieval Theories: Properties of Terms," in *The Stanford Encyclopedia of Philosophy*, http://plato.stanford.edu/entries/medieval-terms.

10. Spade, *Thoughts, Words, and Things,* 83. While signification is transitive, reference or meaning is not. Thus signification cannot be synonymous with meaning.

11. While most medieval thinkers could use the terms *subordinate* and *correspond* interchangeably with "immediate signification," this was not universal. Ockham, for instance, denies that written words immediately signify spoken ones, though he holds that they are subordinate (ibid., 68ff.). Thinkers could hold that a concept "establishes an understanding" of the object by *being* that understanding of the object. Accordingly, Buridan frequently uses the language of the concept "conceiving" rather than immediately signifying the thing. For Peter of Spain a concept is the "representation of the thing by the word in accordance with convention."

12. Ibid., 69.

13. Ibid., 84–85. Spade points out that the Aristotelian-Boethian view emphasizes the social role of language in transmitting concepts, but fails to model the fact that people mostly use language to talk about things, not concepts. Conversely, the Ockhamist-Burleyite view grants that words mostly refer to things but ignores the pragmatic and interpersonal role of language.

14. See Reed, "Medieval Theories."

15. Common personal supposition further divides between determinate and confused, with the confused between the distributively confused and the merely confused. Burley, Ockham, and followers generally hold that a general term in a proposition has determinate supposition when one can move validly back and forth from the proposition in which the term is present to the complete disjunction of its singulars with respect to that term. It is confused and distributive if one can validly move from the proposition to the indefinite conjunction of its singulars with respect to that term. Otherwise it is merely confused.

16. See Reed, "Medieval Theories." The distinctions among personal, simple, and material supposition were useful to explain what goes wrong in syllogisms like: *Homo est*

dignissima creaturarum, Sortes est homo; Ergo Sortes est dignissima creaturarum. The solution claims that *homo* in the major premise is used with simple supposition—*homo* refers to a form—while in the minor premise it has personal supposition with *homo* referring to an individual man.

17. *Supposita* are the entities that terms in propositions supposit. The class of these entities is determined by the *significance* of the terms plus elements within the proposition, e.g., verbal tense and mode. See Novaes, "Medieval Theories of Truth," 9.

18. I first wrote about this in "Luther, Metaphor, and Theological Language," *Modern Theology* 6/2 (January 1990): 121–35.

19. WA 39/II:370, 8-14: *Nequaquam; si personaliter sumimus, verum est: Deus generat Deum; sed si essentialiter, tunc Deus non generat nec se ipsum nec alium. Essentia non generat, sed persona. Si vero non personaliter accipatur, non generat.*

20. See my appendix translating and annotating Luther's three trinitarian disputations from 1543 to 1545 in Dennis Bielfeldt, Paul Hinlicky, and Mickey Mattox, *The Substance of Faith* (Minneapolis: Fortress Press, 2008), 191–209.

21. WA 39/II:4, 24-25: *Iste syllogismus epositorius: Pater in divinis generat. Pater est essentia divina. Ergo essentia divina generat, est bonus.* See LW 38:240.

22. The Fourth Lateran Council had, in fact, denied that the essence generates the essence, so the matter was settled.

23. WA 39/II:4, 28–29: *Iste syllogismus communis: Omnis essentia divinis est pater. Filius est essentia divinis. Ergo filius est pater, est bonus.*

24. WA 39/II:287, 31–32: *Quin M. Sententiarum, non satis recte docuit, Essentiam divinam nec generare nec generari.*

25. Lombard uses this reductio in Book I, d. 5 of the *Sentences.*

26. WA 39/II:291, 22—292, 2.

27. WA 39/II:17, 9—18, 2; LW 38:251–52.

28. Joachim of Flora was condemned at the 1215 Lateran Council because his allowance that the essence generates seemed to compromise the unity of God. Allowing it was perhaps to follow the Eastern church in its supposed emphasis on the ontological priority of the persons of the Trinity over its unity. For a critique of this putative East/West difference see Richard Cross, "Two Models of the Trinity," *Heythrop Journal* 43 (2002): 275–94.

29. WA 39/II:295, 15-16.

30. See Graham White, *Luther as Nominalist* (Helsinki: Luther-Agricola-Society 1994), 201ff.

31. WA 9:34, 35-37; 35, 1-5.

32. WA 1:226, 19-20: "*Frustra fingitur logica fidei, Suppositio mediate extra terminum et numerum.*" Also (Disputation *verbum caro factum est*) WA 39/II:4, 15-16; LW 38:240.

33. WA 39/II:11, 19-20; LW 38:246.

34. See d'Ailly, *Sent*, qu. F, art. 2, not. 3, in Theodor Dieter, *Der junge Luther und Aristotles: Eine historisch-systematische Ubntersuchung zum Verhaeltnis von Theologie und Philosophie* (Berlin: de Gruyter 2001), 384.

35. Ibid., 387ff.

36. See Dieter's excellent discussion, ibid., 380ff. See also my own work at clarifying the actual logical situation in *The Substance of Faith*, 192–94.

37. WA 39/II:288, 1-2.

38. WA 39/II:28, 28; LW 38:260.

39. Dieter, *Der junge Luther und Aristotles*, 399. See WA 39/II:316, 24: *"Res ergo ipsa aequiv-ocatur."* See also WA 39/II:4, 32-33; LW 38:240–41. I have argued in the past that it is precisely because the *res ipsa aequivocatur* that the *nova lingua* of theology arises, and that the new meanings in this language demand an intensional as well as extensional treatment, e.g., WA 39/II:94, 17ff. See my "Luther on Language," *Lutheran Quarterly* 16, no. 2 (Summer 2002): 195–220 and "Luther and the Strange Language of Theology: How New is the *Nova Lingua?*" in *Caritas et Reformatio: Essays on Church and Society in Honor of Carter Lindberg*, ed. David M. Whitford (St. Louis: Concordia Academic, 2002), 221–44. Abridged in *Luther Digest*, 13 (Fort Wayne: Luther Academy, 2005).

Chapter 8: Philipp Melanchthon

1. A shortened version of this paper was published in *Lutheran Forum* 43/2 (Summer 2009): 46–51.

2. A particularly concise treatment of this history is in Timothy Wengert, "Beyond Stereotypes: The Real Philipp Melanchthon," in Scott H. Hendrix and Timothy J. Wengert, eds., *Philipp Melanchthon Then and Now (1497–1997): Essays Celebrating the 500th Anniversary of the Birth of Philipp Melanchthon, Theologian, Teacher, and Reformer* (Columbia, S.C.: Lutheran Theological Southern Seminary, 1999), 9–32. For Wengert's treatment of the history of scholarship on Melanchthon's relationship to Erasmus and Renaissance humanism, see his *Human Freedom, Christian Righteousness: Philipp Melanchthon's Exegetical Dispute with Erasmus of Rotterdam* (New York: Oxford University Press, 1998), esp. 5–14. For the history of scholarship on Melanchthon's relationship to Luther see Wengert, *Philipp Melanchthon's* Annotationes in Ioanem *in Relation to its Predecessors and Contemporaries* (Genève: Librairie Droz S.A., 1987), 143–65. See also Walter Bouman, "Melanchthon's Significance for the Church Today," in Hendrix and Wengert, *Philipp Melanchthon Then and Now,* 33–56.

3. Bouman, "Melanchthon's Significance," 34.

4. Some of these are translated in Sachiko Kusukawa, ed., *Philip Melanchthon: Orations on Philosophy and Education,* trans. Christine Salazar (Cambridge: Cambridge University Press, 1999). Kusukawa has also produced the fullest account of Melanchthon's natural philosophy available in English: *The Transformation of Natural Philosophy: The Case of Philipp Melanchthon* (Cambridge: Cambridge University Press, 1995).

5. The standard edition of Melanchthon's works is the *Corpus Reformatorum Philippi Melanchthonis Operae quae Supersunt Omnia* (hereafter CR), ed. C. D. Bretschneider and H. E. Bindseil (Brunswick, 1834–60; reprinted New York: Johnson, 1963), 28 vols. Ralph Keen's *A Melanchthon Reader* (New York: Peter Lang, 1988) contains English translations of Melanchthon's "Commentary on Aristotle's Ethics, Bk. 1," 179–202, and "Summary of Ethics," 203–38. For Melanchthon's early critiques of scholasticism, see his essays "Paul and the Scholastics, 1520," and "Luther and the Parish Theologians, 1521," in *Melanchthon: Selected Writings,* trans. Charles Leander Hill (Minneapolis, Augsburg, 1962), 31–38, 69–88.

6. See Gunter Frank, "Melanchthon and the Tradition of Neoplatonism," in *Religious Confessions and the Sciences in the Sixteenth Century,* ed. Jürgen Helm and Annette Winkelmann (Leiden: Brill, 2001), 4. The fullest recent account of Melanchthon's philosophy as a whole is Frank's *Die theologische Philosophie Philip Melanchthons (1497–1560)*, Erfurter Theologische Studien, Band 67 (Leipzig: Benno, 1995).

7. CR 7, Col. 475; CR 13, cols. 183f.; cf. Frank, "Melanchthon and the Tradition of Neoplatonism," 6.

8. Quoted in Clyde Manschrek, *Melanchthon: The Quiet Reformer* (New York: Abingdon, 1958), 37; cf. Heinz Scheible, *Melanchthon* (München: Beck, 1997), 20, 25.

9. *Response ad Picum. Mirand.,* CR 9:687–703, here 688; trans. here from Quirinius Breen, "Melanchthon's Reply to G. Pico Della Mirandola," *Journal of the History of Ideas* 13/3 (June 1952): 414.

10. Tr. Kusukawa, *Orations,* "On the distinction between the Gospel and philosophy," 25; CR XII, 689–91.

11. Ibid., "On Philosophy (1536)," 130–31; CR 11:278–84.

12. Ibid., "On Plato (1538)," 202; CR 11:413–25.

13. Ibid., "On Galen (1540)," 218; CR 11:495–503.

14. Cf. Wengert, *In Ioannum,* 174, 178, 192.

15. Tr. Kusukawa, *Orations,* "Dedicatory Letter to Melanchthon's *Epitome of Moral Philosophy,*" 141; CR 3:359–61.

16. Ibid., "On the Distinction between the Gospel and Philosophy," 25; CR 12:689≠91.

17. For a good introduction to general trends in Renaissance approaches to philosophy, see Caesare Vasoli, "The Renaissance Concept of Philosophy," in *The Cambridge History of Renaissance Philosophy,* ed. C. Schmidt, et al. (Cambridge: Cambridge University Press, 1988), 57–74.

18. See, for example, the numerous references to him throughout Charles Schmitt and Quentin Skinner, eds., *The Cambridge History of Renaissance Philosophy* (Cambridge: Cambridge University Press, 1988).

19. Bruce Kimball, *Orators and Philosophers: A History of the Idea of a Liberal Education* (New York: Teacher's College Press, 1986), 12–42; also Ernest Grassi, *Rhetoric as Philosophy* (University Park: Pennsylvania State University Press, 1980), esp. 1–18.

20. Tr. Breen, *Reply to G. Pico,* 414; CR 9:688.

21. Ibid., 417–18; CR 11:692.

22. Cf. Robert Stupperich, *Der unbekannte Melanchthon* (Stuttgart: Kohlhammer, 1961).

23. Keimpe Algra, et al., *The Cambridge History Of Hellenistic Philosophy* (London: Cambridge University Press, 1999), xiii–xiv.

24. Kusukawa, "Introduction," in *Orations,* xviii.

25. Jonathan Barnes, "Logic and Language: Introduction," in Algra, et al., *Cambridge History,* 65–67.

26. Wengert demonstrates the importance of rhetorical theory for Melanchthon's Biblical interpretation in *In Ioannum,* 167–212. John Schneider claims that rhetoric is fundamental to Melanchthon's theology generally in *Philipp Melanchthon's Rhetorical Construal of Biblical Authority: oratio sacra* (Lewiston, N.Y.: Edwin Mellon, 1990); see also his "The Hermeneutics of Commentary: The Origins of Philipp Melanchthon's Integration of Dialectic into Rhetoric,"

in Timothy Wengert and Patrick Graham, eds., *Philipp Melanchthon (1497–1560) and the Commentary* (Sheffield: Sheffield Academic, 1997), 20–47. See also Quirinius Breen, "The Subordination of Philosophy to Rhetoric in Melanchthon: A Study of his Reply to G. Pico della Mirandola," *Archiv für Reformationsgeschichte* 43 (1952): Heft 1, 13–28.

27. Frank, *Neoplatonism*, 5. See also Frank, *Die theologische Philosophie*, 15–30.

28. *Loci communes theologici*, trans. Lowell J. Satre with revisions by Wilhelm Pauck, in Wilhelm Pauck, ed., *Melanchthon and Bucer* (Philadelphia: Westminster, 1969), 50; CR 21:117.

29. Tr. Kusukawa, *Orations*, "On the distinction between the Gospel and philosophy," 23; CR 12:689.

30. Ibid., 24; CR 12:690.

31. Quoted in Kusukawa, *Transformation*, 66; CR 12:692.

32. See with Melanchthon's presentation of these in the 1521 edition of *Loci Communes, Theologicici*, CR 21:117ff.; Pauck, *Melanchthon and Bucer*, 50 .

33. Trans. Kusukawa, *Orations*, "On Plato," 203; CR 11:425.

34. Ibid, 201; CR 11:422–23.

35. Ibid., "On the Life of Avicenna (1549?)," 220; CR 11:826.

36. Ibid., "On Plato," 202; CR 11:424.

37. Hans Engelland, "Introduction," in Clyde L.Manschrek, trans. and ed., *Melanchthon on Christian Doctrine: Loci communes 1555* (New York: Oxford University Press, 1965), xxx.

38. Ibid.

39. Jaroslav Pelikan, *From Luther to Kierkegaard: A Study in the History of Theology* (St. Louis: Concordia, 1950), 115.

40. Bouman, "Melanchthon's Significance," 39.

41. Tr. Kusukawa, *Orations*, "On Philosophy," 127–28; CR 11:280. Cf. Heinze Scheible, "Philip Melanchthon," in *The Reformation Theologians: An Introduction to Theology in the Early Modern Period* (Oxford: Blackwell, 2002), 73.

42. In Clyde L. Manschrek, trans. and ed., *Melanchthon on Christian Doctrine: Loci Communes 1555* (New York: Oxford University Press, 1965), 141; CR 21:732–33.

43. *De corrigendis adolescentiae studentiis 1518*, CR 11:15–25, trans. in Keen as "On Correcting the Studies of Youth," 47–57; cf. Wengert, *Beyond Stereotypes*, 19.

44. In Kusukawa, *Orations*, 256–64, esp. 258; CR 11:726–34, esp. 728.

45. See, for example, Pelikan's treatment of Melanchthon on justification, *From Luther to Kierkegaard*, 42–43.

46. Kusukawa, *Orations*, "On Plato," 203; CR 11:424–25.

Chapter 9: Reasoning Faithfully

1. Gottfried Wilhelm Leibniz, *Theodicy: Essays on the Goodness of God, the Freedom of Man, and the Origin of Evil* (La Salle, Ill.: Open Court, 1993), 76.

2. Paul Hinlicky's recent work addresses a number of these themes in depth and provides a fine example of history of philosophy in this double mode of "'mirror'" and "'window.'" See Paul R. Hinlicky, *Paths Not Taken: Fates of Theology from Luther through Leibniz* (Grand Rapids: Eerdmans, 2009).

3. Maria Rosa Antognazza, *Leibniz: An Intellectual Biography* (Cambridge: Cambridge University Press, 2009), 27.

4. In addition to the exceptionally fine biography by Antognazza (ibid.), the classic English-language biography has been E. J. Aiton, *Leibniz: A Biography* (Bristol: A. Hilger, 1985).

5. Cited in Ursula Goldenbaum, "Leibniz as a Lutheran," in *Leibniz, Mysticism, and Religion*, ed. Allison Coudert, Richard H Popkin, and Gordon M Weiner (Dordrecht: Kluwer, 1998), 170. Goldenbaum also sees Leibniz's Lutheran heritage as an important part of his philosophical theology; for a more detailed analysis of some of the themes considered here, her article is highly recommended.

6. In addition, as Jaroslav Pelikan asserts, Leibniz's *Théodicée* gives a clear sense of his Lutheran influences. For more, see Jaroslav Pelikan, *From Luther to Kierkegaard: A Study in the History of Theology* (St. Louis: Concordia, 1950), 85–86.

7. Leibniz, *Theodicy*, 101.

8. Ibid., 81.

9. Ibid., 96.

10. LW 44:336.

11. Leibniz, *Theodicy*, 123.

12. Goldenbaum also claims that Leibniz has a positive strategy that includes the entirety of his metaphysical project. This is a very interesting suggestion; unfortunately, it is beyond the scope of this essay. For more, see Ursula Goldenbaum, "Spinoza's Parrot, Socinian Syllogisms, and Leibniz's Metaphysics: Leibniz's Three Strategies of Defending Christian Mysteries," *American Catholic Philosophical Quarterly* 76/4 (Fall 2002): 551–74.

13. For more on this strategy, see ibid., 562–63.

14. From more on the presumption of truth, see Maria Rosa Antognazza, "The Defence of the Mysteries of the Trinity and Incarnation: An Example of Leibniz's 'Other' Reason," *British Journal for the History of Philosophy* 9/2 (2001): 289–93.

15. Leibniz, *Theodicy*, 99.

16. B. A. Gerrish, *Grace and Reason: A Study in the Theology of Luther* (Oxford: Clarendon, 1962), 25–26.

Chapter 10: The Means of Revolution

1. Immanuel Kant, *Religion within the Limits of Reason Alone* (hereafter RWL), trans. Theodore M. Greene and Hoyt H. Hudson (New York: Harper Torchbooks, 1960), 43.

2. Ibid., 32.

3. Ibid., 43.

4. Immanuel Kant, *Critique of Practical Reason* (hereafter KpV), trans. Mary Gregor (Cambridge: Cambridge University Press, 1997), 62–75.

5. Martin Luther, *The Large Catechism* (hereafter LC), in *The Book of Concord*, trans. Theodore Tappert (Philadelphia: Fortress Press, 1959), I:311.

6. LW 45:88.

7. LW 26:344.

8. LW 45:90.

9. LW 26:336.

10. LW 26:337.

11. LW 45:90.

12. Ibid.

13. LW 26:321, 4, 6 respectively.

14. LW 34:151.

15. LW 26.321.

16. LW 26:343.

17. Quoted in Paul Althaus, *The Theology of Martin Luther* (Philadelphia: Fortress Press, 1966) 143–44.

18. *KpV,* 75.

19. Ibid., 69, 75.

20. Ibid., 62.

21. Roger J. Sullivan distinguishes a "public" and a "private" realm in Kant's ethics. While both operate on the basis of "universal principles" such as "justice," the former deals exclusively with external actions, while the latter deals with both actions and motivation. Sullivan, *Introduction to Kant's Ethics* (Cambridge: Cambridge University Press, 1994), 24.

22. *KpV*, 62.

23. Ibid., 75, 63; *RWL*, 24–28.

24. *KpV*, 63.

25. *RWL*, 22.

26. *KpV*, 63.

27. Ibid., 62–63.

28. *RWL*, 25–26, see also *KpV*, 62.

29. *KpV*, 70.

30. LW 31:53.

31. *The Smalcald Articles* III.2. See *The Smalcald Articles by Martin Luther,* trans. and ed. William R. Russell (Minneapolis: Fortress Press, 1995).

32. LW 26:345.

33. LW 26:335.

34. LW 26:339.

35. See Althaus, *The Theology of Martin Luther,* 173. I read Luther as using "strange" in two ways. First, as in confusing or unexpected, where God's action appears, by human standards, unreasonable. Second, as in "alien," or that which is not proper to God's merciful nature.

36. LW 26:339.

37. LW 26:345.

38. See *The Freedom of a Christian* (hereafter *FC*), in *Three Treatises from the American Edition of Luther's Works* (Philadelphia: Fortress Press, 1970), 297.

39. *KpV*, 63, 64, 68.

40. *RWL*, 33,

41. *KpV*, 64.

42. In this vein, Kant echoes Luther's sentiments as depicted, for example, in *The Freedom of a Christian* (see n.80). To further make this point, Kant, in good Lutheran form, cites Romans 14:23: "Whatever is not of this faith is sin" (*RWL*, 26).

43. The punchline of *The Freedom of a Christian*: "We conclude, therefore, that a Christian lives not in himself, but in Christ and in his neighbor. . . . He lives in Christ through faith, in his neighbor through love" (309).

44. In light of the longstanding intra-Lutheran debate on the "third use" of the law, I invite the reader, at least for the purposes of this essay, to consider the following: (1) There is a reasonable case that Luther himself did have something like a third use; (2) it is likely that Kant's early religious education assumed a third use.

45. LW 26:321.

46. *LC* II:67–69.

47. *LC* II:311.

48. *KpV*, 74–75.

49. See Barbara Herman, "Transforming Incentives: Feelings and the Making of the Kantian Moral Agent," in *Philosophical Aspects on Emotions*, ed. Asa Carlson (Stockholm: Thales, 200); see also Barbara Herman, *Moral Literacy* (Cambridge: Harvard University Press, 2007).

50. *KpV*, 74.

51. *KpV*, 69.

52. See *KpV*, 70.

53. *RWL*, 19n; *KpV*, 73.

Chapter 11: Faith, Freedom, Conscience

1. See Martin Luther, *Luther deutsch: Die Werke Martin Luthers in neuer Auswahl für die Gegenwart*, vol. 2, ed. Kurt Aland (Göttingen: Vandenhoeck und Ruprecht, 1991), 251 [if not noted otherwise I modified the standard translations].

2. The German word here is *gewisslich*, the translation of which could refer to either "certainty" or "conscience," which is important for what I shall develop in the next sections of this paper.

3. Luther, *Luther deutsch*, 256.

4. Ibid, 263.

5. Thomas S. Hoffmann, „Gewissen und Staat bei Luther, Fichte und Hegel," in *Realität und Begriff: Festschrift für Jakob Barion* (Würzburg: Königshausen und Neumann, 1993), 81.

6. Heinrich Bornkamm, *Luther im Spiegel der deutschen Geistesgeschichte* (Heidelberg: Quelle und Meyer, 1955), 138.

7. Ibid., 140.

8. For this see also Emanuel Hirsch, *Fichtes, Schleiermachers und Hegels Verhältnis zur Reformation* (Göttingen: Vandenhoeck und Ruprecht, 1930), 13.

9. Bornkamm, *Luther im Spiegel*, 140.

10. Fichte's doctrine of the state, however, comes close to Luther's two-world doctrine. For this see Hoffmann, *Gewissen und Staat*, 95.

11. G. W. F. Hegel, *Vorlesungen zur Geschichte der Philosophie III*, Werke, vol. 20 (Frankfurt: Suhrkamp, 1986), 120.

12. Johann G. Fichte, *The Vocation of Man*, trans. Peter Preuss (Indianapolis: Hackett, 1987), 71.

13. Ibid., 72. I will come back to this point.

14. See Luther, *Luther deutsch*, 363 (thesis 32).

15. Johann G. Fichte, *Addresses to the German Nation*, trans. Reginald Foy Jones and George Henry Turnbull (Chicago: Open Court, 1922), 100.

16. Fichte, *The Vocation of Man*, 79.

17. Johann G. Fichte, *The System of Ethics according to the Principles of the Wissenschaftslehre*, trans. Daniel Breazeale and Günter Zöller (Cambridge: Cambridge University Press, 2005), 140.

18. Karl Löwith, "Phänomenologische Ontologie und protestantische Theologie," in *Heidegger: Perspektiven zur Deutung seines Werkes*, ed. Otto Pöggeler (Königstein: Athenäum, 1984), 54–77, here 74.

Chapter 12: Hegel and Luther on the Finite and the Infinite

1. Letter to Tholuck, July 3, 1826, in Johannes Hoffmeister, ed., *Briefe von und an Hegel*, vol. 4, 2d ed., ed. Rolf Flechsig (Hamburg: Felix Meiner, 1961), 29.

2. WA 39/II:112, 11-21.

3. Hegel's fullest discussion of the relation between the finite and the infinite is found in the sub-sections entitled "Finitude" and "Infinity" in book 1, section 1, chap. 2 of his *Science of Logic*.

4. G. W. F. Hegel, *Vorlesungen über die Philosophie der Religion*, vol. 3, ed. Walter Jaeschke (Hamburg: Felix Meiner, 1995), 88, 91, 93; trans. by author.

5. Hegel, *Philosophie der Religion*, vol. 3, 166–67, 260–61.

Chapter 13: "Faith Creates the Deity"

1. Ludwig Feuerbach, *Preliminary Theses on the Reform of Philosophy*, in Zawar Hanfi, trans., *The Fiery Brook: Selected Writings of Ludwig Feuerbach* (New York: Anchor, 1972), 153, 169. Here and in other citations, the emphases are Feuerbach's.

2. Ludwig Feuerbach, *The Essence of Christianity*, trans. George Eliot (New York: Harper Torchbooks, 1957), 181, xliv. This edition includes Karl Barth's famous critique of Feuerbach.

3. Ludwig Feuerbach, *Lectures on the Essence of Religion*, trans. and with introduction by Melvin Cherno (New York: Harper & Row, 1967), 285, see also 23. By this time Feuerbach had been dismissed from his post at the University of Erlangen and had to give these lectures in the Heidelberg town hall because the University of Heidelberg refused the student petition for his appointment as professor of philosophy. In an earlier essay I suggested structural parallels in the developments of Luther and Feuerbach especially in their struggles to free faith from philosophy (viz., Aristotle and Hegel). See Carter Lindberg, "Luther and Feuerbach," *The Sixteenth Century Journal* 1 (1970): 107–25.

4. See Karl Marx, "Luther als Schiedrichter zwischen Strauss und Feuerbach," in *Marx/Engels Werke* (Berlin, 1976), 26–27; and Stephen P. Thornton, "Facing Up to Feuerbach," *International Journal for Philosophy of Religion* 39 (April 1996): 103–20.

5. John Glasse, "Why Did Feuerbach Concern Himself with Luther?" *Revue internationale de Philosophie* 26 (1972): 373–78.

6. "Why Did Feuerbach Concern Himself with Luther?" 380ff. See also John Glasse, "Feuerbach und die Theologie: Sechs Thesen über den Fall Luther" in Hermann Lübbe

and Hans-Martin Sass, eds., *Atheismus in der Diskussion: Kontroversen um Ludwig Feuerbach* (Munich: Kaiser, 1975), 28–35. Glasse's argument is maintained by Van A. Harvey, *Feuerbach and the Interpretation of Religion* (Cambridge: Cambridge University Press, 1995), 148–50; and Harvey, "Feuerbach on Luther's Doctrine of Revelation: An Essay in Honor of Brian Gerrish," *The Journal of Religion* 78/1 (1998): 9. See also Marilyn Chapin Massey, "Censorship and the Language of Feuerbach's *Essence of Christianity* (1841)," *The Journal of Religion* 65 (1985): 173–95.

7. Heinz-Hermann Brandhorst, *Lutherrezeption und bürgerliche Emanzipation: Studien zum Luther- und Reformationsverständnis im deutschen Vormärz (1815–1848) unter besonderer Berücksichtigung Ludwig Feuerbachs* (Göttingen: Vandenhoeck & Ruprecht, 1981), 10: "On 10 March 1843, at the high point of his grappling with Luther's theology, Feuerbach wrote to Arnold Ruge: 'By the way, I agree: theology is for Germany the only practical and successful vehicle of politics, at least for the moment.'" See also Peter C. Caldwell, *Love, Death, and Revolution in Central Europe: Ludwig Feuerbach, Moses Hess, Louis Dittmar, Richard Wagner* (New York: Palgrave Macmillan, 2009), 1–11, 14–17, 31–33.

8. Glasse, "Why Did Feuerbach Concern Himself with Luther?" 385.

9. Eugene Kamenka, *The Philosophy of Ludwig Feuerbach* (London, 1970), 150, cited by Udo Kern, *Der andere Feuerbach: Sinnlichkeit, Konkretheit und Praxis als Qualität der 'neuen Religion' Ludwig Feuerbachs* (Münster: Lit, 1998), 5. In the foreword to his study, Kern states that by "the other Feuerbach" he means the "forgotten Feuerbach, the Feuerbach who expressis verbis will not destroy religion, but interpret it." Kern provides an incisive literature review of Feuerbach studies from Müller to the present and a useful discussion of the editions of Feuerbach's collected works on p. 1, n, 1, and their contents on 169–76. Unfortunately, I was unable to access both Kern's "Zu Ludwig Feuerbachs Lutherverständnis," *Neue Zeitschrift für Systematische Theologie und Religionsphilosophie* 26 (1984): 29–44, also in *Communio viatorum* 26 (1983): 223–38, and Arve Brunvoll, *"Gott ist Mensch": Die Luther-Rezeption Ludwig Feuerbachs und die Entwicklung seiner Religionskritik* (Frankfurt/M., 1996).

10. Thornton, "Facing up to Feuerbach," 108.

11. Barth's view of Feuerbach is widely available: the introductory essay to *Essence* (cf. n.1 above, refs. to pp. xxii–xxiv); *Theology and Church: Shorter Writings 1920–1928* (New York: Harper & Row, 1962); *Protestant Thought from Rousseau to Ritschl* (New York: Harper & Row, 1952), reprinted in *Protestant Theology in the Nineteenth Century* (Valley Forge: Judson, 1973). See John Glasse, "Barth on Feuerbach," *Harvard Theological Review* 57/2 (1964): 69–76.

12. Paul Althaus, *The Theology of Martin Luther* (Philadelphia: Fortress Press, 1966), 45.

13. Cf. Feuerbach, *The Essence of Christianity*, 127 n. †.

14. WA 40/I:360, 5; LW 26:227.

15. For a partial collection of these citations and their discussion see Albrecht Peters, *Kommentar zu Luthers Katechismen, Bd. 1: Die Zehn Gebote* (Göttingen: Vandenhoeck & Ruprecht, 1990), 110–12. See also *The Book of Concord*, ed. Robert Kolb and Timothy Wengert (Minneapolis: Fortress Press, 2000), 386–90; and Oswald Bayer, *Theology the Lutheran Way*, trans. Jeffrey Silcock and Mark Mattes (Grand Rapids: Eerdmans, 2007), 20–21.

16. Cited by Melvin Cherno in his introduction to his translation of Feuerbach, *The Essence of Faith according to Luther* (New York: Harper & Row, 1967), 15.

17. Ibid., 92.

18. Ibid., 13.

19. Feuerbach, *The Essence of Christianity*, 127.

20. Ibid., xxxvi.

21. Feuerbach, *Lectures on the Essence of Religion*, 22.

22. Feuerbach, *The Essence of Christianity*, 21.

23. Ibid., 15. See also *Lectures on the Essence of Religion*, 166.

24. Ibid., 89.

25. Manfred Vogel, "Introduction," in Ludwig Feuerbach, *Principles of the Philosophy of the Future* (Indianapolis: Bobbs-Merrill, 1966), liii–liv.

26. WA 5:163, 28-29.

27. Feuerbach, *The Essence of Faith according to Luther*, 48.

28. Ibid., 51.

29. Feuerbach, *Principles of the Philosophy of the Future*, 5.

30. Ibid., 72; see also 71: "The essence of man is contained only in the community and unity of man with man; it is a unity, however, which rests only on the reality of the distinction between I and thou."

31. It would be interesting to search Feuerbach's writings to see if he was aware of the contemporary Inner Mission movement and Wichern's speech to the 1848 Wittenberg Kirchentag proclaiming that love is the mark of the church.

32. Feuerbach, *The Essence of Christianity*, 66. See Caldwell, *Love, Death, and Revolution*, 24–26.

33. See Kern, *Der andere Feuerbach*, 76–81. *The Essence of Christianity*, chap. 6, "The Mystery of the Trinity."

34. Feuerbach, *The Essence of Christianity*, 92; *Principles of the Philosophy of the Future*, 53–59.

35. Feuerbach, *The Essence of Christianity*, 53. See my *Love: A Brief History through Western Christianity* (Oxford: Blackwell, 2008), 135, 153–54, 161.

36. Feuerbach, *Principles of the Philosophy of the Future*, 52.

37. Feuerbach, *The Essence of Christianity*, 287ff.; xlff.

38. Ibid., 149.

39. Feuerbach, *Principles of the Philosophy of the Future*, 52–53, 67. See Paul Tillich, "Existential Philosophy: Its Historical Meaning" in his *Theology of Culture* (New York: Oxford University Press, 1959), 76–111.

40. Kern ends his study with the hope it might animate theologians to stop demonizing Feuerbach and perceive his positive meaning for theology in terms of his undivided attention to the real world, a necessary cathartic corrective in theology. The way to this goal is tireless detailed study. "Whoever does not shy away from this effort to concern himself painstakingly with the whole work of Ludwig Feuerbach will not return empty-handed from the effort," *Der andere Feuerbach*, 166–68.

41. In his 1981 study, *Lutherrezeption und bürgerliche Emanzipation* (26), Brandhorst notes that Bayer's work "is to date the most comprehensive and sophisticated contribution to Feuerbach's reception of Luther." Although my grasp of the literature since then is admittedly meager, I concur.

42. Oswald Bayer, "Gegen Gott für den Menschen: Zu Feuerbachs Lutherrezeption," *Zeitschrift für Theologie und Kirche* 69/1 (1972): 34–71; reprinted with an addendum in his

Leibliches Wort: Reformation und Neuzeit im Konflikt (Tübingen: Mohr, 1992), 205–41, in which he notes this essay was an important factor in his *Was ist das: Theologie? Eine Skizze* (Stuttgart: Calwer, 1973), especially in the first chapter, "Theologie als Religionssoziologie und Religionspsychologie?" References will be to the *Leibliches Wort* reprint.

43. *Leibliches Wort*, 210, and n.19.
44. Ibid., 223.
45. Ibid., 235. See also Bayer, *Theology the Lutheran Way*, 133.
46. Feuerbach, *The Essence of Faith according to Luther*, 102, 112.
47. Bayer, *Theology the Lutheran Way*, 138.
48. See *Leibliches Wort*, 240–41; and Bayer, "Toward a Theology of Lament," in David M. Whitford, ed., *Caritas et Reformatio* (St. Louis: Concordia, 2002), 211–20, here 214–15.

Chapter 14: Søren Kierkegaard

1. This essay was published in a shortened form in *Lutheran Forum* 43/3 (Fall 2009): 53–55.
2. Jaroslav Pelikan, *From Luther to Kierkegaard: A Study in the History of Theology* (St. Louis: Concordia, 1950), 118, 120.
3. C. Stephen Evans, *Kierkegaard on Faith and the Self: Collected Essays* (Waco: Baylor University Press, 2006), 117, 118, 129, 299–309.
4. Søren Kierkegaard, *Either/Or, Part I*, ed. and trans. Howard V. Hong and Edna H. Hong (Princeton: Princeton University Press, 1987), 32.
5. Søren Kierkegaard, *Søren Kierkegaard's Journals and Papers*, ed. and trans. Howard V. Hong and Edna H. Hong, assisted by Gregor Malantschuk, 7 vols. (Bloomington: Indiana University Press, 1967–78), vol. 3, entry 2461.
6. Ibid.
7. Ibid., vol. 3, entry 2467.
8. Søren Kierkegaard, *Philosophical Fragments*, ed. and trans. Howard V. Hong and Edna H. Hong (Princeton: Princeton University Press, 1985).
9. Ibid., 54.
10. LW 31:53.
11. *King Lear* 1.4.99-100.
12. See again Evans, *Kierkegaard on Faith and the Self*, and also Merold Westphal, *God, Guilt, and Death: An Existential Phenomenology of Religion* (Bloomington: Indiana University Press, 1984), xi, 12, 15.
13. Richard Rorty, *Philosophy and the Mirror of Nature* (Princeton: Princeton University Press, 1979).
14. Søren Kierkegaard, *Concluding Unscientific Postscript to "Philosophical Fragments,"* ed. and trans. Howard V. Hong and Edna H. Hong (Princeton: Princeton University Press, 1992), 1:205.
15. Pelikan, *From Luther to Kierkegaard*, 113-14.
16. Søren Kierkegaard, *"The Moment" and Late Writings*, ed. and trans. Howard V. Hong and Edna H. Hong (Princeton: Princeton University Press, 1998), 341.
17. Edward F. Mooney, ed., *Ethics, Love, and Faith in Kierkegaard: Philosophical Engagements* (Bloomington: Indiana University Press, 2008), 5.

18. See *The Paul L. Holmer Papers*, ed. David J. Gouwens and Lee C. Barrett (Eugene, Ore.: Cascade, forthcoming 2011).

19. Paul L. Holmer, *Making Christian Sense*, Spirituality and the Christian Life, (Philadelphia: Westminster, 1984). Reprinted as *Making Sense of Our Lives* (Minneapolis: MacLaurin Institute, n.d.). See also Paul L. Holmer, *The Grammar of Faith* (San Francisco: Harper & Row, 1978).

20. Holmer, *Making Christian Sense*, 100.

Chapter 15: Delicious Despair and Nihilism

1. I owe this description to Mark C. Taylor's *After God* (Chicago: University of Chicago Press, 2009), where he also adds a discussion of vocation as deregulation. Taylor's analysis of how Luther paves the way for our own internet-obsessed context is also extremely insightful. Because of space limitation, however, I do not have time to discuss the specifics of Taylor's understanding.

2. Luther's relationship to philosophy, despite his acerbic barbs, can be extended to what I am here calling the "task of living philosophically." Such a notion, moreover, is not mutually exclusive to the work of theology itself. For a good beginning to Luther's relationship to philosophy, see "Disputation concerning Man," LW 34:133–44.

3. Luther as quoted in Mark Kolden, "Luther on Vocation," *Word & World*, 3/4 (1983): 387.

4. I am thinking here to the work of Pierre Hadot who traces the way philosophy, especially in the ancient world (and inclusive of Christianity), is more of a spiritual exercise than a discourse about philosophy. See *What Is Ancient Philosophy?* (Cambridge: Belknap Press of Harvard University Press, 2004), and *Philosophy as a Way of Life: Spiritual Exercises from Socrates to Foucault* (Oxford: Wiley-Blackwell, 1995).

5. I am indebted to both Martin Marty's *Martin Luther: A Life* (New York: Vintage Adult: 1990) and Alister McGrath's *Luther's Theology of the Cross* (Oxford: Blackwell, 1990) for their insights into *Anfechtung*.

6. LW 54:234.

7. LW 54:50.

8. E.g., "The Heidelberg Disputation," thesis 18, LW 31:56.

9. LW 34:286.

10. McGrath, *Luther's Theology of the Cross*, 171.

11. To be sure, I am not suggesting that *Anfechtung* no longer refers to things like spiritual assault or temptation, nor am I denying the role of grace and faith as ways Luther clearly believes we use to approach *Anfechtung*. I am, rather, arguing for the ontological primacy of *Anfechtung*.

12. Steven D. Paulson, "Luther on the Hidden God," *Word & World* 19, no. 4 (Fall 1990): 363.

13. See McGrath, *Luther's Theology of the Cross*, 172. He further points out the helpful distinction in Luther between "satanic" and "divine" *Anfechtung*. He writes that the former "relates particularly to fundamental matters of faith, such as doubt about one's election, or

whether Christ really did die *pro nobis*. The latter, however, is much more closely associated with the doctrine of justification and is specifically linked with the dialectic of law and gospel." This is a helpful distinction, but I am still willing to make the strong claim that both satanic and divine *Anfechtungen* are ultimately not a result of something we do or do not do but the very condition that makes the question of vocation possible. One way of also linking my stronger claim is when McGrath, rightly I think, notes that "Luther considers all *Anfechtung* to originate from God whether directly or indirectly" and in doing so brings *Anfechtung* closer to what I am saying.

14. Ronald Thiemann, "Luther's Theology of the Cross: Resource for a Theology of Religions," as quoted in Christine Helmer, *The Global Luther: A Theologian for Modern Times* (Minneapolis: Fortress Press, 2009), 232.

15. Friedrich Nietzsche, *Basic Writings of Nietzsche*, ed. Walter Kaufman and Peter Gay (New York: Modern Library, 2000), 137.

16. For a good discussion on the ambivalence, see Kathleen M. Higgins, *Comic Relief: Nietzsche's Gay Science* (New York: Oxford University Press, 2000). I am indebted to her for helping me to understand some of Nietzsche's relationship to Luther.

17. Friedrich Nietzsche, *The Gay Science*, trans. Walter Kaufman (New York: Vintage, 1974), §343.

18. Ibid., §125. The idea of the death of God originates with Luther in one of his hymns. However, as Eric Von der Luft has argued, this is misleading. The hymn in question, "Ein trauriger Grabgesang," was written by the Lutheran pastor Johann Rist. According to Von der Luft the phrase *Gott ist tot* ("God is dead") appears nowhere in Luther. He does, however, agree that the sentiment of the death of God is not alien to Luther. See Von der Luft, "Sources of Nietzsche's 'God is Dead!' and Its Meaning for Heidegger," *Journal of the History of Ideas* 45/2 (April-June 1984): 263–76.

19. We should note here that Nietzsche is an equal-opportunity critic. While he is stereotyped as being critical of only Christianity, he criticizes, for example, scientific materialism and aesthetic judgments that function the same way. This is one way to link the earliest reference to the death of God in *The Gay Science* §108, where Nietzsche refers to the shadows of God (other stand-ins) and claims that they have to be vanquished.

20. Nietzsche would reject what appears as a democratic movement in Luther's decentralizing of vocation (see Nietzsche, *Beyond Good and Evil*, trans. Walter Kaufman [New York: Vintage, 1966], in particular §203 where he calls democracy a "decadent form of political organization"). I do not have the space to pursue this line of thought. I am interested in not whether they might be in agreement on something like democracy, but what this turn away is (decentralization and God) and what our task is in its wake.

21. Gianni Vattimo, *After Christianity* (New York: Columbia University Press, 2002), 5–6.

22. I borrow this phrase from Gianni Vattimo, which I find helpful in this context. For a recent treatment of this, see his *The Responsibility of the Philosopher*, ed. Franca D'Agostini, trans. William McCuaig (New York: Columbia University Press, 2010).

23. Nietzsche, "European Nihilism," in *The Nietzsche Reader*, ed. Keith Ansell Pearson and Duncan Large (Oxford: Blackwell, 2006), 385. Emphasis in the original.

24. Nietzsche, *The Will to Power*, trans. Walter Kaufman (New York: Vintage, 1967), 9.

25. Simon Critchley, *Infinitely Demanding: Ethics of Commitment, Politics of Resistance* (New York: Verso, 2007), 4. I am indebted in my discussion to Critchley along with Robert Pippin's *Nietzsche, Psychology, and First Philosophy* (Chicago: University of Chicago Press, 2010).

26. Nietzsche as quoted in Pippin, *Nietzsche, Psychology, and First Philosophy*, 52.

27. Critchley, *Infinitely Demanding*, 5.

28. Nietzsche as quoted in Pippin, *Nietzsche, Psychology, and First Philosophy*, 52.

29. Ibid., 53–54.

30. Nietzsche, "European Nihilism," in *The Nietzsche Reader*, 343.

31. Pippin, *Nietzsche, Psychology, and First Philosophy*, 52.

32. Lear's analysis is applied to the cultural devastation of the Crow Nation. It is important to make it clear that even though I am appropriating some of Lear's insights, I am not suggesting, even indirectly, that the situation of Europeans like Luther and Nietzsche are remotely similar to the horror that characterizes what happened to the Crow. They are not. What I am suggesting, instead, is that Lear's notion of radical hope, which he derives in large part from Aristotle (among others), is both a way of understanding how Luther and Nietzsche move beyond their own critical analysis and how something like radical hope is a motivating factor despite their (stereotypically claimed) cynicism. In this way, I would, like others, say that both Luther and Nietzsche, and their projects, stand squarely in the prophetic traditions of the Hebrew Bible and Christian New Testament.

33. Jonathan Lear, *Radical Hope: Ethics in the Face of Cultural Devastation* (Chicago: University of Chicago Press, 2008), 103.

34. Ibid., 104.

35. Ibid., 116.

36. Ibid., 117.

37. Ibid., 115.

Chapter 16: Heidegger's Existential Domestication of Luther

1. Hannah Arendt, "Martin Heidegger at Eighty," *New York Review of Books*, Oct. 21, 1971.

2. Quoted in Theodore Kisiel, *The Genesis of* Being and Time (Berkeley: University of California Press, 1993), 452. *Da-sein* is an antiquated German word for existence. Heidegger uses it to refer to beings for whom their being—both what they are and that they are—is a concern. It allows him to emphasize the there-being, as opposed to the here-being of human beings, that is, the idea that *Da-sein* is first, foremost, and fundamentally engaged in the world around it and only secondarily reflective appropriating that world.

3. In his 1921–22 winter-semester lecture course published as *Phenomenological Interpretations of Aristotle* he wrote, "theological anthropology must be traced back to its basic philosophical experiences and motives" (quoted in S. J. McGrath's *The Early Heidegger and Medieval Philosophy: Phenomenology for the Godforsaken* [Washington, D.C.: Catholic University of America Press, 2006], 167).

4. Much of this material has been covered elsewhere and in greater detail. See Theodore Kisiel, *The Genesis of* Being and Time; John van Buren, "Martin Heidegger/Martin Luther," in *Reading Heidegger from the Start: Essays in His Earliest Thought* (Albany: SUNY

Press, 1994), 159–74; John van Buren, *The Young Heidegger: Rumor of a Hidden King* (Bloomington: Indiana University Press, 1994); S. J. McGrath, *The Early Heidegger and Medieval Philosophy: Phenomenology for the Godforsaken*; Karl Clifton-Soderstrom, "The Phenomenology of Religious Humility in Heidegger's Reading of Luther," in *Continental Philosophy Review* 42 (2009):171–200; and Timothy Staley, "Heidegger on Luther on Paul," in *Dialog: A Journal of Theology* 46/1 (2007): 41–45.

5. In the first part of the introduction Heidegger writes, "Theology is searching for a more original interpretation of human being's being toward God, prescribed by the meaning of faith itself and remaining within it. Theology is slowly beginning to understand again Luther's insight that its system of dogma rests on a 'foundation' that does not stem from a questioning in which faith is primary and whose conceptual apparatus is not only insufficient for the range of problems in theology but rather covers them up and distorts them" (*Being and Time*, trans. Joan Stambaugh [Albany: SUNY Press, 1996], 8). His second reference comes in a footnote to the claim that angst and fear are seldom treated existentially. After mentioning the importance of angst and fear for the history of Christian theology, he says that "Apart from the traditional context of an interpretation of *poenitentia* and *contritio*, Luther treated the problem of fear in his commentary on Genesis, here, of course, least of all conceptually but all the more penetratingly by way of edification" (*Being and Time*, 404 n.4). Thus exhausts Heidegger's references to Luther in *Being and Time*.

6. Martin Heidegger, *The Phenomenology of Religious Life*, vol. 1 (Bloomington: Indiana University Press, 2004), 236.

7. "Letter to Father Engelbert Krebs," in Martin Heidegger, *Supplements: From the Earliest Essays to* Being and Time *and Beyond*, ed. John van Buren (Albany: SUNY Press, 2002), 69.

8. Quoted in van Buren, "Martin Heidegger/Martin Luther," 160.

9. Quoted in Kisiel, *The Genesis of* Being and Time, 530.

10. Van Buren, "Martin Heidegger/Martin Luther," 171.

11. See chap. 5, "What Did Heidegger Discover in Aristotle? (1921–23)," in Kisiel, *The Genesis of* Being and Time, for a detailed discussion of this transformation.

12. Heidegger, "The Problem of Sin in Luther" in *Supplements*, 106.

13. Ibid., 108.

14. Van Buren, "Martin Heidegger/Martin Luther," 170.

15. Heidegger, *Being and Time*, 164.

16. Ibid., 168.

17. Ibid.

18. Ibid., 247–48.

19. Gerhard Ebeling, *Luther: An Introduction to His Thought*, trans. R. A. Wilson (London: Collins, 1970), 119–20.

20. Heidegger, *Being and Time*, 249.

21. Ibid., 252.

22. Ibid., 273.

23. LW 42:99.

24. LW 51:70.

25. Heidegger, *Being and Time*, 283.

26. LW 35:30.

27. Quoted in McGrath, *The Early Heidegger*, 171.

28. Heidegger, *Being and Time*, 20.

29. I have in mind interpretations such as John Haugland's, who says that for Heidegger "what conscience really articulates . . . [is] the difference between one's own life 'working' and its breaking down or failing to 'work'" ("Truth and Finitude: Heidegger's Transcendental Existentialism," in *Heidegger, Authenticity, and Modernity,* ed. Mark Wrathall and Jeff Malpas [Boston: MIT Press, 2003], 64). This is a long way from sinfulness *coram deo*.

Chapter 17: The Vocation of the Philosopher

1. Thanks to my colleagues at the Collegeville Institute who provided such sage insight as we discussed a draft of this essay in the fall of 2010: Luigi Bertocchi, Steven Chase, Patricia Dougherty, Stephen Doughty, Ivan Kauffman, Carmen Maier, James Okoye, Donald Ottenhoff, Michael Slusser, and Ann Svennungsen.

2. "The Freedom of a Christian," 1521, quoted in *Martin Luther's Basic Theological Writings,* ed. Timothy Lull and William Russell (Minneapolis: Fortress Press, 2005), 406. Cf. also George Forell, "Why Recall Luther Today?" *Word & World* 3/4 (1983): 341.

3. Forell, "Luther Today," 341.

4. Karlfried Froehlich, "Luther on Vocation," in *Harvesting Martin Luther's Reflections*, ed. Timothy Wengert, Lutheran Quarterly Books (Grand Rapids: Eerdmans, 2004), 123–24.

5. Ibid., 127.

6. Forell, "Luther Today," 341.

7. Sermon on Luke 2:15-20, LW 52:37. Cf. also Froehlich, "Vocation," 126.

8. "Disputation on the Human Person," LW 41:127 (trans. altered, emphases mine); cf. also Robert Fischer, "The Reasonable Luther," in *Reformation Studies: Essays in Honor of Roland Bainton*, ed. Franklin Littell (Richmond: John Knox, 1962), 33.

9. Sermons on John 6:42-44; WA 33:127, LW 23:84 (trans. altered). Cf. also Siegbert Becker, *The Foolishness of God* (Milwaukee: Northwestern, 1982), 75.

10. Explanation to the First Article of the Creed, *The Small Catechism*, in *The Book of Concord,* ed. by Robert Kolb and Timothy Wengert (Fortress Press: Minneapolis, 2000), 354.

11. *The Smalcald Articles* II:2, in *The Book of Concord*, 301. Emphasis mine.

12. We should note that scholars debate whether or not there is a "third use of the law" in Luther.

13. *The Smalcald Articles* III:2, in *The Book of Concord*, 312.

14. "Martin Luther on Preaching the Law," *Word & World* 21/3 (Summer 2001): 254f. Lose also refers to *The Smalcald Articles* III:2.

15. "Sermon on Jesus Christ" (Torgau, 1533); WA 37:39f.; Fischer, "Reasonable Luther," 33f.

16. Explanation to the Third Article of the Creed, *The Small Catechism*, in *The Book of Concord*, 355-356. Translation altered, emphasis mine.

Chapter 18: Lutheran Environmental Philosophy?

1. LW 1:66, 119–20.

2. LW 1:67, 71, 84–86.

3. LW 2:58-59, 70, 132, 43-45.

4. LW 2:132-33.

5. H. Paul Santmire, *The Travail of Nature: The Ambiguous Ecological Promise of Christian Theology* (Philadelphia: Fortress Press, 1985), 130; idem, *Nature Reborn: The Ecological and Cosmic Promise of Christian Theology*, Theology and the Sciences (Minneapolis: Fortress Press, 2000), 84.

6. Santmire, *The Travail of Nature*, 125.

7. LW 37:58–59.

8. LW 37:59.

9. LW 37:60.

10. LW 37:69.

11. Steven Bouma-Prediger and Peter Bakken, eds., *Evocations of Grace: The Writings of Joseph Sittler on Ecology, Theology, and Ethics* (Grand Rapids: Eerdmans, 2000), 7.

12. Bouma-Prediger and Bakken, eds., *Evocations of Grace*, pp. 5, 7, 35, 39–40, 53–56, 80, 85–86, 92–93, 114, 31, 41, 71.

13. Ibid., 53–56, 80, 85–86.

14. Ibid., 10, 34, 37.

15. Lisa Sideris, "Ecotheology," in *Encyclopedia of Environmental Ethics and Philosophy*, ed. J. Baird Callicott and Robert Frodeman (Detroit: Macmillan Reference, 2009); Susan Power Bratton, "Loving Nature: Ecological Integrity and Christian Responsibility," *Environmental Ethics* 15/1 (1993): 93; Espeth Whitney, "Lynn White, Ecotheology, and History," *Environmental Ethics* 15/2 (1993): 160.

16. Robin Attfield, "White, Lynn, Jr. 1907–1987," in *Encyclopedia of Environmental Ethics and Philosophy*; Whitney, "Lynn White, Ecotheology, and History"; Jeane Kay Guelke, "Looking for Jesus in Christian Environmental Ethics," *Environmental Ethics* 26, no. 2 (2004).

17. The subtitle of Santmire's *The Travail of Nature*.

18. Santmire, *The Travail of Nature*; idem, *Nature Reborn*; idem, *Ritualizing Nature: Renewing Christian Liturgy in a Time of Crisis*, Theology and the Sciences (Minneapolis: Fortress Press, 2008).

19. LW 37:58–59.

20. LW 37:62.

21. Santmire, *Ritualizing Nature*, 119–23.

22. James B. Martin-Schramm, *Climate Justice: Ethics, Energy, and Public Policy* (Minneapolis: Fortress Press, 2010), 24–36; "A Social Statement On: Caring for Creation: Vision, Hope, and Justice," Department for Studies of the Division for Church in Society of the Evangelical Lutheran Church in America, http://www.elca.org/socialstatements/environment.

23. See, for example, Harry Rijnen, "Business Travel; Offsetting Environmental Damage by Planes," *The New York Times*, Feb. 18, 2003, http://www.nytimes.com /2003/02/18/business/business-travel-offsetting-environmental-damage-by-planes.html;

Alex Williams and Amy Goetzman with contributions by Catherine Donaldson-Evans, Kate Hammer, Carol Pogash, Rachel Pomerance and Paula Schwartz, "Water, Water Everywhere, but Guilt by the Bottleful," *The New York Times,* Aug. 12, 2007, http://www.nytimes.com/2007/08/12/fashion/12water.html.

24. Martin Luther, *Christian Liberty,* ed. Harold J. Grimm, trans. W. A. Lambert, rev. ed. (Philadelphia: Fortress Press, 1957), 7; Bouma-Prediger and Bakken, eds., *Evocations of Grace,* 53–58, 148, 89.

25. Bryan G. Norton, *Sustainability: A Philosophy of Adaptive Ecosystem Management* (Chicago: University of Chicago Press, 2005).

Chapter 19: Luther and Philosophy in a Scientific Age

1. Cf. Graham White, *Luther as Nominalist: A Study of the Logical Methods Used in Martin Luther's Disputations in the Light of Their Medieval Background* (Helsinki: Schriften der Luther-Agricola-Gesellschaft, 1994).

2. E.g., Alan D. Schrift, *The Logic of the Gift: Toward an Ethic of Generosity* (New York: Routledge, 1997).

3. Alvin Plantinga, "The Reformed Objection to Natural Theology," *Christian Scholar's Review* 11/3 (1982): 187–98; Alvin Plantinga and Nicholas Wolterstorff, eds., *Faith and Rationality: Reason and Belief in God* (Notre Dame, Ind.: University of Notre Dame Press, 1983).

4. Wilhelm Norlind, "Copernicus and Luther: A Critical Study," *Isis* 44 (1953): 273–76. It is important to note that this frequently cited quote of Luther's is of doubtful authenticity, and it is not at all clear it really represents Luther's view. Indeed, there is good reason to suppose his view was more nuanced, and more in keeping with the views later Lutherans developed.

5. For very different philosophical approaches to this, see Philip Clayton, *Mind and Emergence: From Quantum to Consciousness* (New York: Oxford University Press, 2006); Stewart Goetz and Charles Taliaferro, *Naturalism* (Grand Rapids: Eerdmans, 2008).

6. Robert S. Westman, "The Copernicans and the Churches," in *God and Nature: Historical Essays on the Encounter between Christianity and Science,* ed. David C. Lindberg and Ronald L. Numbers (Berkeley: University of California Press, 1986), 76–113.

7. Linda Zagzebski, *The Dilemma of Freedom and Foreknowledge* (New York: Oxford University Press, 1996).

8. The implications of this point for Lutheran theologians is slightly larger, since it is sometimes argued that theology and science represent separate discourses or concern distinct ontological categories. But while it may be legitimately argued that, to the extent that we understand God as distinct from the world, theology and science are completely separate domains of inquiry, this claim seems to break down quickly once we move to theological anthropology. To be human is to be embodied, and bodies are amenable to scientific inquiry. For an exploration of some of these themes, see Gregory R. Peterson, *Minding God* (Minneapolis: Fortress Press, 2003).

9. Cf. Robert Kane, ed., *The Oxford Handbook of Free Will* (New York: Oxford University Press, 2005).

10. Thomas Hobbes, *Leviathan,* ed. Richard Tuck (New York: Cambridge University Press, 1996).

11. Cf. Aristotle, *Nicomachean Ethics*, Book 7; Donald Davidson, *Essays on Actions and Events*, 2d ed. (New York: Oxford University Press, 2001).

12. Stanley Milgram, "Behavioral Study of Obedience," *Journal of Abnormal and Social Psychology* 67 (1963): 371–78; for a recent review of subsequent experimental work, see Dominic J. Packer, "Identifying Systematic Disobedience in Milgram's Obedience Experiments: A Meta-Analytic Review," *Perspectives on Psychological Science* 3/4 (2008): 301–4.

13. Philip Zimbardo, *The Lucifer Effect: Understanding How Good People Turn Evil* (New York: Random, 2007). It is important to note, however, that Zimbardo's experiment in particular has important interpretive issues, though it is consistent with subsequent literature supporting situationism.

14. John M. Darley and C. Daniel Batson, "'From Jerusalem to Jericho': A Study of Situational and Dispositional Variables in Helping Behavior," *Journal of Personality and Social Psychology* 27/1 (1973): 100–108.

15. G. Harman, "Moral Philosophy Meets Social Psychology: Virtue Ethics and the Fundamental Attribution Error," *Proceedings of the Aristotelian Society* 99 (1999): 315–31; John M. Doris, "Persons, Situations, and Virtue Ethics," *Nous* 32/4 (1998): 504–30.

16. Jonathan Haidt, "The Emotional Dog and Its Rational Tail: A Social Intuitionist Approach to Moral Judgment," *Psychological Review* 108 (2001): 814–34.

17. S. Schnall, S., J. Haidt, G. Clore, and A. Jordan, "Disgust as Embodied Moral Judgment," *Personality and Social Psychology Bulletin* 34 (2008): 1096–109.

18. Jonathan Haidt and Fredrik Bjorklund, "Social Intuitionists Answer Six Questions about Moral Psychology," in *Moral Psychology*, vol. 2, ed. Walter Sinnott-Armstrong (Cambridge: MIT Press, 2008).

19. Candace L. Upton, "Virtue Ethics and Moral Psychology: The Situationism Debate," *The Journal of Ethics* 13/2 (2009): 103–15; Hagop Sarkissian, "Minor Tweaks, Major Payoffs: The Problem and Promise of Situationism in Moral Philosophy," *Philosopher's Imprint* 10/9 (2010): 1–15; Jesse Prinz, "The Normativity Challenge: Cultural Psychology Provides the Real Threat to Virtue Ethics," *The Journal of Ethics* 13/2 (2009): 117–44.

20. cf. Antonio Damasio, *Descartes' Error: Emotion, Reason, and the Human Brain* (New York: Quill, 1994); Martha Nussbaum, *Upheavals of Thought: The Intelligence of the Emotions* (New York: Cambridge University Press, 2001); Jesse J. Prinz, *Gut Reactions: A Perceptual Theory of Emotion* (New York: Oxford University Press, 2004).

Chapter 20: Queering Kenosis

1. Marcella Althaus-Reid, *Indecent Theology: Theological Perversions in Sex, Gender, and Politics* (New York: Routledge, 2000); Robert Goss, *Queering Christ: Beyond Jesus Acted Up* (Cleveland: Pilgrim, 2002). "'Queer,' then, demarcates not a positively but a positionality vis-à-vis the normative—a positionality that is not restricted to lesbians and gay men but is in fact available to anyone who is or who feels marginalized because of his or her sexual practices," David Halperin, *Saint Foucault: Toward a Gay Hagiography* (New York: Oxford, 1995), 62.

2. For an overview of kenotic Christology, see Sarah Coakley, "*Kenōsis* and Subversion: On the Repression of 'Vulnerability' in Christian Feminist Writing," in *Swallowing a Fishbone? Feminist Theologians Debate Christianity*, ed. Daphne Hampson (London: SPCK, 1996), 82–111.

3. Martin Luther, "Palm Sunday: Christ an Example of Love: Sermon on Philippians 2, 5-11," trans. Nicholas Lenker, in *Complete Sermons of Martin Luther*, vol. 7 (Grand Rapids: Baker, 1983), 176.

4. "Two Kinds of Righteousness," LW 31:301.

5. Luther, "Palm Sunday," 178; See also "Psalm 8," LW 12:123.

6. Paul Althaus, *The Theology of Martin Luther*, trans. Robert C. Schultz (Philadelphia: Fortress Press, 1966), 194.

7. "Two Kinds of Righteousness," LW 31:302; see also "Lectures on Romans," LW 25:140.

8. Kyle Pasewark compared Luther and Foucault's theories of power, and he concludes that Luther viewed power as ubiquitous communicated efficacy. Pasewark sees similarities between Luther and Foucault's theories of power that I do not. Kyle A. Pasewark, *A Theology of Power: Being beyond Domination* (Minneapolis: Fortress Press, 1993).

9. "The Magnificat," LW 21:328.

10. See "Psalm 2," LW 14:309.

11. "Temporal Authority," LW 45:120.

12. "Against the Robbing and Murdering Hordes," LW 46:50.

13. "Treatise on Good Works," LW 44:104.

14. Michel Foucault, *Society Must Be Defended: Lectures at the Collège de France, 1975–76*, ed. Mauro Bertani and Alessandro Fontana, trans. David Macey (New York: Picador, 2003), 13.

15. On Foucault and power, see Hubert L. Dreyfus and Paul Rabinow, *Michel Foucault: Beyond Structuralism and Hermeneutics*, 2d ed. (Chicago: University of Chicago Press, 1983); Joseph Rouse, "Power/Knowledge," in *The Cambridge Companion to Foucault*, 2d ed., ed. Gary Gutting (Cambridge: Cambridge University Press, 2003); for a critique of Foucault's analytic of power, see Sandra Bartky, *Femininity and Domination: Studies in the Phenomenology of Oppression* (New York: Routledge, 1990).

16. Michel Foucault, "Powers and Strategies," in *Michel Foucault: Power, Truth, Strategy*, ed. Meaghan Morris and Paul Patton (Sydney: Feral, 1979), 55.

17. Michel Foucault, *An Introduction*, vol. 1 of *The History of Sexuality*, trans. Robert Hurley (New York: Vintage, 1976), 93.

18. Michel Foucault, *Discipline and Punish: The Birth of the Prison*, trans. Alan Sheridan (New York: Vintage, 1995), 27.

19. Michel Foucault, "Sex, Power, and the Politics of Identity," in *Ethics: Subjectivity and Truth*, ed. Paul Rabinow, trans. Robert Hurley and Others (New York: New Press, 1997), 167.

20. "Psalm 110," LW 13:252.

21. See Daphne Hampson, *Theology and Feminism* (Cambridge: Blackwell, 1990), 155; Delores Williams, "Black Women's Surrogacy Experience and the Christian Notion of Redemption," in *After Patriarchy: Feminist Transformations of the World Religions*, ed. Paula M. Cooey, William R. Eakin, and Jay B. McDaniel (Maryknoll, N.Y.: Orbis, 1991).

22. "Temporal Authority," LW 45:112.

23. "Psalm 82," LW 13:44.

24. "Lectures on Romans," LW 25:473.

Chapter 21: Philosophical Kinship

1. See Brian A. Gerrish, "Doctor Martin Luther: Subjectivity and Doctrine in the Lutheran Reformation," in *Seven-Headed Luther: Essays in Commemoration of a Quincentenary, 1483–1983*, ed. Peter Newman Brooks (Oxford: Clarendon, 1983), 18–20.

2. Jaroslav Pelikan, *From Luther to Kierkegaard: A Study in the History of Theology* (St. Louis: Concordia, 1963) 115.

3. It can be argued that Kierkegaard may certainly have been more closely aligned with Luther's self-described *Anfechtung* (angst) that shapes the rift Luther understood there to be between God and humanity.

4. Friedrich Schleiermacher, *The Christian Faith: English Translation of the Second German Edition*, 1822, trans. H. R. Mackintosh and J. S. Stewart (Edinburgh: T & T Clark, 1989), §3.4.

5. Ibid., §§3, 4.

6. Ibid., §4.

7. Some Lutheran theologians have been skeptical about Schleiermacher's primacy of feeling, yet his shared concern with Luther over reason's nonprimacy in seeking truth is a compelling link between the two thinkers.

8. "Lecture on the Epistle to the Romans, 1522," LW 25:361.

9. Sally Haslanger, "On Being Objective and Being Objectified," in *A Mind of One's Own: Feminist Essays on Reason and Objectivity*, ed. Louise M. Antony and Charlotte E. Witt, 2d ed. (Boulder: Westview, 2002), 209–53.

10. Genevieve Lloyd, "Maleness, Metaphor, and the 'Crisis' of Reason," in *A Mind of One's Own*, ed. Antony and Witt, 82–83.

11. Ibid., 82–83.

12. Ibid., 76.

13. Ibid., 81.

14. Ibid., 82.

15. Ibid., 86–87.

16. Gerrish, "Doctor Martin Luther," 18–20.

17. See Pelikan, *From Luther to Kierkegaard*, esp. 4–12.

18. See Wolfhart Pannenberg, "A Theology of the Cross," *Word & World* 8/2 (Spring 1988): 162–63.

19. Gerrish, "Doctor Martin Luther," 20.

20. Ibid., 22.

21. The reference here is to these fields broadly defined.

22. See Haslanger, "On Being Objective," 210.

23. Ibid., 211.

24. See ibid., 211–26, for her full argument.

25. Ibid., 215.

26. Ibid., 216.

27. Ibid., 216–21.

28. Ibid., here referring to Aristotle on natures, 229.

29. Ibid., 232.

30. Ibid., 234.

Chapter 22: Provocateur for the Common Good

1. Martin Luther, "An Open Letter to The Christian Nobility of the German Nation concerning the Reform of the Christian Estate: Proposals for Reform Part III" (1520) trans. C. M. Jacobs, *Project Wittenberg*, http://www.iclnet.org/resources/text/wittenberg/luther/web/nblty.
2. Gustaf Wingren, *Luther on Vocation*, trans. Carl Rasmussen (Philadelphia: Muhlenberg Press, 1957), 2.
3. Quoted in ibid., 3.
4. Ibid., 29.
5. Ibid., 178.
6. See Plato's *Phaedo*.
7. See *The Daily Show and Philosophy*, ed. Jason Holt (Malden, Mass.: Blackwell, 2007) esp. chaps. 3, 5–8, all of which deal with this theme.
8. See Ronald Frost, "Aristotle' Ethics: The Real Reason for Luther's Reformation?" *Trinity Journal* 18/2 (Fall 1997): 223–41.
9. David Hume, *Enquiry Concerning Human Understanding*, Section I:9.
10. See Martha Nussbaum, *Not for Profit: Why Democracy Needs the Humanities* (Princeton: Princeton University Press, 2010).

Chapter 23: Luther and the Vocation of Public Philosophy

1. Alex Beam, *A Great Idea at the Time: The Rise, Fall, and Curious Afterlife of the Great Books* (New York: Public Affairs, 2008), 133f.
2. B. A. Gerrish, "Luther, Martin" in *The Encyclopedia of Philosophy*, vols. 5–6 (New York: Macmillan, 1967), 109–13.
3. B. A. Gerrish, *Grace and Reason: A Study of the Theology of Luther* (Chicago: University of Chicago, 1979), 52f.
4. H. Richard Niebuhr, *Christ and Culture* (New York: Harper & Row, 1951), on Luther, 170–85.
5. Michael Oakeshott, *Experience and Its Modes* (Cambridge: Cambridge University Press, 1933), 5, 9, 70f., 75f., details aspects of "modal" experience and discourse.
6. Samuel Torvend, *Luther and the Hungry Poor: Gathered Fragments* (Minneapolis: Fortress Press, 2008), 122.
1. Augustine, *Contra Academicos* I.1.3-I.1.4, in *Against the Academicians*, trans. Peter King (Indianapolis: Hackett, 1995), 4–5.
2. LW 38:269.
3. LW 34:143.
4. LW 38:240.
5. Ludwig Wittgenstein, *Tractatus Logico-Philosophicus* 7, trans. D. F. Pears and B. F. McGuiness (London: Routledge and Keegan, 1961), 151.

INDEX

Virgil, 208n3
vocation, 32, 90, 122–26, 143
    vocation of philosophy, 9,
    142–47, 178–83, 186–92, 196,
    198
Von der Loft, Eric, 231n18
Von Staupitz, Johann, 41

Weber, Max, 97
Wengert, Timothy, 69, 72, 221n26
White, Graham, 24
William of Ockham, 4, 20, 34, 25,
    63, 66, 308n5, 318n11, 318n13,
    318n15

William of Sherwood, 63
wisdom, 33–35, 48–49, 52, 58, 66,
    71, 109, 123, 137, 142–43,
    163–64, 195
Wittgenstein, Ludwig, 18, 61, 115,
    197, 217n5
Wolfe, Christopher, 8
Wuchterl, Kurt, 14

Xenophon, 34

Zimbardo, Philip, 159
Zwingli, Huldrich, 60, 147, 217n52